CAMBRIDGE

AMERICAN EMPOWER

STUDENT'S BOOK WITH EBOOK

A1

STARTER

Adrian Doff, Craig Thaine
Herbert Puchta, Jeff Stranks, Peter Lewis-Jones
with Rachel Godfrey

CAMBRIDGE

AMERICAN EMPOWER is a six-level general English course for adult and young adult learners, taking students from beginner to advanced level (CEFR A1 to C1). *American Empower* combines course content from Cambridge University Press with validated assessment from the experts at Cambridge Assessment English.

American Empower's unique mix of engaging classroom materials and reliable assessment enables learners to make consistent and measurable progress.

Content you'll love.
Assessment you can trust.

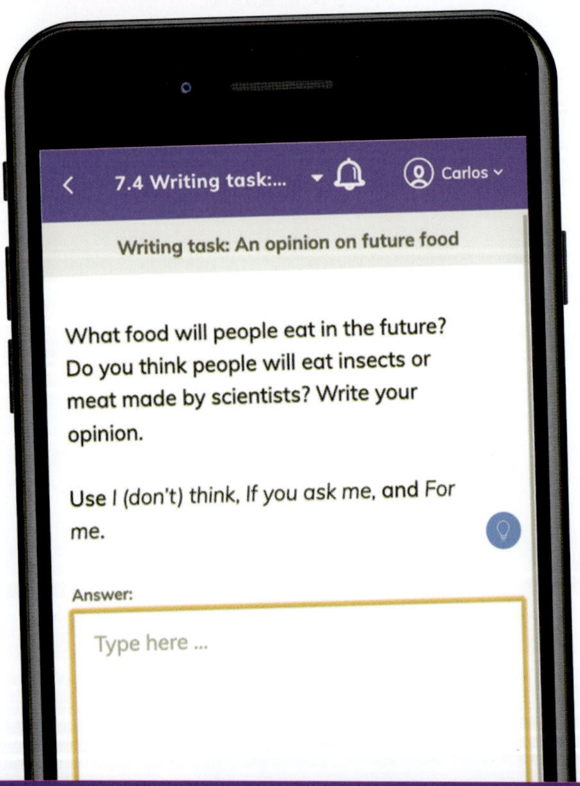

Better Learning with *American Empower*

Better Learning is our simple approach where **insights** we've gained from research have helped shape **content** that drives **results**.

Learner engagement

1 Content that informs and motivates

Insights
Sustained motivation is key to successful language learning and skills development.

Content
Clear learning goals, thought-provoking images, texts, and speaking activities, plus video content to arouse curiosity.

Results
Content that surprises, entertains, and provokes an emotional response, helping teachers to deliver motivating and memorable lessons.

8A I WAS ON TOUR WITH MY BAND

Learn to talk about past events
G Simple past: *be*
V Past time expressions

1 READING

a Look at the events in pictures a–d. Choose one you like and one you don't like. Tell a partner. Say why.

a party | a sports game | a concert | a meeting

b Read about Cara, Antonio, and Ava. Which events in 1a do they talk about?

c Read the texts again. Which cities does each person talk about?

d Talk about Cara, Antonio, and Ava's lives with a partner. Who would you like to meet? Why?

My name's Cara. I'm a photographer. I was in New York three days ago for work, and then I was in Chicago yesterday at a meeting about newspaper photography. Life's busy right now!

"Yesterday I was in Chicago."

"I was at a game in Los Angeles. It was the Finals!"

The people on our team …
My name's Antonio Marotto. I'm the doctor for our team. It's a great job – I really like helping our players. I often go away with the team. We were in Miami two weeks ago for a game, and we were in Cleveland last week. It's fun to travel with the team.

Ava on the road …
Hi everyone, it's Ava. Last week I was on tour with my band in the U.S. – three cities in five days. We were in Seattle on Wednesday, and then we were in Portland on Thursday. But Saturday was the best night. We were in San Francisco, and about 1,000 people were at our concert.

"In this photo, we were in San Francisco."

64

UNIT 8

2 GRAMMAR Simple past: *be* affirmative

a Complete the chart. Find examples of the simple past of *be* in the texts about Cara, Antonio, and Ava.

+	
I [1]______	we [3]______
you were	you were
he/she/it [2]______	they were

b 08.01 Pronunciation Listen to sentences 1–4. Are *was* and *were* stressed? Practice saying the sentences.

1 We were in Seattle.
2 I was in Los Angeles.
3 We were in Miami.
4 I was in New York.

c Now go to Grammar Focus 8A Part 1 on p. 128.

d Write sentences about where you were:
- this morning
- last night
- yesterday afternoon

e Compare your sentences in 2d with a partner. Were you in the same places?

Juan and I were at the supermarket yesterday.

3 VOCABULARY Past time expressions

a Today is Friday of week 3. Put the number of sentences 1–4 in the correct place on the timeline.

week 1 | week 2 | week 3
Monday Tuesday Wednesday Thursday Friday

1 We were in Seattle on Wednesday.
2 We were in Miami two weeks ago.
3 … we were in Cleveland last week.
4 I was in Chicago yesterday.

b Look at the underlined words in 3a. Replace them with words in the box.

months this morning Saturday year

c Now go to Vocabulary Focus 8A on p. 149.

d Work in pairs.
Student A: Say a past time expression.
Student B: Say where a person you know was.
Then switch roles.

last weekend
My parents were in London last weekend.
two years ago
My friend Marco was in Ecuador two years ago.

4 LISTENING AND GRAMMAR Simple past: *be* negative and questions

a 08.06 Review the texts about Cara, Antonio, and Ava again. Then listen to them talking to friends. Write the correct name for each conversation.

Conversation 1 ______
Conversation 2 ______
Conversation 3 ______

b 08.06 Match events 1–3 with adjectives a–c. Listen again and check.

1 the meeting — a exciting
2 the game — b interesting
3 the concert — c fun

c 08.07 Listen to Conversation 1 again. Complete the conversation with the words in the box.

was (x2) were (x2) wasn't

WILL ______ you at work yesterday?
CARA Yes, I ______, but I ______ here in the office.
WILL Where ______ you?
CARA I was at a meeting in Chicago.
WILL Oh, ______ it interesting?
CARA Yes, it was really interesting.

d Now go to Grammar Focus 8A Part 2 on p. 128.

e 08.11 Complete the conversation with *was*, *were*, *wasn't*, or *weren't*. Listen and check.

A You ______ at work yesterday.
B No, I ______ off yesterday.
A Nice. ______ you at home all day?
B No, I ______. I ______ in town in the morning, and then I ______ at a party last night.
A ______ the party good?
B Yes, it ______ a lot of fun.

f Practice the conversation in 4e with a partner. Change some of the information.

I was at a baseball game in the morning and then at the movies last night.
Was the movie good?

5 SPEAKING

a Communication 8A Student A go to p. 113. Student B go to p. 111. Student C go to p. 115.

65

2 Personalized and relevant

Insights
Language learners benefit from frequent opportunities to personalize their responses.

Content
Personalization tasks in every unit make the target language more meaningful to the individual learner.

Results
Personal responses make learning more memorable and inclusive, with all students participating in spontaneous spoken interaction.

> *"There are so many adjectives to describe such a wonderful series, but in my opinion it's very reliable, practical, and modern."*

Zenalde Brianez, Director of Studies, Instituto da Língua Inglesa, Brazil

Measurable progress

1 Assessment you can trust

Insights
Tests developed and validated by Cambridge Assessment English, the world leaders in language assessment, to ensure they are accurate and meaningful.

Content
End-of-unit tests, mid- and end-of-course competency tests, and personalized CEFR test report forms provide reliable information on progress with language skills.

Results
Teachers can see learners' progress at a glance, and learners can see measurable progress, which leads to greater motivation.

Results of an impact study showing % improvement of Reading levels, based on global *Empower* students' scores over one year.

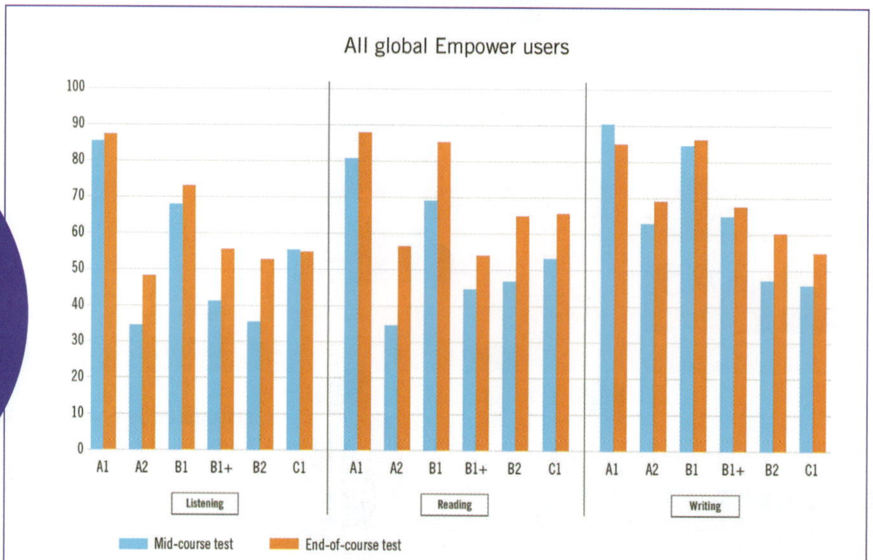

Average score for listening, reading, and writing in the mid-course test and end-of-course test.
Based on global students' scores from August 2016 to July 2017.

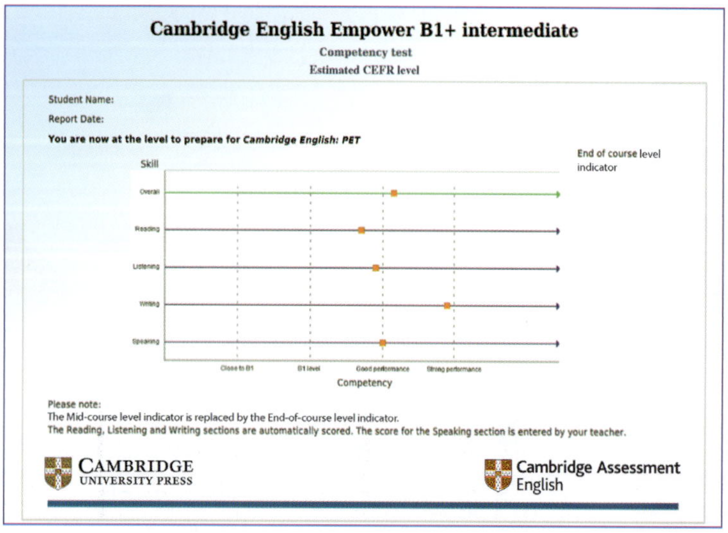
Cambridge English Empower B1+ intermediate

Competency test

Estimated CEFR level

Student Name:

Report Date:

You are now at the level to prepare for *Cambridge English: PET*

Please note:
The Mid-course level indicator is replaced by the End-of-course level indicator.
The Reading, Listening and Writing sections are automatically scored. The score for the Speaking section is entered by your teacher.

CAMBRIDGE UNIVERSITY PRESS

Cambridge Assessment English

"We started using the tests provided with Empower *and our students started showing better results from this point until now."*

Kristina Ivanova, Director of Foreign Language Training Centre, ITMO University, Saint Petersburg, Russia

2 Evidence of impact

Insights
Schools and colleges need to show that they are evaluating the effectiveness of their language programs.

Content
Empower (British English) impact studies have been carried out in various countries, including Russia, Brazil, Turkey, and the UK, to provide evidence of positive impact and progress.

Results
Colleges and universities have demonstrated a significant improvement in language level between the mid- and end-of-course tests, as well as a high level of teacher satisfaction with *Empower*.

Manageable learning

1 Mobile friendly

Insights
Learners expect online content to be mobile friendly but also flexible and easy to use on any digital device.

Content
American Empower provides easy access to Digital Workbook content that works on any device and includes practice activities with audio.

Results
Digital Workbook content is easy to access anywhere, and produces meaningful and actionable data so teachers can track their students' progress and adapt their lesson accordingly.

> *I had been studying English for 10 years before university, and I didn't succeed. But now with* Empower *I know my level of English has changed.*

Nikita, *Empower* Student, ITMO University, Saint Petersburg, Russia

2 Corpus-informed

Insights
Corpora can provide valuable information about the language items learners are able to learn successfully at each CEFR level.

Content
Two powerful resources – Cambridge Corpus and English Profile – informed the development of the *Empower* course syllabus and the writing of the materials.

Results
Learners are presented with the target language they are able to incorporate and use at the right point in their learning journey. They are not overwhelmed with unrealistic learning expectations.

Rich in practice

1 Language in use

Insights

It is essential that learners are offered frequent and manageable opportunities to practice the language they have been focusing on.

Content

Throughout the *American Empower* Student's Book, learners are offered a wide variety of practice activities, plenty of controlled practice, and frequent opportunities for communicative spoken practice.

Results

Meaningful practice makes new language more memorable and leads to more efficient progress in language acquisition.

8B HE SAW A BEAR

Learn to describe events in the past
- G Simple past: affirmative
- V Free time activities

1 READING

a Look at pictures 1–3 below. Match the pictures to the animal names. Where do they usually live? What do you know about them?

___ deer ___ bear ___ hippo

b Read the stories below. Write the story titles next to the sentences.
1 Hippos were on a rugby field. ___
2 Three deer were in a woman's apartment. ___
3 A bear was in a man's backyard. ___

c Read the stories again. Complete the information.

	Where?	When?	Animal activity?
Andrew from Utah	at home		
Ben from South Africa		evening	
A woman from Indiana			jump

d Talk about the questions.
1 Which story do you like?
2 Which animals sometimes come into houses in your country?

cat dog bird snake

3 What do you do if a wild animal comes to your house?

WILD STORIES!

1 CURIOUS CREATURE

Andrew Singer from Utah was at home in his house on a farm. One evening he was in the kitchen, and he heard something strange in the backyard, so he looked out the window. He saw a bear in the backyard. The bear walked around the backyard and looked in the windows of the house. It tried to open the kitchen door, and the man was really scared. It wasn't possible for the bear to get in, so it went away. The man thinks the bear was hungry, but it's not a good idea to give bears food.

2 SURPRISE VISITORS

A woman from Indiana had an apartment with a yard. In the evening, she went into her living room and watched TV. She heard something in her bedroom, so she went to look. She saw three deer near her bed. They came into the living room and jumped on her sofa, then they went into the bathroom. The woman called 911, and the police came to catch the deer. She had an exciting night with her three new friends!

3 READY TO PLAY

Ben Kruger from South Africa loves playing rugby. He has a business in Limpopo, a city in the north of South Africa. One night after work, he went to a rugby field nearby. It was dark, and he saw something on the field. It was large, but it wasn't a person – it was a hippopotamus (hippo)! Then he saw another hippo and then another – there were a lot of them. The hippos ate some grass and then went away. Ben thinks the hippos were from a river near the rugby field.

66

2 GRAMMAR Simple past: affirmative

a 08.12 Read the stories again and find the simple past forms of the verbs in the chart. Listen and check.

A		B	
Verb	Past form	Verb	Past form
look	looked	have	had
watch		hear	
call		eat	
jump		see	
walk		go	
try		come	

b Answer the questions about the chart in 2a.
1 What do we add to the verbs in A to make the past form?
2 Do the verbs in B all change in the same way or in different ways?

c Sound and spelling /t/ and /d/
1 08.13 Listen and practice these sounds.
1 /t/ talk**ed** 2 /d/ liv**ed**
2 08.14 Listen to the past forms in the box. Which *-ed* endings sound ... ?
- more like /t/
- more like /d/

looked watched called tried walked played finished

3 Practice saying the words.

d Cover the chart in 2a. Test a partner.
Student A: Say a verb.
Student B: Say the past form.
Then switch roles.

e Now go to Grammar Focus 8B on p. 128.

f Complete the sentences so they are true for you.
1 Yesterday I called ___ (a person)
2 Last month I saw ___ (a TV show)
3 Last weekend I went to ___ (a place)
4 Last night I ate ___ (food)

Tell your partner about your sentences.

3 LISTENING AND VOCABULARY
Free time activities

a 08.17 Listen to three conversations about the three stories. In each conversation, some information is incorrect. What is the wrong information?
1 ___
2 ___
3 ___

UNIT 8

b 08.18 Listen to the sentences from the conversations. Use the correct verb in the box.

read (x2) talked went had watched heard

1 I just ___ to a café.
2 I ___ a large coffee.
3 And I ___ the newspaper.
4 I ___ this funny story.
5 I ___ this story on a podcast.
6 I ___ to my friend Katie last night.
7 She ___ the video online.

c Match verbs 1 to 6 with a word or phrase in the box to make more simple past phrases.

a book to my parents home dinner a movie for a walk breakfast a song on the radio to my friend

1 went ___, ___
2 had ___, ___
3 read ___
4 heard ___
5 talked ___, ___
6 watched ___

d 08.19 Listen to Emily talk about the things she did yesterday. Put pictures a–e in the correct order.

e 08.19 Complete what Emily says with phrases from 3c. Then listen again and check.

Yesterday I [1] ___ at about 9:00, and then I went to a café and had coffee with my friend Karen. After that, I went to work and was there all day. I [2] ___ with my brother, and then I [3] ___ and called my parents. I [4] ___ Rosie in Brazil on Skype. After, I [5] ___ online, and then I went to bed and [6] ___ before going to sleep.

f Now go to Vocabulary Focus 8B on p. 150.

g Complete the sentences about free time activities.
1 When I was a child, I ___.
2 After work / school, I often ___.
3 On weekends, I like to ___.

h Tell other students your sentences in 3g. What free time activities were/are popular ... ?
a when everyone was a child
b after work / school
c on weekends

4 SPEAKING

a Communication 8B Student A go to p. 113. Student B go to p. 111.

67

2 Beyond the classroom

> "There are plenty of opportunities for personalization."
>
> **Elena Pro, Teacher, EOI de San Fernando de Henares, Spain**

Insights

Progress with language learning often requires work outside of the classroom, and different teaching models require different approaches.

Content

American Empower is available with a print workbook, online practice, documentary-style videos that expose learners to real-world English, plus additional resources with extra ideas and fun activities.

Results

This choice of additional resources helps teachers to find the most effective ways to motivate their students both inside and outside the classroom.

Unit overview

Unit Opener

Getting started page – Clear learning objectives to give an immediate sense of purpose.

Lessons A and B

Grammar and Vocabulary – Input and practice of core grammar and vocabulary, plus a mix of skills.

Digital Workbook (online, mobile): Grammar and Vocabulary.

Lesson C

Everyday English – Functional language in common, everyday situations.

Digital Workbook (online, mobile): Listening, Speaking, Reading, and Writing

Unit Progress Test

Review

Extra practice of grammar, vocabulary, and pronunciation. Also a "Review your progress" section for students to reflect on the unit.

Mid- / End-of-course test

Additional practice

Further practice is available for outside of the class with these components.

Digital Workbook (online, mobile)

Workbook (printed)

Components

Resources – Available on cambridgeone.org

- Audio
- Video
- Unit Progress Tests (Print)
- Unit Progress Tests (Online)
- Mid- and end-of-course assessment (Print)
- Mid- and end-of-course assessment (Online)
- Digital Workbook (Online)
- Photocopiable Grammar, Vocabulary, and Pronunciation worksheets

CONTENTS

Contents

Contents

CLASSROOM LANGUAGE

00.02 Listen and read.

CAN DO OBJECTIVES

- Say your name and country
- Talk about people you know
- Meet and greet new people

UNIT 1

HELLO!

GETTING STARTED

a Look at the picture. What country flags do you see?

b What other countries do you know in English?

1A I'M FROM MEXICO

Learn to say your name and country

G *be: I / you / we*

V Countries

1 READING AND GRAMMAR

be: *I / you / we* affirmative and questions

a 01.01 Listen. Then say *Hi, I'm …* or *Hello, I'm …* and say your name.

b 01.02 Read and listen to conversations 1–3. Match the conversations with groups of people a–c in the picture below.

c Complete the sentences in the chart.

I/we	you
I ______ Camila. (= *I am …*) We ______ from Ecuador. (= *we are …*)	______ you from the U.S.? How ______ you?

d Now go to Grammar Focus 1A Part 1 on p. 116.

e Sound and spelling *I'm, we're*

1 01.06 Listen to the sound of *I'm* and *we're*.
   a I am b I'm c we are d we're
2 Practice saying *I'm* and *we're*.

f Practice the conversations in 1b.

1 Work in pairs. Practice Conversation 1.
2 Work in groups of three. Practice Conversation 2.
3 Work with a new partner. Practice Conversation 3.

g Practice the conversations in 1b again. Use your own name.

1
V Hi, I'm Vilma. What's your name?
C I'm Camila.
V Hi, Camila. Nice to meet you.

2
H Hello, I'm Harumi.
K Hi. I'm Katia.
P And I'm Pablo. Hi.
H Are you from the U.S.?
P No, we're from Ecuador.

3
L Hi, Rubén. How are you?
R Hi, Li. I'm fine. How are you?
L Fine, thanks.

2 LISTENING AND GRAMMAR *be: I / you / we* negative

a 01.07 Read and listen to the conversation. Choose the correct answers.

KELLY Are you Rubén?
RUBÉN Yes, I am.
KELLY Hi, I'm Kelly.
RUBÉN Oh, hi. Are you a student here?
KELLY No, I'm not a student. I'm your teacher!
RUBÉN Oh … sorry.

1 Rubén is:
a a student. **b** a teacher.
2 Kelly is:
a a student. **b** a teacher.

b Complete the sentences in the chart.

Affirmative (+)	Negative (–)
I'm a student. (= *I am*) We _____ from England. (= *we are*)	I'm _____ a student. (= *I am not*) We're not from England. (= *we are not*)

c Now go to Grammar Focus 1A Part 2 on p. 116.

d Read the sentences. Make them true for you.

1 I'm a student.
2 We're teachers.
3 I'm from the U.S.
4 I'm Laura.
5 We're from Tokyo.

e Tell a partner your sentences in 2d. Are they the same?

3 VOCABULARY AND READING Countries

a 01.09 Match the countries in the box with maps 1–8. Listen and check.

the United Kingdom / the U.K. China the United States / the U.S. Spain Japan Ecuador Brazil Mexico

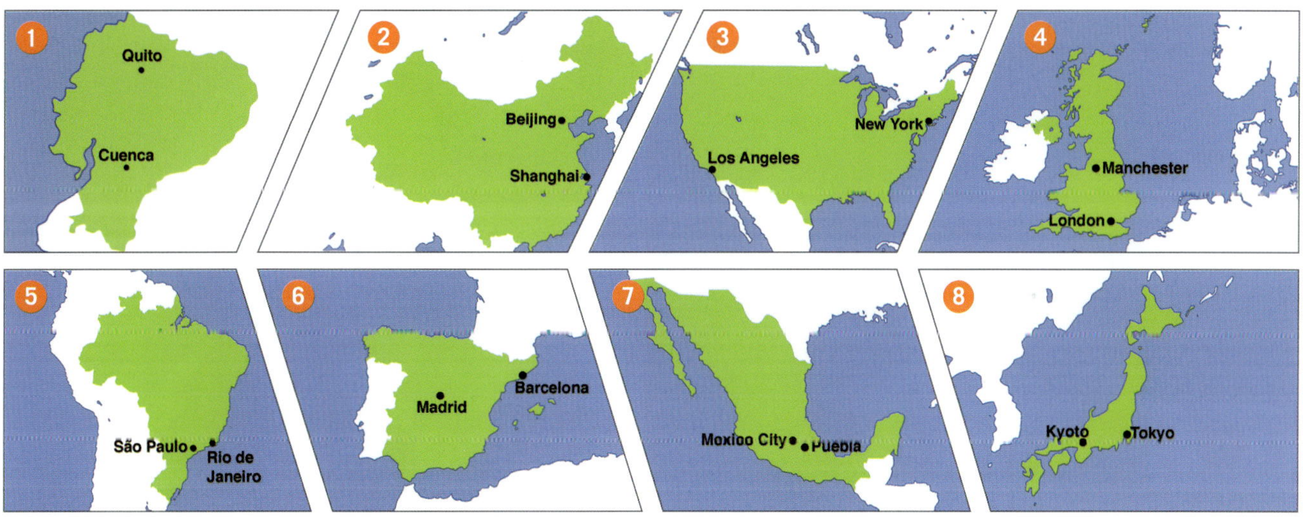

b 01.10 Complete the sentences with the correct country. Listen and check.

OUR GROUP

Vilma 17:02
I'm Vilma. I'm from Rio de Janeiro, in [1]_______.

Pablo 17:02
Hi, I'm Pablo. I'm from [2]_______. I'm from Cuenca.

Camila 17:03
Hello. I'm from Puebla, in [3]_______, and my name's Camila.

Li 17:03
Hi, I'm Li. I'm from Beijing, in [4]_______. But I'm not in Beijing now. I'm a student in Shanghai.

Harumi 17:03
My name's Harumi. I'm from Tokyo, in [5]_______.

Michael 17:03
I'm Michael. I'm from [6]_______. I'm a teacher in London.

Rubén 17:03
I'm from Barcelona, in [7]_______, and my name's Rubén.

Kelly 17:03
Hello. I'm a teacher, and my name's Kelly.
I'm from New York, in [8]_______.

c Now go to Vocabulary Focus 1A on p. 136.

d Choose a city and a country in 3a. Write it on a piece of paper.

Puebla, Mexico

e Give your piece of paper to the teacher and take a new one. Try to find the student with the information on your piece of paper.

Are you from Puebla?
No, I'm not. I'm from Mexico City.

4 SPEAKING

Communication 1A
Student A go to p. 104.
Student B go to p. 106.

1B HE'S ECUADORIAN

Learn to talk about people you know

G *be: he / she / they*

V Nationalities

1 VOCABULARY Nationalities

a Do you know the people in pictures a–h? Ask your partner.

Do you know Serena and Venus Williams?

b Match the nationalities with pictures a–h.

A|mer|i|can   Chi|nese   Mex|i|can   Ec|ua|do|ri|an
Span|ish   Brit|ish   Jap|a|nese   Bra|zil|ian

c 01.12 **Pronunciation** Listen to the words in 1b. How many syllables are in each word?
A|mer|i|can = 4 syllables

d 01.13 Listen and notice the stressed syllable.

e 01.12 Listen to the words in 1b again. Underline the stressed syllables. Then listen and repeat.

f Now go to Vocabulary Focus 1B on p. 136.

a Ricky Rubio – basketball player

b Shohei Ohtani – baseball player

c Serena and Venus Williams – tennis players

d Antonio Valencia – soccer player

e Neymar - soccer player

f Heather Watson – tennis player

g Zhu Ting – volleyball player

h Javier Hernández and Guillermo Ochoa – soccer players

2 GRAMMAR *be*: *he* / *she* / *they* affirmative

a 01.15 Match 1–3 with a–c. Listen and check.

1 Heather Watson is a tennis player.
2 Shohei Ohtani is a baseball player.
3 Serena and Venus Williams are tennis players.

a He's Japanese.
b They're American.
c She's British.

b Complete the chart.

+	
she is …	she's …
he is …	[1] ______ …
they are …	[2] ______ …

c Now go to Grammar Focus 1B Part 1 on p. 116.

d Write two sentences about the people below.

1 Ricky Rubio
2 Zhu Ting
3 Javier Hernández and Guillermo Ochoa

e Tell a partner your sentences in 2d. Are they the same?

3 LISTENING

a 01.17 Look at the photo below. Read and listen to Mia talk about the people on her vacation. Complete 1–6 with the words in the box.

American Luis Lucía Colombian Mexican Anna

MIA This is [1] ______. She's my friend from Chicago. She's [2] ______.
NOAH OK. And who's this?
MIA This is [3] ______. He's a teacher in Brazil.
NOAH Is he Brazilian?
MIA No, he's not Brazilian. He's [4] ______.
NOAH Oh, really.
MIA And these are my friends [5] ______ and Mateo. They're married.
NOAH Are they American?
MIA No, they're not American. They're [6] ______ – from Veracruz.

b Tell a partner about two of your friends. What nationality are they?

4 GRAMMAR *be*: *he* / *she* / *they* negative and questions

a Complete the charts with the words in the box.

they 's not is are 're not she

+	–
She's Spanish.	She ______ Spanish.
They're Chinese.	They ______ Chinese.

?
______ ______ Spanish?
______ ______ Chinese?

b Now go to Grammar Focus 1B Part 2 on p. 116.

c 01.21 Complete the sentences. Listen and check.

1 **A** ______ he Mexican?
B No, ______ ______.
2 **A** ______ they American?
B Yes, ______ ______.
3 **A** ______ she Chinese?
B No, ______ ______.
4 **A** ______ they Brazilian?
B No, ______ ______.
5 **A** ______ he British?
B Yes, ______ ______.

d Practice saying 1–5 in 4c with a partner.

Language Plus *this / these*

***This is** Anna.*
this = one person

***These are** my friends Lucía and Mateo.*
these = two or more people

5 SPEAKING

Communication 1B Student A go to p. 104. Student B go to p. 106.

1C EVERYDAY ENGLISH
Nice to meet you

Learn to meet and greet new people

P Intonation

W A personal profile

1 LISTENING

a Look at picture a. Is she in an office?

b 01.22 Listen to Part 1 and check your answer in 1a.

c 01.22 Listen to Part 1 again. Complete the sentences with words in the box.

Hi   Good morning

RECEPTIONIST ______, welcome to Blue Web Technology.
SOPHIA ______, my name's Sophia Taylor. It's my first day.

2 USEFUL LANGUAGE Greeting people

a Complete 1–3 with the words in the box.

evening   morning   afternoon

7 a.m.–12 p.m. = [1]______
12 p.m.–5 p.m. = [2]______
5 p.m.–10 p.m. = [3]______

b 01.23 **Pronunciation** Listen. How many syllables are in the words and expressions?

hi (1)   good | mor | ning   good | eve | ning
hel | lo   good | af | ter | noon

c 01.23 Listen to the words and expressions in 2b again. Underline the stressed syllables.

hel<u>lo</u>

d Look at the times with a partner. Use the correct expression.

1 8 p.m.   3 11 a.m.   5 6 a.m.
2 3 p.m.   4 10 p.m.   6 1 p.m.

Good morning.

Good afternoon.

3 LISTENING AND USEFUL LANGUAGE
Meeting new people 1

a 01.24 Listen to Part 2. Sophia meets the manager of Blue Web Technology. What's his name?

☐ Daniel   ☐ Darren   ☐ David

b 01.25 Listen to the sentences. Underline the words you hear. Are both options in 1–2 possible?

1 *I'm / My name's* Sophia Taylor.
2 *I'm / My name's* David.

c 01.26 **Pronunciation** Listen and notice the stressed words.

A How are <u>you</u>?
B I'm <u>good</u>, thank you. And <u>you</u>?
A I'm <u>fine</u>, thanks.

d Practice the conversation in 3c with a partner.

e 01.27 Listen to the expressions. Complete them with the words in the box.

not bad   I'm   morning   thank you

1 **A** How are you?
B I'm fine, [1]______ ______.

2 **A** Hi! How are you?
B Oh, [2]______ ______, thanks.

3 **A** My name's Jack.
B [3]______ Chloe.

4 **A** Good [4]______. How are you?
B I'm OK, thank you.

f Practice the conversations in 3e with a partner.

4 LISTENING AND USEFUL LANGUAGE Meeting new people 2

a 01.28 Listen to Part 3. Are Sophia and Isaac friends?

b 01.28 Listen to Part 3 again. Underline the correct answer.

1 **ISAAC** Nice to *meet* / *see* you too, Sophia.
2 **DAVID** So, this is your *home* / *office*.
3 **ISAAC** OK. So, ... this is your *desk* / *chair*.

c 01.29 Put the conversation in the correct order. Listen and check.

☐ **ISAAC** Nice to meet you, too, Sophia.
☐ **SOPHIA** Nice to meet you, Isaac.
☐ **DAVID** This is Isaac Jackson.

d Work in groups of three. Practice the conversation in 4c. Use your names.

This is Hassan.

Nice to meet you, Hassan.

5 PRONUNCIATION Intonation

a 01.30 Listen to phrases 1–5. Does the intonation change or stay the same →?

1 Hello.
2 How are you?
3 I'm good.
4 Nice to meet you.
5 Thank you.

b 01.30 Listen to the phrases in 5a again and repeat.

6 SPEAKING

a 01.31 Complete the conversation. Listen and check.

MICHELLE Hi.
LEE Good afternoon.
JORGE Hello.
MICHELLE I'm Michelle, and this [1]______ Lee.
JORGE Nice to meet you. I'm Jorge.
LEE Nice to [2]______ you, too. How are you?
JORGE I'm good. And [3]______ ?
LEE I'm good.
MICHELLE I'm [4]______, too.

b Work in groups of three. Practice the conversation in 6a. Use your names.

7 WRITING

a Read Sophia's profile. What information about her is new?

b Now go to Writing Plus 1C on p. 158 for Capital letters and periods.

c Write a profile about you and your English class. Here are some ideas:

Hi/Hello, my ...
I'm from ... in ...
I'm in a class with ... in room ...

d Read other students' profiles. Is everyone from the same place?

UNIT PROGRESS TEST

→ **CHECK YOUR PROGRESS**

YOU CAN NOW DO THE UNIT PROGRESS TEST.

UNIT 1
Review

1 GRAMMAR

a Underline the correct answer.

1 Hello. I *'m* / *are* Anna.
2 "Are you students?" "Yes, *we're* / *we are*."
3 You *am not* / *'re not* a teacher.
4 "*Am I* / *I am* right?" "Yes, you are."
5 Where *are you* / *you are*?
6 We *'re* / *am* at home.

b Add *is*, *'s not*, *are*, or *'re not*.

1 "Is your name Sandy?" "No, it ________."
2 "Are Javier Hernández and Guillermo Ochoa from Mexico?" "Yes, they ________."
3 "Is Ricky Rubio Spanish?" "Yes, he ________."
4 "________ New York and Washington in the U.S.?" "Yes, they are."
5 "Are your friends soccer players?" "No, they ________."
6 "________ your teacher English?" "No, she ________."

c Ask and answer the questions in 1b.

d Correct the sentences.

> They's Spanish.
They're Spanish.

1 No, he 're not from China.
2 You are OK?
3 Yes, I'm.
4 She is Colombian?
5 I not am Brazilian.
6 They are from the U.S.?

2 VOCABULARY

a Write the names of the countries.

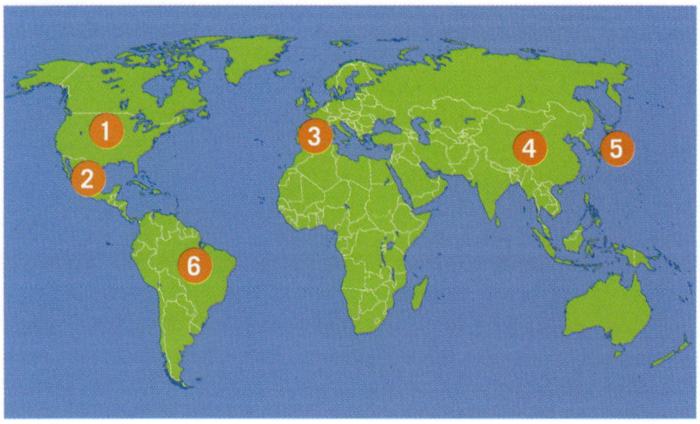

1 e n d i U t s S a t t e ________
2 e i x M c o ________
3 i p S a n ________
4 h i C a n ________
5 a n a J p ________
6 l a r B i z ________

b Complete the nationalities.

> Spa nish ________

1 Canad________

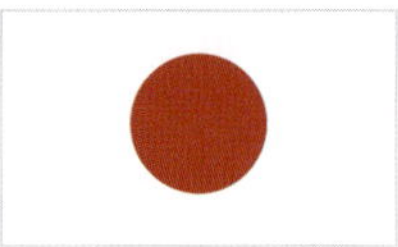

4 Jap________

2 Brazil________

5 Brit________

3 Amer________

6 Ital________

3 SOUND AND SPELLING

a Write the short forms in the chart.

Full forms	Short forms
I am	I'm
They are	They're
She is	______
We are	______
It is	______
I am not	______ not
He is not	He ______

b 01.32 Listen and practice saying the short forms.

c 01.33 Listen to these phrases. Underline the stressed word or syllable.

1 Good morning.
2 How are you?
3 They're American.
4 We're teachers.
5 Nice to meet you.

d 01.33 Listen again to check. Practice saying the sentences.

REVIEW YOUR PROGRESS

How well did you do in this unit? Write 3, 2, or 1 for each objective.
3 = very well 2 = well 1 = not so well

I CAN ...	
say my name and country	☐
talk about people I know	☐
meet and greet new people	☐

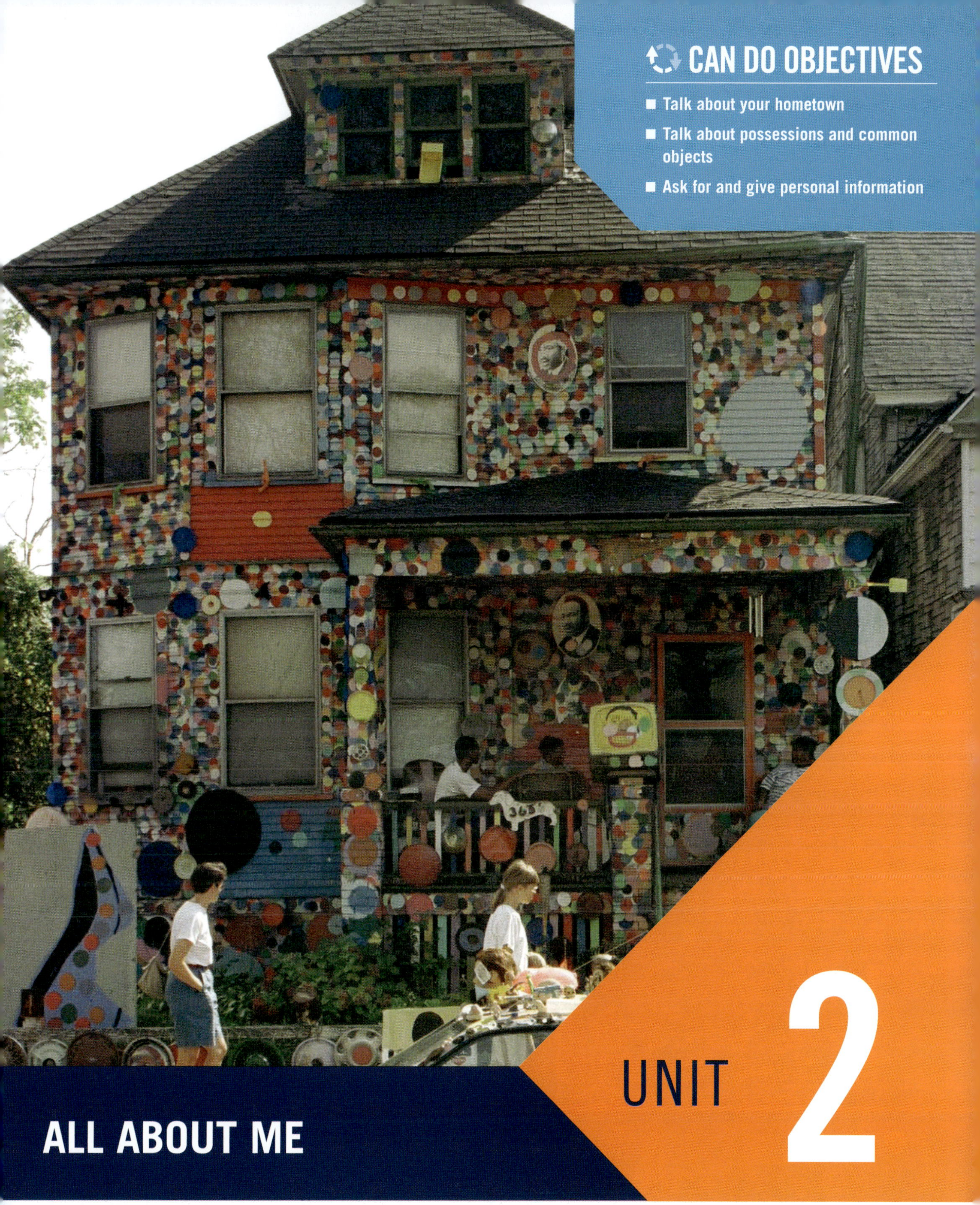

CAN DO OBJECTIVES

- Talk about your hometown
- Talk about possessions and common objects
- Ask for and give personal information

UNIT 2

ALL ABOUT ME

GETTING STARTED

a Look at the picture and answer the questions.

1. Is it a ... ?
   - hot country
   - big city
   - new house
2. What country do you think it is?
3. Count (1, 2, 3, ...):
   - the windows on the house
   - the people in the picture

b What colors do you see on the house?

2A IT'S A BIG CITY

Learn to talk about your hometown

G *be: it's / it's not*; Possessive adjectives

V Common adjectives

1 LISTENING

a 02.01 Match the words in the box with pictures a–b. Listen and check.

town city

Which are you from?

b 02.02 Listen and match pictures a–b with the names in the box.

Rocío Carlo

c 02.02 Listen again. Complete the sentences with the words in the box.

is it it's it's not

Conversation 1

A Is [1]______ a big city?

B No, no. [2]______ a city.

Conversation 2

A [3]______ it a city?

B Yes, it is. ______[4] a big city.

2 GRAMMAR *be: it's / it's not*

a Complete the chart with *it* or *it's*.

+	Ravello is in Italy.	______ in Italy.
–	Ravello's not in Mexico.	______ not in Mexico.
?	Is Ravello in Italy?	Is ______ in Italy?

b Complete the sentences with *he's*, *she's*, or *it's*.

1 Giovanna's from Ravello in Italy. ______ a town near Naples.
2 Aaron's from Blue Bell, Pennsylvania. ______ American.
3 Ricardo's Spanish. ______ from Madrid.
4 Akira's from Sōka in Japan. ______ a city near Tokyo.
5 Vanessa's from Zapopan in Mexico. ______ a big city near Guadalajara.

c 02.03 Listen and check.

d Now go to Grammar Focus 2A Part 1 on p. 118.

Language Plus *in / near*

*Naples is **in** Italy.*

*Ravello is **near** Naples.*

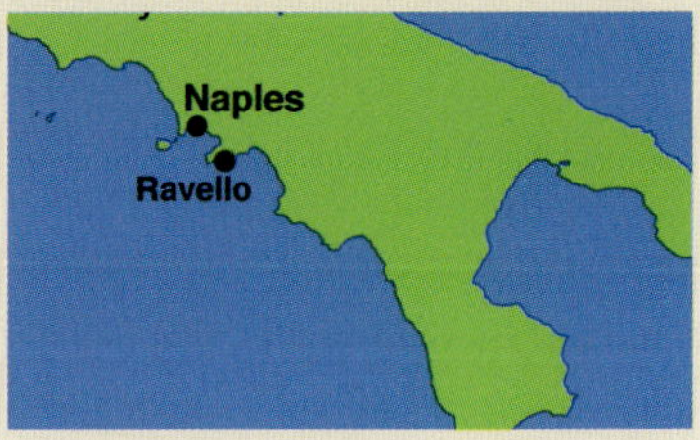

e Write sentences about you.

I'm from … It's a (town / city) (in / near) …

f Tell a partner your sentences.

3 READING AND VOCABULARY
Common adjectives

a 02.06 Read and listen to *Our Homes*. Complete the chart.

	home		home
Rocío	big apartment	Miguel	
Carlo		Pietro and Susanna	
Aaron		Sophia	

b Sound and spelling /h/ and /w/

1 02.07 Listen to the words. Which words have a /h/ sound? Which words have a /w/ sound?

home hi who what how hotel where

2 Practice saying the words.

c 02.08 Complete the sentences with the words in the box. Listen and check.

big small old new

1 It's a ______ house.

2 It's a ______ apartment.

3 It's a ______ city.

4 It's an ______ house.

d Now go to Vocabulary Focus 2A on p. 137.

Our Homes

My apartment is in a new part of Quito. It's very big. My friend Miguel is from Otavalo. It's a beautiful town near Quito. This is his home – it's a small house. **Rocío**

My apartment in Ravello is big, old, and beautiful. My friends Pietro and Susanna are from Naples. This is their home. It's a big apartment in a nice part of town. **Carlo**

My home is a small house in Blue Bell. It's an old town. My friend Sophia is from Philadelphia. This is her home. It's a small apartment, and it's new and beautiful. **Aaron**

4 GRAMMAR
Possessive adjectives

a Read *Our Homes* again. Complete the chart.

Pronoun	Possessive adjective
I	______
you	your
he	______
she	her
we	our
they	______

b Complete the sentences.

1 Javier is from Barcelona. ______ home is in a nice part of the city.
2 Are you from Berlin? Where's ______ apartment?
3 We're from Bogotá. ______ home is near a big hotel.
4 Sarah is from England. ______ town is near Hastings.
5 Pedro and Eva are from Mexico City. ______ apartment is very big.

c Now go to Grammar Focus 2A Part 2 on p. 118.

d Complete the sentences about a friend.

My friend ______ is from ______. His / Her home is ______.

e Tell a partner about your friend's home.

5 SPEAKING

Communication 2A

Student A go to p. 104.
Student B go to p. 106.
Student C go to p. 108.

2B DO YOU HAVE A PHONE?

Learn to talk about possessions and common objects

G Plural nouns; *have*

V Common objects 1; Numbers 1

1 VOCABULARY Common objects 1

a 02.11 Match 1–10 in picture a with the words in the box. Listen and check.

a computer a newspaper a knife a phone a key a watch an umbrella a ticket a book a bottle of water

b Two objects in 1a are not OK at an airport. What are they?

Language Plus *a* / *an*

We use *a* before most nouns.	• *a key*	• *a book*
We use *an* before *a, e, i, o, u*.	• *an **a**pple*	• *an **u**mbrella*

c Cover the words in the box in 1a. Ask a partner questions about the objects in the picture.

What's this?

It's a watch.

d Now go to Vocabulary Focus 2B Common objects 1 on p. 138.

2 LISTENING AND GRAMMAR Plural nouns

a 02.13 Listen to the conversation with an airport customs official. Check (✓) the words you hear.

- ☐ books
- ☐ computers
- ☐ phones
- ☐ watches
- ☐ umbrellas
- ☐ bottles
- ☐ newspapers
- ☐ knives

b Complete the chart.

Singular (= 1)	Plural (= 2+)
a key	keys
a newspaper	______
a watch	______
a knife	______

c Most nouns add *-s* in the plural. How are the plurals of *watch* and *knife* different?

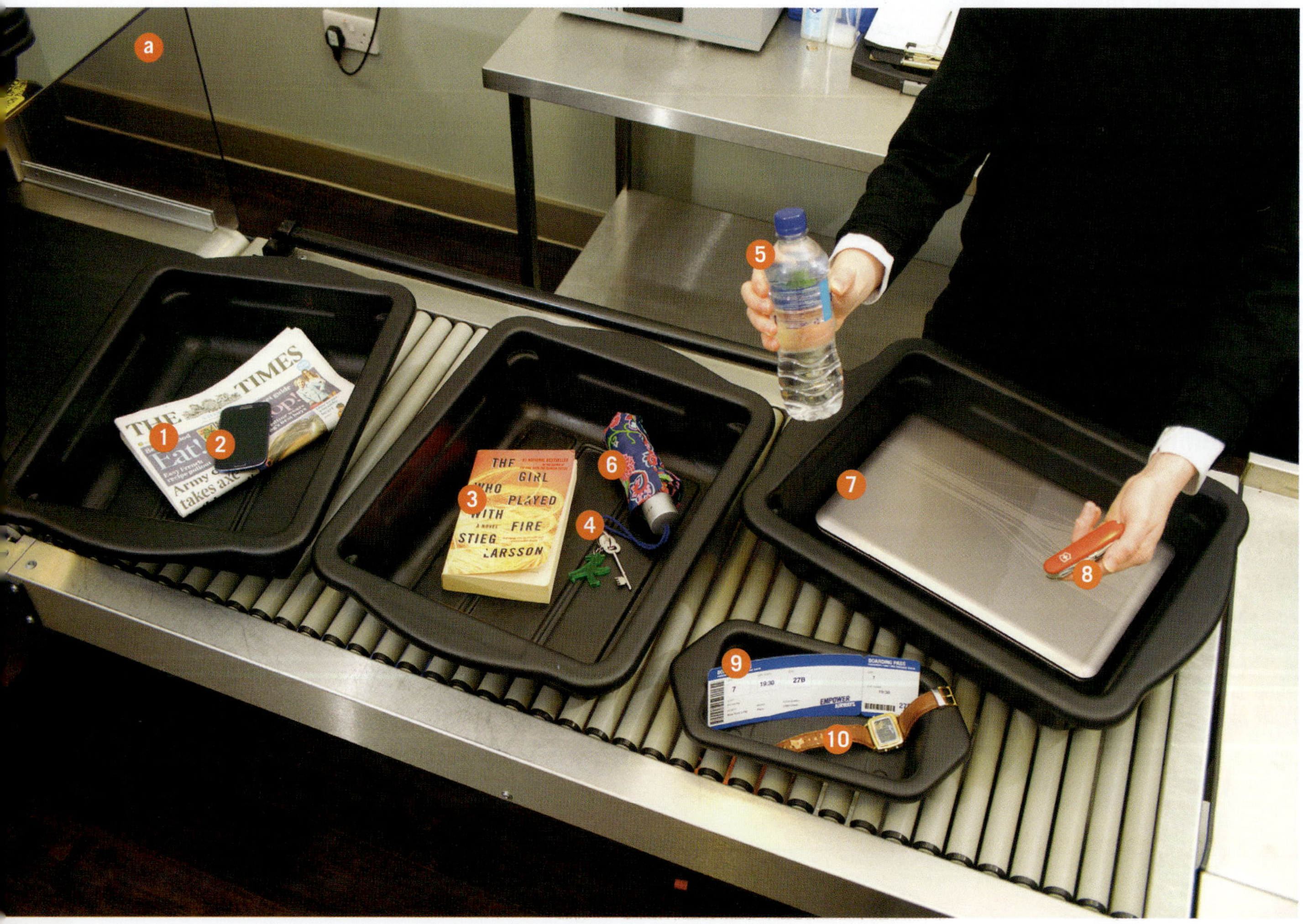

d **Sound and spelling** /s/, /z/, and /ɪz/

1 **02.14** Listen and practice these sounds. Which word has an extra syllable in the plural?
1 /s/ book**s** 2 /z/ key**s** 3 /ɪz/ watch**es**

2 **02.15** Listen to these words. Which word has an extra syllable in the plural? Listen again and repeat.

knives bottles tickets apples houses phones

e Work in pairs.

Student A: Say a singular word.
Student B: Say the plural.

Then switch roles.

f Now go to Grammar Focus 2B on p. 118.

3 GRAMMAR *I have / you have*

a **02.16** Look at the X-ray picture and complete the conversation. Listen and check.

A What's in your bag?
B Mm, I have a [1]b______, and my [2]k______s, and an [3]u______.
A Do you have a [4]p______?
B Yes. Oh, and a [5]b______of w______. Sorry!

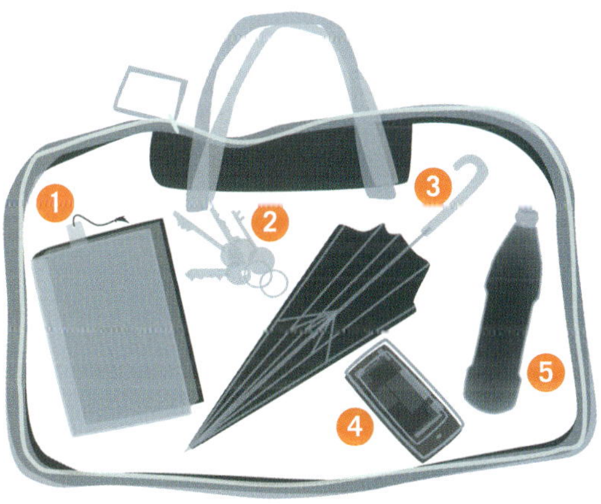

b **02.17** Listen to the forms of *have*.

+	?
I **have** a book.	**Do** you **have** a book?

c **02.17** **Pronunciation** Listen again. Practice saying the sentences.

d Ask a partner about objects 1–5 in 3a. Ask about:

1 here (in class)
2 at home

Do you have an umbrella here?
No.
Do you have an umbrella at home?
Yes.

4 VOCABULARY Numbers 1

a **02.18** Listen and repeat the numbers.

b Match the words in the box with numbers 1–12 in 4a.

seven two nine four eight eleven
three six one ten twelve five

c Work in pairs.

Student A: Say a number.
Student B: Say the next number.

Then switch roles.

d **Communication 2B** Student A go to p. 104. Student B go to p. 106.

e Now go to Vocabulary Focus 2B Numbers 1 on p. 141.

5 SPEAKING

a Write three things you have in your bag.

a bottle of water

an apple

a computer

b Guess what is in your partner's bag.

Do you have a phone?
Yes.
Do you have a knife?
No!

2C EVERYDAY ENGLISH

What's your address?

Learn to ask for and give personal information

- **p** Intonation in questions
- **w** A form

1 LISTENING

a Think about a good home for you. Check (✓) four boxes.

1 ☐ a house
☐ an apartment
2 ☐ in a small town
☐ in a city
3 ☐ big
☐ small
4 ☐ near a park
☐ near stores

b Tell a partner about your home in 1a.

A good home for me is …

c 02.21 Listen to Part 1. Answer the questions.

1 Who asks questions, Juan or the woman?
2 What kind of home does Juan need, an apartment or a house?

d 02.21 Listen to Part 1 again. Check (✓) the correct answer.

1 Juan's last name:
a ☐ Hays b ☐ Hayes
2 His address in Seattle:
a ☐ 55 Park Street b ☐ 5 Park Street
3 His phone number:
a ☐ 760 264 7893 b ☐ 760 264 7389

2 USEFUL LANGUAGE Asking for and giving personal information

a 02.22 Underline the correct answer. Listen and check.

1 A What's your last name?
B *It's / I'm* Robinson.
2 A What's your address?
B *It's / It's on* 7 King Street.
3 A What's your phone number?
B *They're / It's* 421 505 2738.
4 A What's your email address?
B *He's / It's* chrisrobinson@travelmail.com.

b 02.23 Listen to the answers to questions 3 and 4 in 2a again. Check (✓) the correct answer.

1 a ☐ four-two-one-five-oh-five-two-seven-three-eight
b ☐ four-two-fifteen-oh-five-two-seven-three-eight
2 a ☐ chris-robinson-from-travelmail-point-com
b ☐ chris-robinson-at-travelmail-dot-com

c 02.24 Underline the correct word. Listen and check your answer.

AGENT Juan Hayes. *What / How* do you spell that?
JUAN J-U-A-N.

d 02.25 **Pronunciation** Listen to the questions. Notice the stressed part in each question.

1 How do you spell that?
2 Can you spell that?
3 Sorry, what's the spelling?

02.25 Listen again and repeat.

e Now go to Writing Plus 2C Part 1 on p. 158 for The alphabet.

f Ask a partner his/her last name. Then ask how to spell it.

g **Communication 2C** Student A go to p. 105. Student B go to p. 108.

3 LISTENING

a 02.27 Listen to Part 2. What does Juan think? Check (✓) the correct sentence.

1 ☐ The apartment's really nice.
2 ☐ The apartment's not very nice.

b 02.27 Listen to Part 2 again. Check (✓) the correct information about the apartment.

1 ☐ small ☐ big
2 ☐ good for one person ☐ good for two people
3 ☐ near a supermarket ☐ near a park

4 PRONUNCIATION Intonation in questions

a 02.28 Listen to the questions. Does the intonation go up ↗ or down ↘ at the end?

1 What's your last name?
2 What's your phone number?

b 02.28 Listen again and repeat the questions.

c 02.29 Practice asking the questions with a partner. Then listen and check the intonation.

1 What's your address?
2 Where are you from?
3 What's the spelling?

5 SPEAKING

a Talk to different students. Ask about:

- names (first name and last name)
- phone number
- address
- email address

Write down the information. Ask about the spelling.

What's your last name?

It's Mishkin.

Can you spell that, please?

M-I-S-H-K-I-N.

6 WRITING

a Read about Juan. What's the new information?

Local Rentals: Customer Information

First name:	Juan
Last name:	Hayes
Address:	55 Park Street
Phone number:	760 264 7893
Email:	juanh@travelmail.com

b Now go to Writing Plus 2C Part 2 on p. 158 for Spelling.

c Complete the form with your information.

Local Rentals: Customer Information

First name:	
Last name:	
Address:	
Phone number:	
Email:	

UNIT PROGRESS TEST

CHECK YOUR PROGRESS

YOU CAN NOW DO THE UNIT PROGRESS TEST.

UNIT 2
Review

1 GRAMMAR

a Correct the underlined word.

> It's big houses. *They're*
1 This is Katia, and this is she house.
2 "Excuse me! Is this you bag?" "Yes, it is! Thank you."
3 Hiro's from Sōka. She's a city in Japan.
4 It not a big apartment.
5 They live in Madrid. This is they home.
6 "Hi, we're from New York. We city is big!"

b Complete the sentences with the plural form of the nouns in parentheses.

1 They're my __________. (key)
2 Are they your __________? (knife)
3 I have two __________. (watch)
4 Are they your __________? (bottle of water)
5 San Francisco and Seattle are __________ in the U.S. (city)
6 Where are the __________? (book)

c Complete the sentences with the words in the box.

are his is they
they're it's it's not

1 I'm from Ravello. __________ a town in Italy.
2 The men __________ at home.
3 "Are they big houses?" "Yes, __________ are."
4 __________ my books.
5 __________ it a city?
6 This is John and this is __________ apartment.
7 "Is Madrid in Italy?" "No, __________."

2 VOCABULARY

a Match 1–6 with the opposite adjectives in the box.

boring difficult good
happy old ~~small~~ wrong

> big *small*
1 easy __________
2 bad __________
3 right __________
4 sad __________
5 interesting __________
6 new __________

b Complete the crossword with the objects in pictures 1–8.

3 SOUND AND SPELLING

a 02.31 Look at the words in the box. Is the final sound /s/, /z/, or /ɪz/? Complete the chart. Practice saying the words.

~~phones~~ watches keys addresses houses
apartments umbrellas tickets books computers

/s/	/z/	/ɪz/
	phones	

b 02.32 Check (✓) the words with a /h/ sound. Practice saying the words.

☐ hello ☐ is ☐ how ☐ watch
☐ her ☐ home ☐ who ☐ happy
☐ our ☐ house ☐ she ☐ right
☐ his ☐ where ☐ phone

REVIEW YOUR PROGRESS

How well did you do in this unit? Write 3, 2, or 1 for each objective.
3 = very well 2 = well 1 = not so well

I CAN ...	
talk about my hometown	☐
talk about possessions and common objects	☐
ask for and give personal information	☐

CAN DO OBJECTIVES

- Say what you eat and drink
- Talk about food and meals
- Order and pay in a café

UNIT 3

FOOD AND DRINK

GETTING STARTED

a Look at the picture and answer the questions.

1 What food can you see in the shopping cart?
2 Which food in the shopping cart do you like?
3 Which food in the shopping cart don't you like?
4 What food do you buy?

b What other food do you know in English?

3A DO YOU LIKE FISH?

Learn to say what you eat and drink

G Simple present: *I / you / we / they*

V Food 1

1 VOCABULARY Food 1

a 03.01 Match pictures 1–7 with the words in the box. Then listen and check.

fruit rice meat bread vegetables eggs fish

1 

2 

3 

4 

5 

6 

7 

b 03.01 **Pronunciation** Listen to the words in 1a again. Which word has more than one syllable? Underline the stressed syllable.

c Say two things you like ☺.

I like fruit, and I like fish.

d **Sound and spelling** /i/, /ɪ/, and /aɪ/

1 03.02 Listen and practice these sounds.
1 /i/ m**ea**t 2 /ɪ/ f**i**sh 3 /aɪ/ **I**'m

2 03.03 Look at the words in the box. What sounds do the letters in **bold** have? Listen and add the words to the sound groups below.

b**i**g **ea**t n**i**ne s**i**ster **i**t's m**e** m**i**lk
Ch**i**na f**i**ve h**i**s t**ea**cher h**i** ch**ee**se

Sound 1 /i/	Sound 2 /ɪ/	Sound 3 /aɪ/
meat	fish	I'm

3 Practice saying the words.

e Now go to Vocabulary Focus 3A on p. 139.

2 READING AND GRAMMAR
Simple present: *I / you / we / they* affirmative and negative

a Which words in 1a can you see in pictures 1–3? Which word isn't in the pictures?

b 03.06 Read and listen to texts a–c. Match them with the families in pictures 1–3.

FOOD
FOR ONE WEEK

a They eat a lot of fruit and vegetables every day. And they eat meat with rice. They like eggs, but they don't eat bread or fish. They don't like fish. They drink a lot of water.

b They eat meat and eggs every day, but they don't eat fish. And they don't eat vegetables, but they eat fruit. They really like bread.

c They eat a lot of rice and vegetables. They like fruit, and they eat bread. They don't eat fish or meat. They are vegetarians.

1 ☐

Tang family, China

c Complete the chart.

+			–		
I We They	eat like	meat. fish.	I We They	________ eat ________ like	meat. fish.

d <u>Underline</u> the correct words.

1 The Tangs *eat* / *don't eat* fish.
2 The Delgados *eat* / *don't eat* bread.
3 The Donatis *like* / *don't like* meat.
4 The Tangs *eat* / *don't eat* a lot of eggs.
5 The Donatis *like* / *don't like* vegetables.

e Which family's food would you like to have for a week? Why?

2 ☐

Donati family, Italy

3 ☐

Delgado family, Guatemala

3 LISTENING AND GRAMMAR Simple present: *I / you / we / they* questions

a 03.07 Listen to a conversation with Rajit. Check (✓) the different food he eats.

- [x] bread
- [ ] vegetables
- [ ] meat
- [ ] fish
- [ ] rice
- [ ] fruit

Rajit

b 03.07 Listen again. Complete the conversation.

A Rajit, what do you eat in a week?
B Oh, a lot of things. I eat rice every day, and bread. I eat a lot of fruit. I eat fish …
A [1]________ you eat meat?
B No, I don't like meat.
A Do you [2]________ vegetables?
B Oh yes, I like vegetables. I eat a lot of vegetables.
A Do you [3]________ them every day?
B Yes. They're very good for me.

c 03.08 Complete the questions in the chart. Then listen and check.

+	–	?
I eat fish. We like fruit.	I don't eat fish. We don't like fruit.	____ you ____ fish? ____ you ____ fruit?

d Now go to Grammar Focus 3A on p. 118.

e Practice the conversation in 3b with a partner.

4 SPEAKING

a Ask and answer questions with a partner. Complete the chart with their answers.

Do you eat meat?
Yes, (I do).
Do you eat bread every day?
No, not every day.
Do you like fish?
No, I don't like fish.

	yes / no?	every day?	like?
meat			
fish			
rice			
bread			
vegetables			
fruit			
eggs			

b Write three words for drinks. Then ask your partner questions.

Do you drink soda?
Do you like milk?

3B I USUALLY HAVE DINNER EARLY

Learn to talk about food and meals

G Adverbs of frequency

V Food 2; Time

1 READING

a Check (✓) the boxes about your breakfast.

For my breakfast, I have ...

	YES	NO		YES	NO
coffee			tea		
bread			fruit		
ice cream			fish		
cold pizza			nothing		

b Talk about your answers in 1a with a partner.

> I have coffee – I don't have ice cream.

c Look at the pictures. What's the number one breakfast in the U.S.? Make a guess below.

☐ fruit

☐ cereal

☐ toast

☐ eggs

d Read the text and find the answer to 1c.

THE NUMBER ONE BREAKFAST

In the U.S., people like different food for breakfast. They sometimes eat cereal with cold milk, but eggs are the number one breakfast food. They also like fruit with toast and bacon or sausage.

e What's the number one breakfast food in your country? What's the number one drink?

> I think ______ is the number one breakfast food in my country.

2 VOCABULARY Food 2; Time

a Match sentences 1–3 with pictures a–c.

1 I have lunch at *twelve* / *one* o'clock.
2 They have dinner at *six* / *seven* o'clock.
3 In my family, we have breakfast at *seven* / *eight* o'clock.

a in the morning

b in the afternoon

c in the evening

b Now go to Vocabulary Focus 3B Food 2 on p. 140.

c 03.13 Listen to sentences 1–3 in 2a. Underline the correct words.

d 03.14 Match the clocks with the times. Listen and check.

☐ (a) quarter after four
☐ four o'clock
☐ (a) quarter to five
☐ four thirty

e Point to a clock in 2d for a partner to say the time.

f Now go to Vocabulary Focus 3B Time on p. 141.

g **Sound and spelling** /æ/ and /ɔ/

1 03.16 Listen and practice these sounds.
1 /æ/ **a**fter f**a**mily 2 /ɔ/ f**our** qu**ar**ter

2 03.17 Look at the words in the box. What sounds do the letters in **bold** have? Listen and add the words to the sound groups below.

cl**a**ss **a**ll **a**pple **a**fternoon w**a**ter **o**range

Sound 1 /æ/	Sound 2 /ɔ/
after	four

3 Practice saying the words.

h **Communication 3B** Student A go to p. 105. Student B go to p. 107.

3 LISTENING

a 03.18 Listen to three people talk about dinner. Match 1–3 with a country in the box.

Ecuador Spain the U.S. Brazil Mexico China

b 03.18 Listen again. Complete the chart.

Name	Dinner time	Food
Julie		
Lucas		
Monica		

c Do you like the same food as Julie, Lucas, and Monica?

4 GRAMMAR Adverbs of frequency

a 03.19 Listen and complete the sentences with the words in the box.

always usually sometimes never

1 **JULIE** We ________ have dinner early.
2 **LUCAS** I ________ have fish for dinner.
3 **MONICA** People ________ have dinner early in Spain.
4 **MONICA** I ________ have bread and cheese.

b Complete 2 and 4 with words in the box in 4a.

1 always (100%)
2 ________ (80%)
3 sometimes (50%)
4 ________ (0%)

c Now go to Grammar Focus 3B on p. 120.

d Put the words in parentheses in the correct place in the sentences.

1 I have breakfast at 9:00 on the weekends. (sometimes)
2 I have a sandwich for lunch. (usually)
3 I have breakfast. (never)
4 In the evening, I have dinner at about 7:00. (always)

e Which sentences in 4d are true for you?

Language Plus *What time ... ? / When ... ?*

What time *do you have dinner?* = ***When*** *do you have dinner?*

5 SPEAKING

a Answer questions 1–4. Write another question with your own idea.

1 In the morning, do you eat breakfast?
2 In the evening, do you eat a big dinner?
3 What time do you have lunch?
4 What do you eat for lunch?

b Ask and answer the questions in 5a with other students. Who has the same answers as you?

Jaime and I never eat breakfast.

3C EVERYDAY ENGLISH
I'd like a large coffee, please

Learn to order and pay in a café

P Stressed and unstressed words

W A text message

1 LISTENING

a What food and drinks on the menu do you like? Tell a partner.

b 03.21 **Pronunciation** Listen. This word has two syllables:

cof|fee

03.22 Which words have two syllables? Listen and check.

sandwich banana orange vegetable

c 03.22 Listen to the words in 1b again. Underline the stressed syllable.

coffee

d Practice saying the words in 1b with a partner.

e Find 1–3 in pictures a–c.

1 a piece of chocolate cake 2 a watch 3 money

f 03.23 Listen. Put pictures a–c in the correct order.

g 03.23 Listen again. Are the sentences true or false?

1 Tracy has a new watch.
2 They order two large coffees.
3 Tracy likes her watch.
4 Hannah never has coffee at lunch.

2 PRONUNCIATION Stressed and unstressed words

a 03.24 Listen to 1–4. Is the pronunciation of *of* the same?

1 of
2 a piece of cake
3 a bottle of water
4 a slice of pizza

b 03.25 Listen to these phrases. Which word isn't stressed?

a large coffee a large tea a small orange juice

c Practice saying the phrases in 2b.

d Work in pairs. Practice more phrases with *a large* / *a small* / *a piece of* … . Use the menu in 1a or your own ideas.

a ☐

b ☐

c ☐

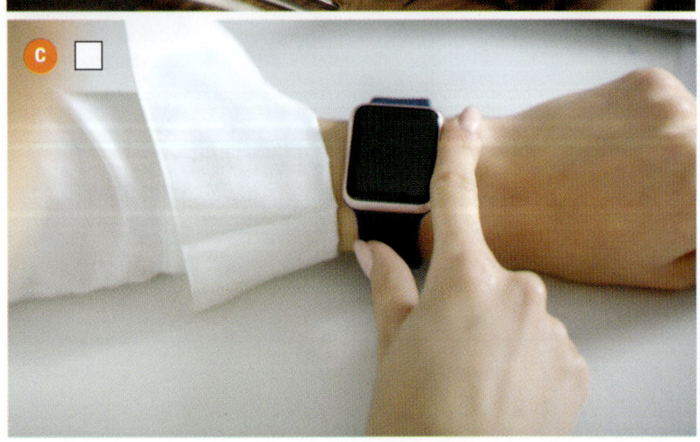

3 USEFUL LANGUAGE Ordering and paying in a café

a 03.26 Listen and complete the sentences.

1 **HANNAH** I'd ________ a large coffee, please.
2 **TRACY** Can we ________ two pieces of chocolate cake, please?

03.26 Listen again and repeat.

b 03.27 Put the words in the correct order. Listen and check.

1 have / I / a small / can / coffee, / please ?
2 please / a vegetable sandwich, / I'd like .
3 two / can / have / we / banana cake / pieces of ?

c Practice saying the sentences in 3b with a partner.

d 03.28 Put the conversation in the correct order. Listen and check.

- [ ] A slice of cheese pizza, please.
- [ ] Of course. That's five dollars, please.
- [ ] Sure. And to eat?
- [ ] Here you go.
- [ ] Can I have a bottle of water, please?
- [ ] Thank you.

e Practice the conversation in 3d with a partner. Change the drink, food, and price.

Can I have a small orange juice, please?

4 SPEAKING

a Work with a partner. Student A: You work in a café. Student B: You're a customer. Use the menu on p. 28 and the conversation map below.

A	B
Hello	Hello. I'd like … (*a drink*)
And something to eat?	Can I … ?
Of course. That's …	Here you go.
Thank you.	

b Switch roles and repeat the conversation.

5 WRITING

a Read the text message Tracy sends from her new smartwatch. Who is it for?

Hi, Brian. I'm at a café with Hannah. She's my friend from work. This message is from my new smartwatch. I love it! Talk to you later!

Delivered

b Now go to Writing Plus 3C on p. 159 for Contractions.

c Write a text message to a friend. Here are some ideas:

Hi, …
I'm … (*at school* / *at work* / *at a café* / *at a restaurant*) with …
He's / She's … (*Spanish* / *a student* / *very nice*)
Talk (to you) / See you soon / later.

d Read a partner's text message. Who does he/she write about?

UNIT PROGRESS TEST

CHECK YOUR PROGRESS

YOU CAN NOW DO THE UNIT PROGRESS TEST.

UNIT 3
Review

1 GRAMMAR

a Write simple present sentences and questions with the words and phrases.

> (–) I / have / lunch at home.
I don't have lunch at home.

1 (?) you / like / eggs
2 (+) we / eat / bread every day.
3 (–) I / drink / juice.
4 (–) we / eat / meat.
5 (+) you / like / fruit.
6 (?) they / eat / fish

b Underline the correct answer.

1 *Always I* / *I always* have a sandwich for lunch.
2 I *drink sometimes* / *sometimes drink* soda.
3 I *eat usually* / *usually eat* lunch at home.
4 I *never* / *never don't* drink milk.
5 *Never I have* / *I never have* dinner at 9:00.
6 I *don't sometimes* / *sometimes don't* have breakfast.

c Are the sentences in 1b true or false for you? Tell a partner.

d Correct the sentences.

> I not like rice.
I don't like rice.

1 No, we not do.
2 Always I have breakfast.
3 We not eat fish.
4 I drink usually water.
5 You like tea?
6 Yes, do I.

2 VOCABULARY

a Complete the groups with words in the box.

coffee	dinner	fish	cakes	juice	banana

1 water, milk, ____________
2 tea, ____________
3 orange, apple, ____________
4 breakfast, lunch, ____________
5 meat, eggs, ____________
6 ice cream, cookies, ____________

b Which is your favorite group in 2a?

c Look at 1–6 in the picture and complete the food words.

1 b____________
2 r____________
3 m____________
4 a____________s
5 o____________s
6 e____________s

3 SOUND AND SPELLING

a 03.29 Listen to the sentences. Check (✓) the sentence with the same vowel sounds in **bold**.

> T**ea**, pl**ea**se.
a ☐ **I** l**i**ke r**i**ce.
b ☑ H**e** **ea**ts m**ea**t.

1 It's a f**i**sh sandw**i**ch.
a ☐ H**i**s b**i**g sister **i**s s**i**x.
b ☐ I'd l**i**ke **i**ce cream.

2 Sh**e** **ea**ts ch**ee**se.
a ☐ Hi from China!
b ☐ H**e** t**ea**ches m**e**.

3 R**i**ce is n**i**ce.
a ☐ H**i**s b**i**g sister **i**s s**i**x.
b ☐ I'd l**i**ke **i**ce cream.

4 H**i** from Ch**i**na!
a ☐ From n**i**ne to f**i**ve.
b ☐ It's a f**i**sh sandw**i**ch.

b 03.30 Listen to the words. Check (✓) the words with the /ɔ/ sound. Practice saying the words.

1 ☐ water
2 ☐ after
3 ☐ glass
4 ☐ morning
5 ☐ apple
6 ☐ orange
7 ☐ quarter
8 ☐ all

REVIEW YOUR PROGRESS

How well did you do in this unit? Write 3, 2, or 1 for each objective.
3 = very well 2 = well 1 = not so well

I CAN ...	
say what I eat and drink	☐
talk about food and meals	☐
order and pay in a café	☐

CAN DO OBJECTIVES

- Talk about your life and ask about others'
- Talk about your family
- Ask and talk about photos

UNIT 4

MY LIFE AND MY FAMILY

GETTING STARTED

a Look at the picture and answer the questions.

1 Look at person a. Can you see … ?
   - her mother
   - her father
   - her grandparents

2 Do you think this family all lives together in one house?

3 Who in the picture … ?
   - works
   - studies

4 What do you think the people in the picture do next?

b Who lives in your home?

4A WHAT DO YOU STUDY?

Learn to ask and talk about your life

G Simple present: *Wh-* questions

V Common verbs

1 VOCABULARY Common verbs

a 04.01 Match sentences 1–5 with pictures a–e. Listen and check.

1 I **study** in college.
2 I **work** in an office.
3 I **speak** Japanese.
4 We **live** in Los Angeles.
5 We **go** to the gym every day.

b Which sentences in 1a are true for you?

c Now go to Vocabulary Focus 4A on p. 142.

2 READING

a Read Matt's blog. Which sentence is true?

1 "I live and I work in London."
2 "I live in Málaga, and I work in London."
3 "I speak Spanish very well."

b Read Matt's blog again. What does he say about these things?

1 apartments in London
2 beaches in Málaga
3 number of days at work (in London)
4 number of days at work (in Málaga)
5 Spanish classes
6 Málaga

c What do you think of Matt's life?

Language Plus *study*

	... *in college*
	... *at school / at an English language school*
study	... *English / Spanish / Arabic*
	... a subject (*art, math*)

d Write sentences about you.

I live ... I work / study ... I study English ...

e Tell a partner your sentences in 2d.

Breakfast in MÁLAGA and Lunch in LONDON

JUST A NORMAL DAY!

I work in London.

Apartments are very expensive there. In Málaga, Spain, apartments aren't very expensive, and the beaches are beautiful. So I work in London, but I live in Málaga! I fly from Málaga to London on Monday. I work there for three days, and I stay with my sister. Then I fly to Málaga again, and I work from home two days a week. I don't speak Spanish very well, so I study Spanish at a language school and I go to classes on Saturdays. I love Málaga – it's a beautiful city, and it's great to live here!

3 LISTENING

a 04.03 Listen to Justin and Fernanda. Who lives in Ottawa, but works in Québec City?

b 04.03 Listen again. Underline the correct answers.

1 Fernanda is *Brazilian* / *Canadian*.
2 Her home's in *Brazil* / *Canada*.
3 Her job *is* / *isn't* near her home.
4 She *is* / *isn't* married.
5 Fernanda and Bernardo speak *English* / *Portuguese* together.

4 GRAMMAR
Simple present: *Wh-* questions

a 04.04 Complete the questions in the chart. Listen and check.

***Yes/No* questions**	
______ you work from home?	Yes, I work two days from home. No, I work in an office.
***Wh-* questions**	
Where ______ you live? When ______ you have dinner? What ______ you study in college?	I live in Ottawa. I have dinner at 8:00. I study Italian.

b Now go to Grammar Focus 4A on p. 120.

c 04.07 Put the words in the correct order to make questions. Listen and check.

1 you work / do / in an office ?
2 do / where / you work ?
3 where / you live / do ?
4 college / study in / do you / what ?
5 do / speak Spanish / you ?

d 04.07 **Pronunciation** Listen to the questions in 4c again. Notice the stressed words and syllables.

1 *Do you work in an office?*

e 04.07 Check (✓) the words we stress. Then listen to the questions in 4c again and repeat.

1 ☐ question word (e.g., *where*)
2 ☐ *do*
3 ☐ main verb (e.g., *work*)
4 ☐ preposition (e.g., *in*)

f Ask and answer the questions in 4c with a partner.

5 SPEAKING

Communication 4A

Student A go to p. 105.
Student B go to p. 108.

4B SHE HAS A SISTER AND A BROTHER

Learn to talk about your family

G Simple present: *he / she / it* affirmative

V Family and people; Numbers 2

1 READING AND LISTENING

a Match 1–6 with pictures a–f.

1 Soccer player Lionel Messi with his children.
2 Pop star Beyoncé with her husband, Jay-Z, and her sister Solange.
3 Movie star Kate Hudson with her parents.
4 Movie director Alejandro González Iñárritu with his wife, his son, and his daughter.
5 Actor Colin Hanks and his father, Tom Hanks.
6 Singer Camila Cabello with her mother.

b 04.08 Listen and check.

c What other things do you know about the people in the pictures?

2 VOCABULARY Family and people

a Complete the chart. Use words from 1a.

female	male
mother	father
______	son
wife	______
______	brother

b Which word in the sentences in 1a means … ?

1 mother and father 2 boys and girls

c Look at the family tree. Which people … ?

1 are married
2 have a brother
3 have a sister
4 have a child / children

d Work in pairs.

Student A: Choose a person from the family tree.
Student B: Ask questions to guess who Student A is.

Then switch roles.

Are you married? — Yes.

Do you have children? — Yes.

e Now go to Vocabulary Focus 4B Family and people on p. 143.

f **Sound and spelling /ð/**

1 04.11 Listen and practice this sound.
/ð/ mo**th**er

2 04.12 /ð/ is usually spelled *th*. Listen to the words and repeat.

this that father they brother then

3 Practice saying the words.

3 READING AND VOCABULARY Numbers 2

a Read *An International Family*. Are the sentences true or false?

1 Pablo and Alicia have two small children.
2 María is married and lives in Turkey.
3 Pablo and Alicia live in Mexico.

An International Family

Pablo and Alicia Moreno are married. Pablo is from Spain, and Alicia is from Buenos Aires, in Argentina, but they live in New York. Their family is very international!

Alicia has a sister and a brother. Her sister, Daniela, is 46. She lives in Buenos Aires, and her mother lives there, too. Her brother, Carlos, is 37. He lives in Brazil, and he works in São Paulo.

Alicia and Pablo have two children. Their son, Alex, is 19. He's in college in Mexico, and he lives there, too. Their daughter, María, is 24. She lives in Istanbul with her Turkish husband, Mehmet.

b Where do they live? Write the names of the countries.

1 Daniela
2 Carlos
3 Alex
4 María
5 Mehmet

c Daniela is forty-six. How old is … ? (Write the numbers in words.)

1 Carlos 2 Alex 3 María

> **Language Plus** *How old … ?*
>
> ***How old is** she?*
> ***She's** 25.*
>
> ***How old are** her children?*
> ***They're** three and five.*
>
> **Note:** We use *be*, not *have*, to talk about age.

d Now go to Vocabulary Focus 4B Numbers 2 on p. 141.

e Write the names of three famous people. How old are they? If you don't know, guess! Read out the names. What do other students think?

Lady Gaga

I think she's 38.

4 GRAMMAR
Simple present: *he / she / it* affirmative

a Look at the verbs in the chart and answer the questions.

1 How are the verbs in A different from the verbs in B?
2 How is *has* different?

I / we / you / they	he / she / it
A	B
I **work** in an office.	He **works** in São Paulo.
We **have** two children.	She **has** a sister and a brother.
They **live** in New York.	She **lives** in Buenos Aires.

b Complete the sentences with verbs from 4a.

1 He ______ in an office.
2 He ______ at home with his parents.
3 Her mother ______ an apartment in New York.

c Now go to Grammar Focus 4B on p. 120.

d **Communication 4B** Student A go to p. 105. Student B go to p. 109.

5 SPEAKING

a Tell your partner about your family. Use the verbs in the box. Listen, but don't write notes.

have go study live work

My brother has two children – a boy and a girl.

b Say what you remember about your partner's family. Are you correct?

4C EVERYDAY ENGLISH

This is my father

Learn to ask and talk about photos

P Sound and spelling: /tʃ/ and /dʒ/

W Photo captions

1 LISTENING

a Ask and answer the questions.

1 Do you have photos of family and friends with you?
2 Where do you have them, on your phone or in your wallet?
3 How often do you look at them?

b 04.15 Listen to Part 1 and answer the questions.

1 Who writes Hector an email?
2 Where is he/she?

c 04.16 Listen to Part 2. Answer the questions.

1 How many people does Hector talk about?
2 How many people does Toby talk about?

d 04.16 Complete the information about Hector's and Toby's families with the words in the box. Then listen to Part 2 again and check your answers.

sister cousin teacher hotel computers supermarket

Hector's mother's a [1] ______, and his father's the manager of a [2] ______. He has a [3] ______, Isa. Isa has two girls, Yasmin and Gabriela. Toby has a brother, Mike. He works with [4] ______ and is married to Kara. She's the manager of a [5] ______. Troy also has a [6] ______, James.

e Talk about a favorite photo of your family. Who's in it?

2 USEFUL LANGUAGE Asking and talking about photos

a Look at expressions 1–7 from Part 2. Do we use them to … ?

a ask about photos
b talk about your photos
c talk about another person's photos

1 This is my mother.
2 Do you have photos of your family?
3 Nice picture!
4 Can I see them?
5 Who's this?
6 They're cute.
7 This is my sister, Isa.

b 04.17 Look at expressions 1–4. Are they in group a, b, or c in 2a? Listen and check your answers in 2a and 2b.

1 This is a picture of my town.
2 It's really nice.
3 Do you have any pictures of your home?
4 These are my friends Rob and Mona.

c 04.18 **Pronunciation** Listen to the sentence. Answer the questions. Listen again and repeat.

This is my mother.

1 Do the first two words connect?
2 Is the pronunciation of *s* the same in *this* and *is*?

d 04.19 Complete the conversation with expressions in the box. Listen and check.

Great photo!	Can I see them?
He's funny.	
Do you have any photos of your friends?	

A [1] ____________
B Yes, I do.
A [2] ____________
B Sure. This is a photo of my friend Marco.
A [3] ____________
B And this is me with my friend Emilio.
A Yes, I know Emilio. [4] ____________
B You're right – he's really funny.

e Practice the conversation in 2d. Take turns being A and B.

3 PRONUNCIATION Sound and spelling: /tʃ/ and /dʒ/

a 04.20 Listen and practice these sounds.

1 /tʃ/ tea**ch**er pic**t**ure   2 /dʒ/ mana**g**er **J**ames

b 04.21 Listen to the words. Look at the sounds in **bold**. Which one is different in each group?

1 **ch**ips **j**eans ques**t**ion
2 lar**ge** **j**ob **ch**oose
3 oran**ge** **ch**eap mat**ch**
4 pa**ge** **ch**eese **G**ermany

c Practice saying the words in 3b.

4 SPEAKING

Communication 4C Student A go to p. 105. Student B go to p. 108.

5 WRITING

a Read Hector's information about his sister. What information is new?

This is my sister, Isa, with her two beautiful daughters, Yasmin and Gabriela. They live in a new house in Rio de Janeiro – it's very nice. Her husband, Pablo, isn't here, because it's his photo! They're a great family.

b Now go to Writing Plus 4C on p. 159 for Word order.

c Write about your photo from 1e. Here are some ideas:

This is my … with …   He's / She's / They're …
They live … It's nice / great!

d Read about your partner's photo. How many people does he/she write about?

UNIT PROGRESS TEST

CHECK YOUR PROGRESS

YOU CAN NOW DO THE UNIT PROGRESS TEST.

UNIT 4
Review

1 GRAMMAR

a Look at the words and write simple present questions.

> where / you / live *Where do you live?*
1 what / your name
2 when / you / have lunch
3 what time / you / go to work
4 where / your friends / from
5 what / you / study
6 where / your school

b Ask and answer the questions in 1a.

c Correct the underlined words.

> My son like basketball. *likes*
1 Yolanda work in Boston.
2 Our daughter eat rice every day.
3 My city haves two universities.
4 Nacho go to school at 8:30.
5 My dad teachs Spanish.
6 My brother studys Chinese.

d Underline the correct answer.

1 When *are* / *'s* / *do* you work?
2 María *is live* / *live* / *lives* in Sydney.
3 Where *are* / *is* / *do* you from?
4 What *are* / *is* / *do* you have for breakfast?
5 What *are* / *is* / *do* their names?
6 What time do you *gos* / *go* / *goes* to school?

2 VOCABULARY

a Cross out the answer that is NOT possible.

> I work *in a factory* / *in an office* / ~~*tennis*~~.
1 I meet *my friends for coffee* / *to the gym* / *people at work* every day.
2 I play *home* / *baseball* / *the guitar*.
3 I live in *Italian* / *a small house* / *a big city*.
4 I teach *at a university* / *to the movies* / *young children*.
5 I study *English* / *in college* / *to school*.
6 I speak *Spanish* / *Japan* / *Chinese*.

b Which information in 2a is true for you? Tell a partner.

c Complete the numbers.

> 29 *twenty-* nine
1 31 ______ one
2 24 ______ four
3 75 ______ five
4 82 ______ two
5 96 ______ six
6 53 ______ three
7 48 ______ eight
8 67 ______ seven
9 100 a ______

d Match 1–6 with the words in the box.

baby boy girl men woman women

3 SOUND AND SPELLING

a 04.22 Underline ONE or TWO /ð/ sounds in each sentence. Practice saying the sentences.

1 These are my friends.
2 I study there.
3 This is my father.
4 They're at the movies.
5 They teach at the university.
6 She's their daughter.

b 04.23 Look at the information in the chart.

/tʃ/	/dʒ/
tea**ch**	mana**g**er
pic**t**ure	**g**ym
child	**J**ulia

c 04.24 Are the sounds in **bold** the same (S) or different (D)? Practice saying the sentences.

> We're on pa**g**e **s**eventy-two. *D*
> He's a mana**g**er at the **g**ym. *S*
1 **G**ary is a mana**g**er.
2 **J**ohn speaks **G**erman.
3 It's a pic**t**ure of the **g**ym.
4 She tea**ch**es the grammar on pa**g**e three.
5 It's a ques**t**ion about **ch**ildren.

REVIEW YOUR PROGRESS

How well did you do in this unit? Write 3, 2, or 1 for each objective.
3 = very well 2 = well 1 = not so well

I CAN ...	
talk about my life and ask about others	☐
talk about my family	☐
ask and talk about photos	☐

CAN DO OBJECTIVES

- Describe a town
- Talk about hotels and hostels
- Ask about and say where places are

UNIT 5

PLACES

GETTING STARTED

a Look at the picture and check (✓) the things you think are in the museum.

- ☐ art
- ☐ photos
- ☐ a restaurant
- ☐ a phone
- ☐ tickets
- ☐ a store

b Talk about the questions.

1 Who do you think visits this museum?
2 What other buildings do you think are near this museum?
3 Would you like to visit this museum?

5A THERE ARE A FEW STORES

Learn to describe a town

G *there is / there are*: affirmative

V Places in a town

VERY HOT!

Stovepipe Wells, Death Valley, California

Stovepipe Wells is a small town in Death Valley in California. It's in the desert, so it's very dry, and it's also very hot during the day – it's sometimes 50°C in the summer. Only a few people live there, but there's a good road through the town, so there are a lot of tourists. In the town, there's a restaurant, there's a store, and there's a gas station. There are also two big hotels near the town. One of the hotels even has a golf course!

VERY COLD!

Resolute Bay, Canada

Resolute Bay is in the far north of Canada. It's cold in summer (4°C), and it's very cold in winter (–35°C). Also, because it's so far north, it's night from September to April. It's a very small place. Only about 200 people live there, but there's an airport, there are a few stores, there's a school for the children, and there are three small hotels. There are even a few cars, but there's only one good road in Resolute Bay. It goes from the town to the airport!

1 READING

a Look at the pictures of Resolute Bay and Stovepipe Wells. Which place is … ?

- in a desert
- on the ocean
- a good place for tourists

b Read about the two places and check your answers in 1a.

c Are the sentences about Resolute Bay (RB) or Stovepipe Wells (SW)?

1 "We often come here by car."
2 "It's always dark here in the winter."
3 "The school is small. There's only one teacher."
4 "There's a golf course at our hotel."
5 "Boats come here in the summer."

d Do you think Resolute Bay and Stovepipe Wells are … ?

- nice places to live?
- nice places for a vacation?

Why / Why not?

Language Plus *a few, a lot of*

***a few** cars*

***a lot of** cars*

***a few** stores*

***a lot of** stores*

2 GRAMMAR

there is / there are: affirmative

a Complete the sentences. Check your answers in the texts in 1b.

Singular: [1]______ is a school / a good road.
Plural: There [2]______ three small hotels / a lot of tourists.

b 05.01 **Pronunciation** Listen and write the sentences. Tell the sentences to your partner.

c Now go to Grammar Focus 5A on p. 122.

d Cover the texts. Make sentences about the two places:

- hotels
- cars
- an airport
- stores
- schools

e Write two true sentences about your street. Use *there is* or *there are*. Check your partner's sentences.

3 VOCABULARY Places in a town

a 05.03 Match the words in the box with the places in pictures a–f. Listen and check.

café store restaurant
school bank hotel

b Which places in 3a are these?

1 "My daughter goes there every day."
2 "We go there for dinner every Saturday night."
3 "I often drink coffee there with my friends."
4 "You're in room 305. Here's your key."
5 "They have fruit and vegetables and also newspapers and magazines."
6 "I'd like $500, please."

c Now go to Vocabulary Focus 5A on p. 144.

d **Sound and spelling /u/ and /ʌ/**

1 05.05 Listen and practice these sounds.
1 /u/ sch**oo**l 2 /ʌ/ l**u**nch

2 05.06 Look at the words in the box. What sounds do the letters in **bold** have? Listen and add the words to the sound groups below.

s**u**mmer f**oo**d n**ew** tw**o** wh**o** m**o**ther
umbrella b**eau**tiful s**o**metimes p**oo**l

Sound 1 /u/	Sound 2 /ʌ/
school	lunch

3 Practice saying the words.

4 LISTENING

a 05.07 Listen to a conversation about places in a town. Look at the map and match 1–5 with the words in the box.

bookstore café bank restaurant supermarket

b 05.07 Listen again. Are the sentences true or false?

1 There are a lot of stores on 14th Street.
2 Nice people work in the bookstore.
3 The café is Italian.
4 The coffee in the café isn't very good.
5 The restaurant on Main Street has Chinese food.
6 The restaurant is cheap.

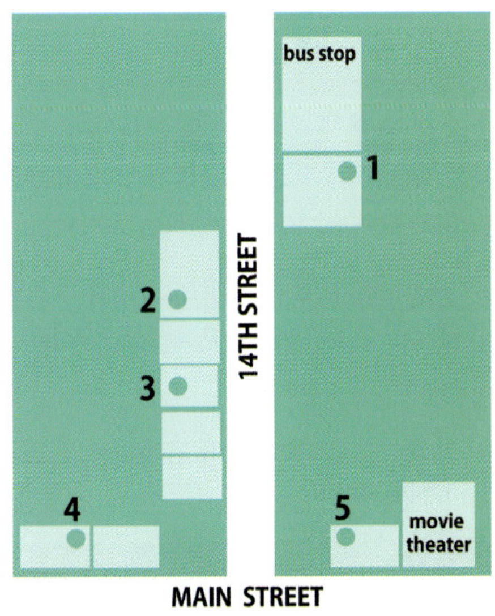

c What is the same about the town on the map and your town?

5 SPEAKING

a Think of a street in the town where you are now. Write notes. Use words from this lesson.

There's a ... There are ... It's in ... It's near ...

b Describe your street, but don't say its name. Do other students know the name of the street?

5B IS THERE A HOSTEL IN YOUR TOWN?

Learn to talk about hotels and hostels

G *there is / there are*: negative and questions

V Hotels

1 VOCABULARY Hotels

a 05.08 Match the words in the box with pictures 1–5. Listen and check.

bathtub room bed TV shower

b Sound and spelling /ʃ/

1 05.09 Listen and practice this sound.
/ʃ/ **sh**ower

2 05.10 Listen to the words in the box. Underline the /ʃ/ sound in each word.

station fish sure ocean

3 Practice saying the words.

c Now go to Vocabulary Focus 5B on p. 138.

d 05.12 **Pronunciation** Listen to the words. Notice the stressed syllables. Practice saying them.

hostel hotel

e Which things in pictures 1–5 in 1a aren't in a hostel room?

2 READING

a Look at pictures 1–3 of Turkey. Choose adjectives to talk about them. Compare your ideas with your partner.

- beautiful
- exciting
- great
- interesting
- nice
- old
- boring
- big

b Read Sandra's review of a hostel in Turkey. Does Sandra like the hostel?

c Read the review again. Check (✓) what's in the hostel.

third floor	☐ small rooms	☐ big rooms	☐ café
second floor	☐ restaurant	☐ TV room	☐ small rooms
first floor	☐ café	☐ kitchen	☐ TV room

d Would you like to stay at the hostel? Why / Why not?

HOSTEL REVIEWS

The Cave Hostel ★★★★★

This is a great hostel in Göreme, in Turkey. It's in Cappadocia, a very old part of the country. You can do a lot of things here. My favorite thing is going in a hot air balloon. You can see really beautiful places from the air.

The hostel has different rooms with different prices. On the second floor, there are small rooms for two people with bathtubs. On the third floor, there are big rooms with six beds in them. They're very cheap, but there isn't a shower or a bathtub in the big rooms. There aren't any blankets or pillows – you pay for those. There isn't a restaurant or café in the hostel, but there's a kitchen on the first floor. There aren't any TVs in the rooms, but there's free Wi-Fi. It's a very simple place to stay, and it's clean. And the people are very friendly. Faruk, the manager, sings karaoke really well!
Sandra

3 GRAMMAR *there is / there are*: negative

a 05.13 Complete the sentences with *isn't* or *aren't*. Listen and check.

1 There ______ any blankets.
2 There ______ a restaurant.

b Find more examples of *there isn't* and *there aren't* in Sandra's review.

c Think about the town or city you're in now. Check (✓) the sentences that are true. Correct the false sentences.

1 ☐ There's a big museum in this town / city.
2 ☐ There are a lot of stores here.
3 ☐ There aren't any hostels.
4 ☐ There are two bus stations.
5 ☐ There aren't any parks.

d Read your sentences and listen to your partner's sentences. Are they the same?

There aren't any museums in this town.

Yes, there is a museum in this town – on Cromwell Road.

4 LISTENING

a 05.14 Listen to a hostel receptionist and George, a guest. Is George happy with the hostel?

b 05.14 Listen again. Check (✓) the things in the hostel.

☐ available rooms ☐ café ☐ Wi-Fi
☐ parking ☐ kitchen ☐ showers

c Why do people like hostels? Why do people like hotels?

5 GRAMMAR *there is / there are*: questions

a 05.15 Complete the questions. Listen and check.

1 Singular: ______ ______ a restaurant here?
Yes, there's a restaurant here.
2 Plural: ______ ______ any cafés near here?
Yes, there are cafés near here.

b Now go to Grammar Focus 5B on p. 122.

c Write questions using *Is there … ?* and *Are there … ?* about your partner's town, city, or street. Here are some ideas:

- cafés
- supermarket
- swimming pool
- hospital
- movie theater
- restaurants

d Ask your partner about their town, city, or street.

Are there any cafés in your town?

Yes, there are two cafés.

Is there a supermarket on your street?

No, but there are two stores.

6 SPEAKING

Communication 5B
Student A go to p. 109.
Student B go to p. 107.

3

2

5C EVERYDAY ENGLISH

Is there a café near here?

Learn to ask about and say where places are

P Emphasizing what you say 1

W An email about a place

1 LISTENING

a Ask and answer the questions.

1 What stores or supermarkets are there near your home?
2 Do you go to these stores or supermarkets? How often?
3 Is the food good / expensive?

b 05.18 Listen to Part 1. Answer the questions.

1 Does Anya like the hotel room?
2 What do Anya and Lily want to drink?
3 Do they know the area near their hotel?

2 PRONUNCIATION Emphasizing what you say 1

a 05.19 Listen to the sentence.

ANYA It's really small, but it's OK.

05.20 Listen to the sentence again. Is *really* more or less stressed the second time?

b Check (✓) the correct rule.

We say *really* with a strong stress to:
1 ☐ speak loudly
2 ☐ make the meaning stronger

c 05.21 Listen to the sentences. Underline one word with strong stress in each sentence.

1 My country is very hot in the summer.
2 James's new car is really fast.
3 This movie is so boring.

d 05.21 Listen again and repeat.

3 LISTENING

a 05.22 Listen to Part 2. Answer the questions.

1 Do Lily and Anya find a café near their hotel?
2 Who do they see on the street?

b 05.22 Listen to Part 2 again. Are the sentences true or false?

1 Lily thinks a store is a café.
2 Sebastien sees Lily and Anya first.
3 Sebastien works in Paris.
4 There's a café near their hotel.
5 There's a café near Sebastien's apartment.

4 USEFUL LANGUAGE Asking and saying where places are

a 05.23 Complete the questions with words in the box. Listen and check.

near where there

1 ______'s our hotel?
2 Is ______ a supermarket near here?
3 Are there any stores ______ here?

b 05.24 Match the two possible answers in a–c with questions 1–3 in 4a. Listen and check.

a Yes, there are. There's one on this street. / No, sorry, there aren't.
b Yes, there's one near the bank. / No, sorry, there isn't.
c It's on the next street. / It's on this street.

c 05.25 Put the conversation in the correct order. Listen and check.

A ☐ Great, thank you. And is there a good restaurant in this part of town?
A 1 Excuse me, can you help me?
A ☐ OK, thanks for your help.
A ☐ Are there any good cafés near here?
B ☐ Yes, there's one on the next street – Park Café.
B ☐ No, I'm sorry, there are no restaurants near here. But there's one near the bus station.
B ☐ Yes, of course.
B ☐ No problem.

d Practice the conversation in 4c with a partner.

5 SPEAKING

Communication 5C Student A look at the information below. Student B go to p. 106.

a Conversation 1. You're on a street you don't know. Ask Student B about:

- a hotel
- cafés

b Conversation 2. Now you're on a street you know. Use the information to answer Student B's questions.

- a bank: on the next street
- stores: not near here – near the hospital

6 WRITING

a Read part of an email from Lily to her parents. She writes about her trip to Paris. Does she only write about the good things?

> Paris is great! Our hotel is in a nice part of the city, but it's really small. There's a beautiful park near the hotel, and there are stores on the next street. And guess what! I'm at a café with Sebastien! He is really good! His apartment is nice, but it's not near our hotel. ...

b Go to Writing Plus 5C on p. 160 for *and* and *but*.

c Write about your part of town. Use *there's* / *there isn't* / *there are* / *there aren't*. Use *and* and *but*.

d Read about your partner's part of town. Is it the same?

UNIT PROGRESS TEST

CHECK YOUR PROGRESS

YOU CAN NOW DO THE UNIT PROGRESS TEST.

UNIT 5
Review

1 GRAMMAR

a Correct the sentences.

> There an Italian restaurant. *There's an Italian restaurant.*
1 There is a hotel on this street?
2 Yes, there's.
3 There are a shower.
4 There aren't a available rooms.
5 Is there swimming pool at the hotel?
6 No, there not is.

b Complete the sentences.

1 Is __________ a bank near here?
2 Are there __________ bottles of water in the room?
3 __________ there a supermarket on this street?
4 Is there __________ TV in the room?
5 __________ there any cafés near here?
6 Is there __________ teacher in the room?

c Ask and answer the questions in 1b.

2 VOCABULARY

a What are these places? Use the words to complete the crossword.

1 
2 
3 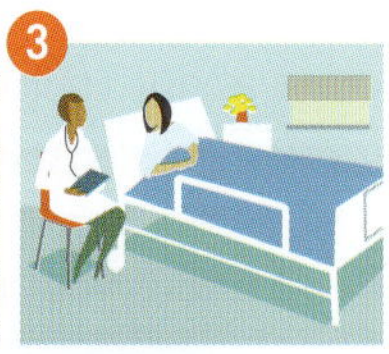
4 
5 
6 
7 
8 

b Write the words.

1 d e b __________

2 w e r h o s __________

3 i p o w l l __________

4 t h t a u b b __________

5 o r o m __________

6 w o t e l __________

7 i W-i F __________

8 k a n b l e t __________

3 SOUND AND SPELLING

a 05.26 Complete the chart with the words in the box. Practice saying the words.

~~**u**p~~ ~~y**ou**~~ **u**mbrella l**u**nch s**u**mmer b**eau**tiful n**ew** br**o**ther sch**oo**l m**o**ther f**oo**d p**oo**l

/uː/	/ʌ/
you	*up*

b 05.27 Look at the information in the chart.

/ɑ/	/aʊ/	/oʊ/
l**o**t	sh**ow**er	pill**ow**
h**o**spital	fl**ow**er	kn**ow**
h**o**t	t**ow**el	h**o**tel

c 05.28 Are the sounds in **bold** the same (S) or different (D)? Practice saying the words.

> t**ow**n – a l**o**t *D*
1 h**o**t – h**o**tel
2 sh**ow**er – h**ow**
3 **O**K – kn**ow**
4 g**o** – pill**ow**
5 h**o**t – t**ow**el
6 fl**ow**er – h**o**spital

REVIEW YOUR PROGRESS

How well did you do in this unit? Write 3, 2, or 1 for each objective.
3 = very well 2 = well 1 = not so well

I CAN ...	
describe a town	☐
talk about hotels and hostels	☐
ask about and say where places are	☐

CAN DO OBJECTIVES

- Talk about people's jobs
- Talk about daily routines and habits
- Make and accept offers

UNIT 6

WORK AND ROUTINES

GETTING STARTED

a Look at the picture and answer the questions.

1 What do the people do?
2 Where do the people work?
3 Would you like to do this job?

b Think of two questions to ask the people in the picture.

6A I DON'T WORK AT NIGHT

Learn to talk about people's jobs

G Simple present: *he / she / it* negative

V Jobs

JOBS INTERNATIONAL   HOME NEWS ABOUT

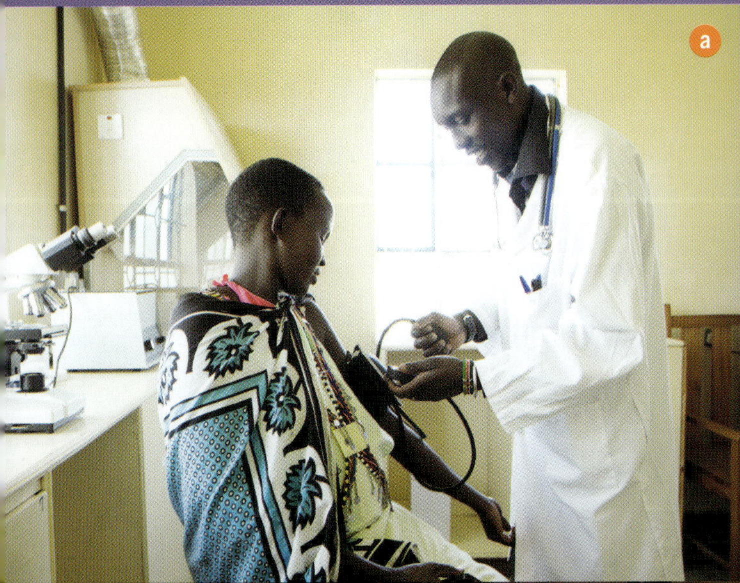

HELP AROUND THE WORLD ...

Welcome to Jobs International. Our people go around the world and help others. Meet two of them.

I'm a doctor from Brazil, and I work in a small hospital in Ghana. I love the work here because it's very interesting. I do different things every day. And the people are so friendly. Life isn't always easy here, but it's great to help people.

I'm a teacher at a school in Samoa, but I'm from Australia. I teach English here and after school, I play sports with the children. They love rugby and volleyball. The children are really happy – a lot of fun. This is a really good job.

1 READING

a Look at pictures a and b. What places are in the pictures? What jobs do people do there?

b Read about Luiza and Fred on the *Jobs International* website. Are your ideas in 1a correct?

c Read the website again. Are the sentences true or false?

1 *Jobs International* people don't work in their home countries.
2 Luiza works in a big hospital.
3 Her work is sometimes boring.
4 She likes the people in Ghana.
5 Fred goes home after classes.
6 His students like playing sports.

d Write questions for Luiza and Fred.

What ... do? → *What do you do?*

1 Where ... work?
2 ... like the people?
3 ... like the job?

e You are Luiza or Fred. Ask and answer the questions in 1d.

What do you do?

I'm a teacher.

Language Plus *work / job*

*I **work** in a hospital.*	*work* = verb
*I like my **work**.*	*work* = noun
*It's a good **job**.*	*job* = noun (*doctor, teacher*)

2 LISTENING AND VOCABULARY Jobs

a Match the words in the box with pictures a–h.

soccer player	student	receptionist	server	taxi driver	factory worker	office worker	sales assistant

b 06.01 **Pronunciation** Listen to the two-word jobs in 2a. Which word is stressed?

1 the first word
2 the second word

Practice saying the words.

c 06.02 Listen to four people talk about their jobs. What do they do?

1 ________ 3 ________
2 ________ 4 ________

d 06.02 Listen again. Complete the sentences with the words in the box.

study	play (x2)	sit	meet (x2)

1 **ANNA** I ________ all day, but I ________ some interesting people and go to a lot of different places. I don't work at night.
2 **FELIPE** I ________ on a team, and the weekend is the most important time of the week in my job. I don't ________ games during the week – well, sometimes on Wednesdays.
3 **MARIA** I ________ business at college. It's really interesting.
4 **JESSICA** I work in a store and ________ a lot of different people.

e Which job do you like in 2c? Which job don't you like? Say why.

f Now go to Vocabulary Focus 6A on p. 145.

3 GRAMMAR Simple present: *he / she / it* negative

a 06.04 Complete the sentences with *does* or *doesn't*. Listen and check.

ANNA I don't work at night.
1 She ________ work at night.
FELIPE I don't play games during the week.
2 He ________ play games during the week.

b Now go to Grammar Focus 6A on p. 124.

c Complete the sentences with the correct form of the verbs in parentheses.

1 Alex is a taxi driver. He ________ in the morning. (not work)
2 Sam is a bank teller. He ________ his job. (not like)
3 Lucy is a sales assistant. She ________ much during the day. (not sit)
4 Matteo is a server. He ________ on Monday. (not work)

d **Sound and spelling** /ʃ/ and /tʃ/

1 06.06 Listen to the words. Do the letters in **bold** have the same sound?

she **ch**ildren recep**ti**onist tea**ch**

2 06.07 Listen to the words in the box. Which words have **sound 1 /ʃ/** and which have **sound 2 /tʃ/**?

short **ch**eap wa**tch** fini**sh** sta**ti**on ki**tch**en

3 Which two letters often make sound 2?

4 Practice saying the words in 2.

4 SPEAKING

Communication 6A Student A go to p. 109. Student B go to p. 107.

6B I WAKE UP AT 4:00

Learn to talk about daily routine and habits

G Simple present: *he* / *she* / *it* questions

V Daily routine

A Good Night's Sleep

People say it's good to sleep for eight hours every night ... but is it true? Some people sleep for only five or six hours, and they feel fine in the morning. And some people sleep twice every night ...

a

b

Anneli Hanka, 24, Finland

I always <u>**wake up**</u> at about 4:00 in the morning. I don't want to sleep, so I <u>**get up**</u>, and I do yoga. Then I <u>**go to bed**</u> again. Then I get up at 8:00 in the morning, and I go to work. I feel fine – I never feel tired.

Beatriz Romero, 32, U.S.

I finish work at 6:00 in the evening, and I arrive home at 6:30. I read the news or text a friend. Then I go to bed for three hours. My husband works at a restaurant, and he gets home at about 12:00 at night. So I get up, we have dinner, and then we watch TV until about 3:00. Then I sleep until 7:00.

1 READING AND VOCABULARY Daily routine

a Talk about when you do these things. Use the phrases in the box.

in the morning | in the afternoon | in the evening | at night

1 have dinner
2 go to English class
3 work
4 have coffee
5 read the news
6 sleep

b Read the text above. Match what Beatriz and Anneli say with pictures a and b.

c Match the <u>underlined</u> words from the text with pictures 1–3.

d Complete the verb phrases with the words in the box. Then read the text again to check your answers.

have | watch | go | arrive / get | finish

1 ______ to work
2 ______ home
3 ______ dinner
4 ______ TV
5 ______ work

e Now go to Vocabulary Focus 6B on p. 146.

f Ask and answer the questions with a partner.

1 Do you sleep ... ?
- for eight hours
- for five or six hours
- twice every night

2 When do you usually ... ?
- wake up
- get up
- go to bed

3 When do you usually ... ?
- go to work or school
- finish work or school
- get home in the evening

Language Plus *for, from ... to ... , until*

8 hours

11:00 p.m. ———————— **7:00 a.m.**

I sleep ***for*** *eight hours.*
I sleep ***from*** *11:00* ***to*** *7:00.*
I sleep ***until*** *7:00.*

g Sound and spelling Consonant clusters

1 06.10 These words start with two consonant sounds together. Listen and practice saying them.
sleep **br**eakfast **tw**elve

2 06.11 Listen to the words in the box. <u>Underline</u> the two consonant sounds that are together.

play | small | bread | fruit | driver | study | speak

3 Practice saying the words.

2 LISTENING

a ▶ 06.12 Listen to an interview with Paul. What are his answers to the questions?

1 Do you go to bed early?
2 When do you wake up?
3 What do you do then?
4 What about your wife? Does she wake up then?

b Talk about the questions with a partner.

1 What do you think about Paul's daily routine?
2 What do you think about his photos? Think of adjectives to talk about them.

3 GRAMMAR Simple present: *he / she / it* questions

a Complete the questions in the chart with *do* or *does*.

you	he/she/it
__Do__ you go to bed early?	______ she wake up?
When ______ you wake up?	When ______ he get up?

b Now go to Grammar Focus 6B on p. 124.

c ▶ 06.15 **Pronunciation** Listen to the questions with *when* in 3a and notice the stressed words. Check (✓) the words we stress.

1 ☐ question word (*when*)
2 ☐ *do*
3 ☐ *up*

d Write questions about Beatriz and Anneli on page 50.

1 What time / Beatriz / finish work?
2 Where / her husband / work?
3 What time / he / get home?
4 When / Anneli / wake up?
5 What / she / do then?
6 How / she / feel in the morning?

e Ask and answer the questions in 3d with a partner.

f Ask about your partner's routine.

- the morning
- meals
- work / school / college
- the evening
- sleep

When do you get up?

I get up at 7:30.

g Work with a new partner. Ask questions about their <u>first</u> partner's routine.

When does Emma get up?

Emma gets up at 7:30.

4 SPEAKING

Communication 6B Student A go to p. 109. Student B go to p. 107.

6C EVERYDAY ENGLISH
I'll come with you

Learn to make and accept offers

P Emphasizing what you say 2

W An email about your day

1 LISTENING

a You want to have a birthday party for your friend. Check (✓) four things you need.

1 ☐ a cake
2 ☐ pizza
3 ☐ cups
4 ☐ ice cream
5 ☐ soda
6 ☐ plates

b Tell a partner your ideas in 1a. Do you need the same things?

c 06.16 Listen to Part 1. Answer the questions.

1 Who does Zoey see on the street?
2 When does Ariana want to go shopping?

d 06.16 Listen to Part 1 again. <u>Underline</u> the correct word.

1 The flowers are for *Zoey / Ariana*.
2 *Zoey / Evan* wants coffee.
3 *Ariana / Zoey* loves to cook.
4 Ariana *wants / doesn't want* a birthday party.

2 USEFUL LANGUAGE Making and accepting offers 1

a 06.17 Complete the conversation with the words in the box. Listen and check.

thanks	please	like

ARIANA Would you ________ some coffee?
EVAN No, that's OK, ________.
ZOEY Yes, ________!

b 06.17 Pronunciation Listen to the mini-conversation in 2a again. What sounds do *would* and *you* make together? Listen again and repeat.

c 06.18 Put A's questions in the correct order in the conversation. Listen and check.

A like / would you / some coffee ?
B Yes, please.
A piece of cake / you like a / and would ?
B No, that's OK, thanks.

d Practice the conversation in 2c with a partner. Ask about different food and drinks.

Would you like a glass of orange juice?

Yes, please.

Would you like a sandwich?

No, thanks.

3 LISTENING AND USEFUL LANGUAGE
Making and accepting offers 2

a 06.19 Listen to Part 2. Answer the questions.

1 What does Evan want to do?
2 Do Ariana and Zoey accept his help?

b 06.20 Complete the sentences with words in the box. Listen and check.

can help I'll

1 I ________ go with you.
2 I'll ________ you buy things.
3 ________ come with you.

c 06.21 Do these replies answer yes or no? Listen and check.

That's great, thanks. Don't worry, that's OK.
Thanks, but I'm fine. Thank you, that's very nice of you.

d 06.22 Complete the conversation with the words in the box. Listen and check.

great can help right supermarket

A I need to go to the [1]________.
B I [2]________ come with you.
A That's [3]________! And I need to make dinner.
B I'll [4]________ you.
A All [5]________, thank you so much.

e Practice the conversation in 3d with a partner.

f Use different words and expressions to make a new conversation.

I need to go shopping.

I'll go with you.

4 PRONUNCIATION
Emphasizing what you say 2

a 06.23 Listen to the sentences and notice the strong stress. Then listen again and repeat.

1 <u>I</u> can go with you. 2 <u>I'll</u> come with you.

b 06.24 Listen to the mini-conversations. Underline the strong stress.

Conversation 1
A I can't do this exercise.
B José can help you.
Conversation 2
C I need to get to the bus station this afternoon.
D I'll drive you.

c Practice the mini-conversations in 4b with a partner.

5 SPEAKING

a You're at a café with your partner. Use the ideas below to make a conversation.

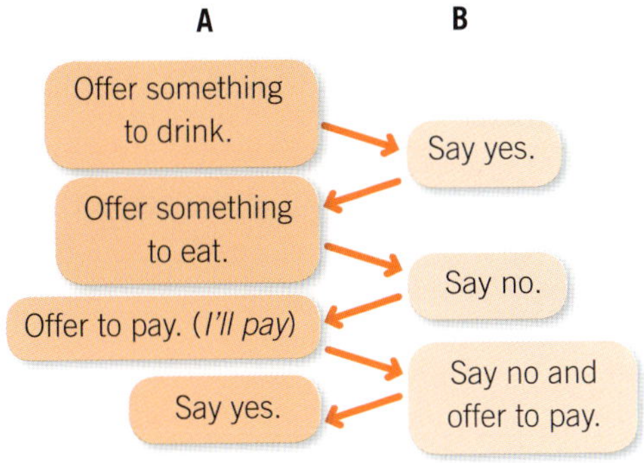

6 WRITING

a Read part of an email from Ariana to her sister. She writes about a day in her life in Los Angeles. Where do Ariana and Zoey have coffee? Why?

I walk to work every day because my apartment is near the office. I start work at 8:30, and I finish at 5:30. I work with Zoey. We go out to a café for coffee every day because the coffee machine in the office isn't very good. We also have lunch there. They have great pizza and chocolate cake – my favorite! Zoey always says, "I'll pay." She's really nice.

b Now go to Writing Plus 6C on p. 160 for *because* and *also*.

c Write about a day in your life. Use *because* and *also*.

d Read about your partner's day. Do you do the same?

UNIT PROGRESS TEST

CHECK YOUR PROGRESS

YOU CAN NOW DO THE UNIT PROGRESS TEST.

UNIT 6
Review

1 GRAMMAR

a Check (✓) the sentences that are correct. Correct the mistakes.

> My sister doesn't lives at home.
My sister doesn't live at home.
> ☑ I don't study Chinese.
1 ☐ She don't like cake.
2 ☐ Marcus doesn't meets many people.
3 ☐ This town doesn't have a university.
4 ☐ I work not on Fridays.
5 ☐ We don't talk much at work.
6 ☐ Isabella speaks not Italian.

b Complete the sentences with *do*, *don't*, *does*, or *doesn't*.

1 ___________ your sister work in a bank?
No, she 2 ___________.

3 ___________ you meet people at work?
Yes, I 4 ___________.

5 ___________ you and your friends play basketball?
No, we 6 ___________.

c Write simple present questions with the words and phrases.

> what time / you / get up
What time do you get up?
1 what / you / eat in the morning
2 where / your brother / work
3 you / speak / English
4 your teacher / speak / Spanish
5 what time / the class / start
6 when / it / end

d Ask and answer the questions in 1c.

2 VOCABULARY

a Complete the job words.

1 s___________r

2 t_____i d_____r

3 d___________r

4 r___________t

5 t___________r

6 c___________f

b Complete the chart with the words and phrases in the box.

arrive get start to bed lunch
shower ~~to school~~ take

go	*to school* / to work 1 ___________
wake 2 ___________	up
3 ___________ finish	work
have	breakfast / 4 ___________ / dinner a coffee
5 ___________ / get	home
6 ___________	a shower

c What do you do every day? Tell a partner.

3 SOUND AND SPELLING

a 06.25 Listen to the sounds in **bold** and put the words in the correct box.

chair informa**ti**on spe**ci**al **ch**icken **ch**eck ma**ch**ine

/ʃ/	/tʃ/

b 06.26 Look at the pair of words. Put the words in the box into similar pairs.

sound 1 /ʃ/ sound 2 /tʃ/
ship – **ch**ip

choose cash wash cheap cheese
watch sheep catch she's shoes

c 06.27 Match the words that start with the same consonant group. Practice saying the words.

bread class ~~drink~~ player sport start twenty

> **dr**iver – *drink*
1 **tw**elve – ___________
2 **st**udy – ___________
3 **pl**ate – ___________
4 **cl**ock – ___________
5 **br**eakfast – ___________
6 **sp**oon – ___________

REVIEW YOUR PROGRESS

How well did you do in this unit? Write 3, 2, or 1 for each objective.
3 = very well 2 = well 1 = not so well

I CAN ...	
talk about people's jobs	☐
talk about daily routines and habits	☐
make and accept offers	☐

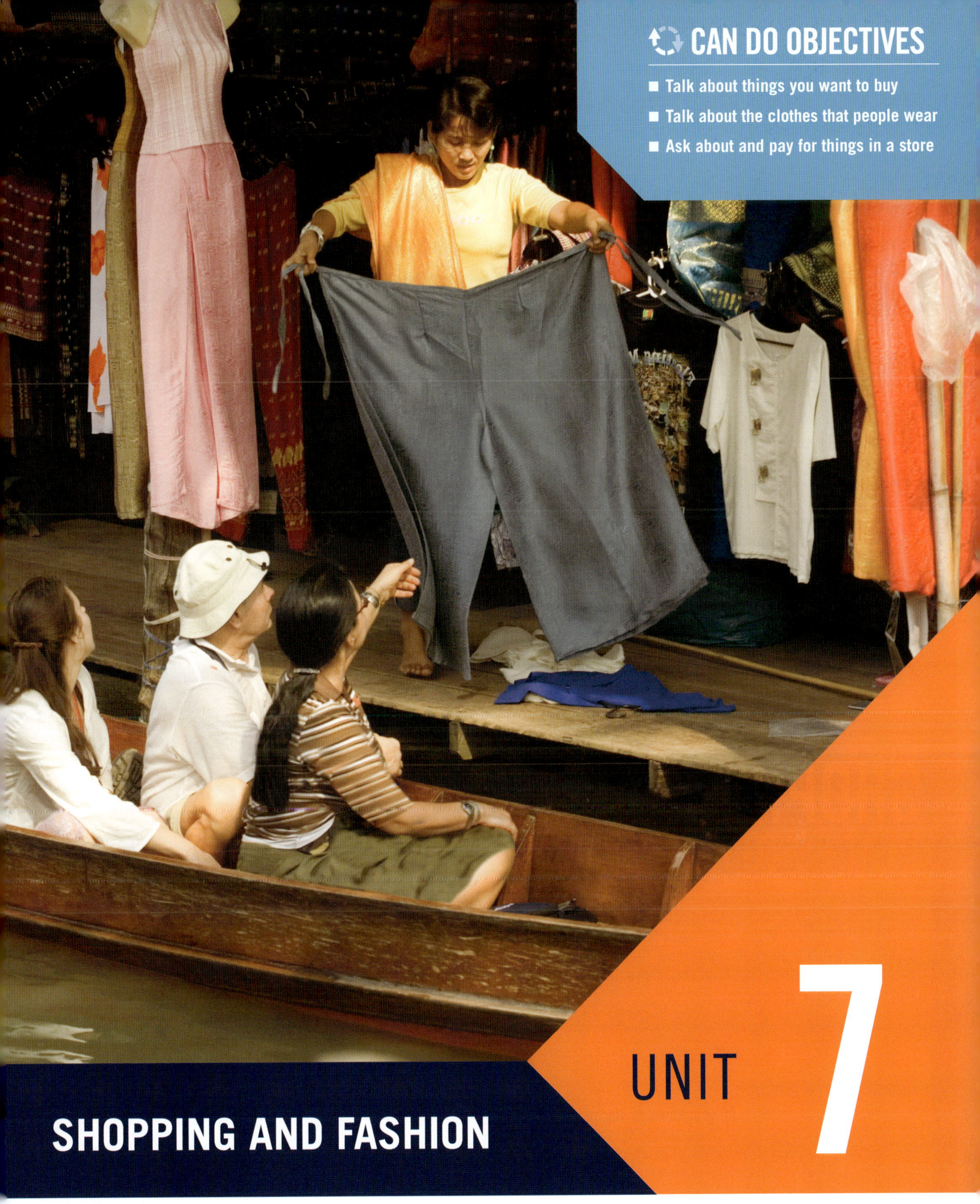

CAN DO OBJECTIVES

- Talk about things you want to buy
- Talk about the clothes that people wear
- Ask about and pay for things in a store

UNIT 7

SHOPPING AND FASHION

GETTING STARTED

a Look at the picture and answer the questions.

1 Are the people in the boat … ?
- ☐ on vacation
- ☐ shopping for food
- ☐ shopping for clothes
- ☐ friends
- ☐ family

2 What question does the woman in the boat ask?

3 What clothes can you see in the picture?

b Talk about the questions.

1 What do you like to buy when you go shopping?

2 What clothes do you have?

3 What color clothes do you like?

7A I LIKE THIS LAMP

Learn to talk about things you want to buy

G *this, that, these, those*

V Common objects 2; Prices

1 READING AND VOCABULARY Common objects 2

a Read about three places to shop. Which place is in the pictures?

b Which place is good for these people?

1 "I want a new bed for my apartment."
2 "I love old books and magazines."
3 "I always finish work at 7:00 p.m."
4 "I think old lamps are beautiful."

c Look at the pictures and read about The Sunday Flea Market again. Match the objects a–f with the words in the box.

suitcase lamp clock guitar picture chair

d Talk with other students about which object you would like to buy in the pictures. Say why. Which object do most people want?

e Now go to Vocabulary Focus 7A on p. 147.

f **Sound and spelling** /b/, /p/, /g/, and /k/

1 Complete the words in the chart. They are all common objects.

Sound 1 /b/	Sound 2 /p/	Sound 3 /g/	Sound 4 /k/
___ag	___lant	___lass	___up
___all	___late	___uitar	suit___ase
	___icture		___lo___ ___

2 07.02 Listen and check.
3 Which sound is spelled in different ways in the chart?
4 Practice saying the words.

g Work in pairs.

Student A: You have a stall at the flea market. Write five things you sell. Don't show Student B.
Student B: What does Student A sell?

Do you sell guitars?
No, sorry.
Do you have glasses?
Yes, I do. Here you go.

SHOPPING
PLACES TO GO

MEGA HOME STORE

Open 8 a.m.–8 p.m.

A great place to buy things for your home. They sell beds, pillows, tables, chairs, and lamps. Everything is new, but it isn't expensive. There's also a good café with drinks, pizza, and sandwiches.

THE SUNDAY FLEA MARKET

Open 6 a.m.–4 p.m.

Here you can buy something for your home, or you can just look around. They sell a lot of old things. You can buy clocks, guitars, suitcases, lamps, pictures, chairs … anything! Just look at these pictures from our readers!

BOOKS & CO.

Open 9 a.m.–6 p.m.

A very interesting bookstore. They sell old and new books, and they also have magazines, pictures, old photographs, and music. If you like old books and pictures, this is the place for you.

2 LISTENING AND GRAMMAR
this, that, these, those

a 07.03 Kate and Edward are at Mega Home Store. Listen to their conversation and answer the questions.

1 Who likes the plant and the chairs?
2 Who likes the phone, Kate or Edward?
3 How much is the speaker?
4 Does Kate think it's a good price?

b 07.04 Listen to Kate and Edward. Complete the sentences with *this*, *that*, *these*, or *those*.

1 "I like ________ plant. What do you think?"
2 "Or ________ chairs. They're really nice."
3 "Oh, look. ________ plates are beautiful."
4 "Look at ________ speaker. That's so cool."

c Complete the chart with the words in 2b.

Singular	this	
Plural		

Which words mean ... ?
1 here, near me
2 there, not near me

d **Sound and spelling** *this*, *that*, *these*, and *those*

1 07.05 Listen to *this*, *that*, *these*, and *those*. Which words ... ?
- end in a /s/ sound
- end in a /z/ sound

2 Practice saying the words.

e Now go to Grammar Focus 7A on p. 126.

f You and your partner are in the store below. Talk about the objects in the box with *this*, *that*, *these*, or *those*.

glasses plates speaker plant chairs phone lamp

3 VOCABULARY Prices

a 07.07 Listen to the prices. Check (✓) the phrase you hear.

1 $3.80
a ☐ three dollar eighty
b ☐ three dollars eighty cents
c ☐ three dollars and eighty cents

2 $25
a ☐ twenty-five dollar
b ☐ twenty-five dollars
c ☐ twenty-five of dollars

b 07.08 Practice saying the prices below. Listen and check.

1 $5.99
2 $16.50
3 $4.50
4 $100

c 07.09 Listen. Then complete the conversation.

A Excuse me. [1]______ ______ is that **clock**?
B [2]______ $13.50.
A Hmm. And [3]______ ______ are these **cups**?
B [4]______ $5 each.

d Practice the conversation in 3c with a partner. Change the words in **bold** and the prices.

e How much are these things in your country?
- a cup of coffee in a café
- a phone
- a pizza
- a bottle of water

4 SPEAKING

Communication 7A

Student A go to p. 113.
Student B go to p. 111.

7B IT'S OSCAR'S T-SHIRT

Learn to talk about clothes that people wear

G Possessive *'s*; Review of adverbs

V Clothes; Colors

They make colorful clothes, but do they wear them?

Fashion designers often make very different and interesting clothes for people, but they don't usually wear colorful clothes. They often wear the same clothes and the same colors.

TOM FORD makes beautiful clothes for men and for women, but he often wears a white shirt and a black or dark gray jacket.

1 VOCABULARY Clothes

a Look at the pictures of the models and the fashion designers. Which clothes do you like?

b 07.10 Match the words in the box with a–h in the pictures. Listen and check.

jacket coat shirt skirt pants T-shirt dress blouse

c Which clothes do you often wear together?

d **Sound and spelling** /ʃ/ and /dʒ/

1 07.11 Listen and practice these sounds.
1 /ʃ/ **sh**irt 2 /dʒ/ **j**acket

2 07.12 Look at the words in the box. What sounds do the letters in **bold** have? Listen and add the words to the sound groups below.

German interna**t**ional fa**sh**ion lar**ge** langua**ge** **g**ym **s**ugar

Sound 1 /ʃ/	Sound 2 /dʒ/
shirt	jacket

3 Practice saying the words.

e **Communication 7B** Student A go to p. 110. Student B go to p. 114.

2 READING

a Read about the fashion designers. What is the same about them?

b Read the text again. Are the sentences true or false? Correct the false sentences.

1 Fashion designers sometimes wear boring clothes.
2 Tom Ford never wears a black jacket.
3 Carolina Herrera often wears a white skirt.
4 Michael Kors usually wears a jacket.

c Is it a good idea for fashion designers to wear their clothes? Why / Why not?

3 VOCABULARY Colors

a Look at the picture of Tom Ford. Complete the sentence about him with colors in the box.

black ● gray ● white ○

Tom Ford often wears a ______ shirt and a ______ or dark ______ jacket.

CAROLINA HERRERA makes clothes with a lot of different colors, but she usually wears a black skirt and a white blouse.

MICHAEL KORS designs colorful clothes, but he often wears a black T-shirt, black jeans, and a black jacket.

Language Plus *dark/light*

***dark** blue*	***light** blue*
***dark** green*	***light** green*

b Now go to Vocabulary Focus 7B on p. 148.

c Work with a partner.

Student A: Choose a picture in 1a. Don't tell your partner! Talk about the colors and the clothes.
Student B: Guess the picture your partner talks about.

Then switch roles.

4 LISTENING

a 07.15 Listen to Isabella and Gonzalo López. Check (✓) the clothes you hear.

- ☐ T-shirt
- ☐ jeans
- ☐ skirt
- ☐ pants
- ☐ shoes
- ☐ shirt

b 07.15 Listen again and complete the information.

Who?	What clothes?	Why?
Oscar	______	*doesn't wear / doesn't like*
Sara	______	*doesn't wear / doesn't like*
Gonzalo	______	*doesn't wear / doesn't like*

5 GRAMMAR Possessive *'s*; Review of adverbs

a 07.16 Complete the sentences with a name from 4b. Listen and check.

1 **GONZALO** Is this my old T-shirt?
ISABELLA No, it's ______**'s** T-shirt. (= It's **his** T-shirt.)
2 **GONZALO** Are these your jeans?
ISABELLA No, they're ______**'s** jeans. (= They're **her** jeans.)

b Now go to Grammar Focus 7B on p. 126.

c Look at the picture of Oscar, Sara, Gonzalo, and Isabella. Ask and answer questions about the López family.

Who's Gonzalo?

He's Isabella's husband.

d 07.18 Isabella talks about the people in her office. Put the word in parentheses in the correct place in the sentences. Listen and check.

"Everyone wears different clothes at work. [1]My boss wears a blouse and pants (always). [2]She wears a skirt (never) – she doesn't like them. [3]John wears jeans and a white shirt (usually), [4]but he wears black pants (sometimes). [5]And Lindsay wears a dress (often), [6]but on Fridays she wears jeans (usually)."

e Think of people you work or study with. What do they usually wear? Tell a partner.

6 SPEAKING

a Put the words and phrases in the correct order to make questions. Write another question with your own idea.

1 wear / at work (or school) / do you / what ?
2 wear / do you / what color clothes ?
3 your brother's (or sister's, father's, mother's) clothes / do you / wear ?
4 at home / do you / wear shoes ?

b Ask and answer the questions in 6a. Add extra information to your answers.

What do you wear to work?

I usually wear a blue or black dress and dark shoes. I like dark colors.

7C EVERYDAY ENGLISH
Can I help you?

Learn to ask about and pay for things in a store

P Connecting sounds

W An email request for information

1 LISTENING

a Number the things you can buy from 1 to 4.
1 = I like going shopping for this/these very much.
4 = I really don't like going shopping for this/these.

☐ food ☐ clothes ☐ things for the home ☐ electronics

b Talk with a partner about your ideas in 1a. Do you like shopping for the same things?

c 07.19 Listen to Part 1. Answer the questions.

1 Who do Alexis and Mia go shopping for?
2 What does Mia buy?

d 07.19 Listen to Part 1 again. Complete the information about the things in the store.

Umbrellas	Bags
price: $______ colors: ______ ______	price: $______ colors: ______ ______

2 USEFUL LANGUAGE Going shopping 1

a 07.20 Who says each expression – the customer (C) or the sales assistant (S)? Listen and check.

1 How much are these umbrellas?
2 I'd like four of these plates, please.
3 They're fifteen dollars each.
4 Sure.
5 Can I look around?
6 Can I help you?
7 Of course.

b 07.21 Put the conversation in the correct order. Listen and check.

☐ It's fifteen dollars.
☐ Of course.
☐ It's ten dollars for the small one.
1 Can I help you?
☐ And how much is the small bowl?
☐ OK, then I'd like the large bowl, please.
☐ Yes, thank you. How much is this large bowl?

c Practice the conversation in 2b with a partner.

d Practice the conversation in 2b again, but ask about glasses. Change the prices.

3 PRONUNCIATION Connecting sounds

a 07.22 Listen and notice the extra sounds in these sentences.

1 We /j/ only have three.
2 I'd like two /w/ of these glasses.

Practice saying the sentences.

b Complete the rules with the sounds in the box.

/w/ /j/

We add a ______ sound between words ending with /i/ and words starting with a vowel.
We add a ______ sound between words ending with /u/ and words starting with a vowel.

c 07.23 Listen to these sentences. Which extra /j/ or /w/ sound can you hear? Listen again and repeat.

1 Would you like two or three?
2 These are for me and you.
3 Would you like three or four?
4 Are they for you or me?

d Practice the sentences in 3c with a partner.

4 LISTENING AND USEFUL LANGUAGE
Going shopping 2

a 07.24 Listen to Part 2. Are the sentences true or false?

1 Mia pays ten dollars.
2 She uses a card to pay.
3 Alexis doesn't buy anything.

b 07.25 Complete the sentences with words in the box. Listen and check.

your that's here's you no

S OK, ________ eight dollars, please.
C Here ________ go.
S Enter ________ PIN, please.
C OK, ________ problem.
S ________ your receipt.

c 07.26 Complete a conversation between a sales assistant and customer. Use phrases in 4b. Listen and check.

C How much … ? (*shoes*)
S Thirty dollars.
C Here …
S Enter …
C OK …
S And … receipt.

d Practice the conversation in 4c with a partner. Change the things you buy and the price.

5 SPEAKING

Communication 7C

Student A go to p. 111.
Student B go to p. 112.

6 WRITING

a Alexis saw an online advertisement.

FOR SALE

Designer women's coats, blouses, jeans, bags – *all in good condition.*
Not expensive!

Email me for more information **stylecarolina@travelmail.com**

Read her email. What information does she want to know?

Dear Carolina,
You have an online ad for things you want to sell. I'd like a bag, a coat, and a blouse. Can I see photos of these things? How much are they? Can I pay by credit card?
Thank you!
Alexis

b Now go to Writing Plus 7C on p. 161 for Commas, exclamation points, and question marks.

c You see these online advertisements.

FOR SALE

Sports T-shirts and balls – lots of different sports – signed by professional players: soccer, basketball, baseball, and more.
Great prices!

Email me for more information **ilovesports@travelmail.com**

FOR SALE

Beautiful things for your home – chairs, lamps, small tables.
All in good condition.

Email me for more information **melissa@travelmail.com**

Write an email to ask about one of the advertisements. Here are some ideas:

You have a / an / some …
I need …
How old … ?
How much … ?
Can I pay … ?

d Read a partner's email. What objects does your partner ask about? Do you ask about the same things?

UNIT PROGRESS TEST

CHECK YOUR PROGRESS

YOU CAN NOW DO THE UNIT PROGRESS TEST.

UNIT 7
Review

1 GRAMMAR

a Complete the sentences with the phrases in the box.

these this those that's

1 ______ is my dad's car.

2 I love ______ flowers.

3 ______ an expensive car.

4 ______ flowers in the windows are nice!

b Underline the correct answers to complete the conversation.

ZOE Hi, Lee. Do you know Kate? [1] *This / That / These* are [2] *Kate's / Kates / Kates'* daughters, Amy and Anna.
LEE Hello! Nice to meet you, girls. Who's who?
ZOE This [3] *is / are* Amy.
ANNA And I'm Anna.
LEE I like your bag, Anna.
ANNA Oh, thanks. It's [4] *Amys / Amys' / Amy's*. Amy and I have a swimming lesson today.
ZOE Yes, the [5] *girl's / girls / girls'* lesson starts at nine.
ANNA And then we go to our favorite restaurant!

c Practice the conversation in 1b in groups of three.

2 VOCABULARY

a Complete the names of these common objects.

1 a p______________e

2 a g______________r

3 a c______________r

4 a g______________s

5 a l______________p

6 a p______________t

b Complete the descriptions using the colors and clothes.

white light blue light brown red green dark blue

shirt coat skirt jeans shoes

1 a ______ dress
2 ______ pants and black ______
3 a gray ______ and a ______ jacket
4 a light green ______ and a ______ hat
5 a ______ blouse and a red ______
6 dark blue ______ and a ______ T-shirt

c How many hats/coats/jackets/shoes do you have? What color are they? Tell a partner.

3 SOUND AND SPELLING

a 07.27 Answer the questions. Practice saying the words.

1 Which words have the /k/ sound? Underline them.

suitcase clock place chair cup jacket coat dark

2 Which words have the /p/ sound? Underline them.

pink lamp photograph picture plate plant

3 Which words have the /g/ sound? Underline them.

magazine bag light gray green thing

b 07.28 Complete the chart with the words in the box. Practice saying the words.

~~shoes~~ sugar international jeans large fashion T-shirt jacket Germany

/ʃ/	/dʒ/
shoes	

REVIEW YOUR PROGRESS

How well did you do in this unit? Write 3, 2, or 1 for each objective.
3 = very well 2 = well 1 = not so well

I CAN ...	
talk about things I want to buy	☐
talk about the clothes that people wear	☐
ask about and pay for things in a store	☐

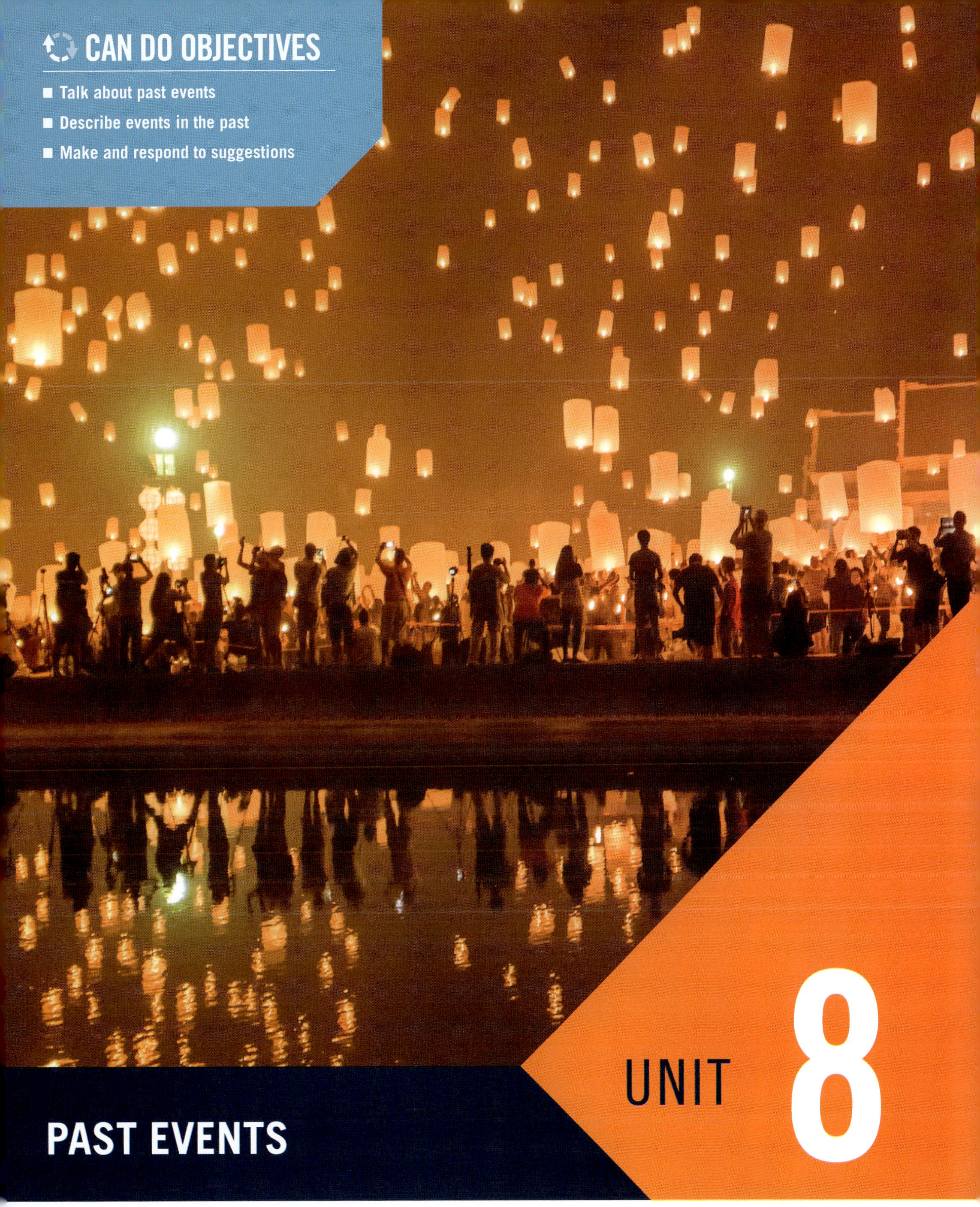

CAN DO OBJECTIVES

- Talk about past events
- Describe events in the past
- Make and respond to suggestions

UNIT 8

PAST EVENTS

GETTING STARTED

a Look at the picture of a New Year's Eve celebration and talk about the questions.

1 Do you want to go there? Why / Why not?
2 What do you think is happening at this New Year's Eve celebration? Here are some ideas:

- ☐ music
- ☐ dancing
- ☐ shopping
- ☐ fireworks
- ☐ eating food
- ☐ meeting friends

b Talk about the questions.

1 Where were you last New Year's Eve?
2 Who were you with?
3 What things did you do?
4 Did you have fun?

8A I WAS ON TOUR WITH MY BAND

Learn to talk about past events

- **G** Simple past: *be*
- **V** Past time expressions

1 READING

a Look at the events in pictures a–d. Choose one you like and one you don't like. Tell a partner. Say why.

a party

a sports game

a concert

a meeting

b Read about Cara, Antonio, and Ava. Which events in 1a do they talk about?

c Read the texts again. Which cities does each person talk about?

d Talk about Cara, Antonio, and Ava's lives with a partner. Who would you like to meet? Why?

My name's Cara. I'm a photographer. I was in New York three days ago for work, and then I was in Chicago yesterday at a meeting about newspaper photography. Life's busy right now!

"Yesterday I was in Chicago."

"I was at a game in Los Angeles. It was the Finals!"

The people on our team ...

My name's Antonio Marotto. I'm the doctor for our team. It's a great job – I really like helping our players. I often go away with the team. We were in Miami two weeks ago for a game, and we were in Cleveland last week. It's fun to travel with the team.

Ava on the road ...

Hi everyone, it's Ava. Last week I was on tour with my band in the U.S. – three cities in five days. We were in Seattle on Wednesday, and then we were in Portland on Thursday. But Saturday was the best night. We were in San Francisco, and about 1,000 people were at our concert.

"In this photo, we were in San Francisco."

2 GRAMMAR Simple past: *be* affirmative

a Complete the chart. Find examples of the simple past of *be* in the texts about Cara, Antonio, and Ava.

+	
I [1] ________ you were he/she/it [2] ________	we [3] ________ you were they were

b 08.01 **Pronunciation** Listen to sentences 1–4. Are *was* and *were* stressed? Practice saying the sentences.

1 We were in Seattle.
2 I was in Los Angeles.
3 We were in Miami.
4 I was in New York.

c Now go to Grammar Focus 8A Part 1 on p. 128.

d Write sentences about where you were:

- this morning
- last night
- yesterday afternoon

e Compare your sentences in 2d with a partner. Were you in the same places?

> Juan and I were at the supermarket yesterday.

3 VOCABULARY Past time expressions

a Today is Friday of week 3. Put the number of sentences 1–4 in the correct place on the timeline.

week 1	week 2	week 3
		Monday Tuesday Wednesday Thursday (Friday)

1 We were in Seattle on <u>Wednesday</u>.
2 We were in Miami two <u>weeks</u> ago.
3 … we were in Cleveland last <u>week</u>.
4 I was in Chicago <u>yesterday</u>.

b Look at the <u>underlined</u> words in 3a. Replace them with words in the box.

months	this morning	Saturday	year

c Now go to Vocabulary Focus 8A on p. 149.

d Work in pairs.

Student A: Say a past time expression.
Student B: Say where a person you know was.

Then switch roles.

> last weekend
> My parents were in London last weekend.
> two years ago
> My friend Marco was in Ecuador two years ago.

4 LISTENING AND GRAMMAR Simple past: *be* negative and questions

a 08.06 Review the texts about Cara, Antonio, and Ava again. Then listen to them talking to friends. Write the correct name for each conversation.

Conversation 1 ____________
Conversation 2 ____________
Conversation 3 ____________

b 08.06 Match events 1–3 with adjectives a–c. Listen again and check.

1 the meeting — a exciting
2 the game — b interesting
3 the concert — c fun

c 08.07 Listen to Conversation 1 again. Complete the conversation with the words in the box.

was (x2)	were (x2)	wasn't

WILL ________ you at work yesterday?
CARA Yes, I ________, but I ________ here in the office.
WILL Where ________ you?
CARA I was at a meeting in Chicago.
WILL Oh, ________ it interesting?
CARA Yes, it was really interesting.

d Now go to Grammar Focus 8A Part 2 on p. 128.

e 08.11 Complete the conversation with *was*, *were*, *wasn't*, or *weren't*. Listen and check.

A You ________ at work yesterday.
B No, I ________ off yesterday.
A Nice. ________ you at home all day?
B No, I ________. I ________ in town in the morning, and then I ________ at a party last night.
A ________ the party good?
B Yes, it ________ a lot of fun.

f Practice the conversation in 4e with a partner. Change some of the information.

> I was at a baseball game in the morning and then at the movies last night.
> Was the movie good?

5 SPEAKING

a **Communication 8A** Student A go to p. 113. Student B go to p. 111. Student C go to p. 115.

8B HE SAW A BEAR

Learn to describe events in the past

G Simple past: affirmative

V Free time activities

1 READING

a Look at pictures 1–3 below. Match the pictures to the animal names. Where do they usually live? What do you know about them?

_____ deer _____ bear _____ hippo

b Read the stories below. Write the story titles next to the sentences.

1 Hippos were on a rugby field. __________
2 Three deer were in a woman's apartment. __________
3 A bear was in a man's backyard. __________

c Read the stories again. Complete the information.

	Where?	When?	Animal activity?
Andrew from Utah	at home		
Ben from South Africa		evening	
A woman from Indiana			jump

d Talk about the questions.

1 Which story do you like?
2 Which animals sometimes come into houses in your country?

cat

dog

bird

snake

3 What do you do if a wild animal comes to your house?

WILD STORIES!

1

CURIOUS CREATURE

Andrew Singer from Utah was at home in his house on a farm. One evening he was in the kitchen, and he heard something strange in the backyard, so he looked out the window. He saw a bear in the backyard. The bear walked around the backyard and looked in the windows of the house. It tried to open the kitchen door, and the man was really scared. It wasn't possible for the bear to get in, so it went away. The man thinks the bear was hungry, but it's not a good idea to give bears food.

2

SURPRISE VISITORS

A woman from Indiana had an apartment with a yard. In the evening, she went into her living room and watched TV. She heard something in her bedroom, so she went to look. She saw three deer near her bed. They came into the living room and jumped on her sofa, then they went into the bathroom. The woman called 911, and the police came to catch the deer. She had an exciting night with her three new friends!

3

READY TO PLAY

Ben Kruger from South Africa loves playing rugby. He has a business in Limpopo, a city in the north of South Africa. One night after work, he went to a rugby field nearby. It was dark, and he saw something on the field. It was large, but it wasn't a person – it was a hippopotamus (hippo)! Then he saw another hippo and then another – there were a lot of them. The hippos ate some grass and then went away. Ben thinks the hippos were from a river near the rugby field.

2 GRAMMAR Simple past: affirmative

a 08.12 Read the stories again and find the simple past forms of the verbs in the chart. Listen and check.

A		B	
Verb	**Past form**	**Verb**	**Past form**
look	*looked*	have	*had*
watch		hear	
call		eat	
jump		see	
walk		go	
try		come	

b Answer the questions about the chart in 2a.

1 What do we add to the verbs in A to make the past form?
2 Do the verbs in B all change in the same way or in different ways?

c **Sound and spelling** /t/ and /d/

1 08.13 Listen and practice these sounds.
1 /t/ talk**ed** 2 /d/ liv**ed**

2 08.14 Listen to the past forms in the box. Which *-ed* endings sound ... ?
- more like /t/
- more like /d/

looked watched called tried
walked played finished

3 Practice saying the words.

d Cover the chart in 2a. Test a partner.
Student A: Say a verb.
Student B: Say the past form.
Then switch roles.

e Now go to Grammar Focus 8B on p. 128.

f Complete the sentences so they are true for you.

1 Yesterday I called ________. (a person)
2 Last month I saw ________. (a TV show)
3 Last weekend I went to ________. (a place)
4 Last night I ate ________. (food)

Tell your partner about your sentences.

3 LISTENING AND VOCABULARY Free time activities

a 08.17 Listen to three conversations about the three stories. In each conversation, some information is incorrect. What is the wrong information?

1 ________
2 ________
3 ________

b 08.18 Listen to the sentences from the conversations. Use the correct verb in the box.

read (x2) talked went had watched heard

1 I just ________ to a café.
2 I ________ a large coffee.
3 And I ________ the newspaper.
4 I ________ this funny story.
5 I ________ this story on a podcast.
6 I ________ to my friend Katie last night.
7 She ________ the video online.

c Match verbs 1 to 6 with a word or phrase in the box to make more simple past phrases.

a book to my parents home dinner a movie
for a walk breakfast a song on the radio to my friend

1 went ________, ________
2 had ________, ________
3 read ________
4 heard ________
5 talked ________, ________
6 watched ________

d 08.19 Listen to Emily talk about the things she did yesterday. Put pictures a–e in the correct order.

a

b

c

d

e

e 08.19 Complete what Emily says with phrases from 3c. Then listen again and check.

Yesterday I [1]________ at about 9:00, and then I went to a café and had coffee with my friend Karen. After that, I went to work and was there all day. I [2]________ with my brother, and then I [3]________ and called my parents. I [4]________ Rosie in Brazil on Skype. After, I [5]________ online, and then I went to bed and [6]________ before going to sleep.

f Now go to Vocabulary Focus 8B on p. 150.

g Complete the sentences about free time activities.

1 When I was a child, I ________.
2 After work / school, I often ________.
3 On weekends, I like to ________.

h Tell other students your sentences in 3g. What free time activities were/are popular ... ?

a when everyone was a child
b after work / school
c on weekends

4 SPEAKING

a **Communication 8B** Student A go to p. 113. Student B go to p. 111.

8C EVERYDAY ENGLISH

Let's go somewhere this weekend

Learn to make and respond to suggestions

P Sentence stress and intonation

W Thank you note

1 LISTENING

a Ask and answer the questions.

1 On the first day at work / school after the weekend, how do you feel?
2 What do you usually talk to your friends about on that day?

b 08.22 Listen to Part 1. Logan and Daniel are at work on Monday morning. Check (✓) the things they talk about:

a ☐ the weekend
b ☐ Boston (the city where they live)
c ☐ work
d ☐ family
e ☐ baseball

c 08.22 Listen to Part 1 again. Are the sentences true or false?

1 Daniel was busy with friends all weekend.
2 Logan likes the city, but he doesn't like the weather.
3 Logan sees his family often.

d What do you like about the town or city where you live? What don't you like?

e 08.23 Listen to Part 2. Who went to a party? Who watched TV?

f 08.23 Listen to Part 2 again and answer the questions.

1 What's difficult for Logan? Is it hard for Daniel, too?
2 What's Daniel's idea for next weekend?
3 Does Logan feel happy or sad at the end of the conversation? Why?

g Talk about the questions.

1 Is it difficult to meet new people in your town / city? Why / Why not?
2 What are good ways to meet new people?

Boston, Massachusetts

2 USEFUL LANGUAGE Making and responding to suggestions

a 08.24 Listen to the conversations. Underline the word you hear. Are both options possible?

1 **DANIEL** *Let's* / *We could* go to Newport.
LOGAN That sounds *nice* / *good*.
2 **DANIEL** So, *do you want to* / *let's* go there on Saturday?
LOGAN Yeah, that's a *nice* / *great* idea.

b 08.25 Complete the conversation with the words in the box. Listen and check.

A Let's ______ for dinner on Saturday.
B Saturday? I'm ______, I can't. I'm out of town on Saturday.
A Do you ______ to go on Sunday?
B Yes, that's a great ______.

want idea go sorry

c Practice the conversation in 2b with a partner.

d Complete the conversation with words or expressions in 2a and 2b. There is sometimes more than one answer.

A ______ go to the movies tonight.
B ______, I'm busy. I have a work dinner.
A ______ go tomorrow night.
B OK, ______.

e Practice the conversation in 2d with a partner. Take turns being A and B.

3 PRONUNCIATION Sentence stress and intonation

a 08.26 Listen to the expressions. Notice the main stress.

1 Yes, that's a great idea. 2 Yes, that's a nice idea.

b 08.26 Listen to the expressions in 3a again. Does the intonation rise ↗ or fall ↘ after the main stress?

c Work with a partner.

Student A: Say sentences 1 and 2.
Student B: Answer with phrases in 3a.
1 Let's have some coffee.
2 Do you want to go for a walk?

Then switch roles.

4 SPEAKING

a Work in pairs. Read the ideas below and think about what you want to say.

A	B
Suggest going to a restaurant on Friday.	You're busy on Friday. You have a work dinner.
Suggest Saturday.	Say yes. Suggest an Italian restaurant.
You went to an Italian restaurant last weekend. Suggest a Mexican restaurant.	Say yes. Suggest a time.
Agree with Student B. Say goodbye.	Thank Student A and say goodbye.

b Have a phone conversation with your partner. Then switch roles.

Do you want to go to a restaurant on Friday?

I'm sorry, I'm busy that night. I have a work dinner.

5 WRITING

a Read Logan's text to Daniel. Why did Logan write it?

Logan M.

Hi Daniel!
Thank you for the tour of Newport yesterday. It was great to see a new town and meet your friends. I had a lot of fun! Here is a picture I took at lunch. I hope we can do it again sometime soon.
See you soon!

b Now go to Writing Plus 8C on p. 161 for Writing short emails, notes, and texts.

c Write a note to a friend to thank them for something. Here are some ideas:

I want to say thank you for …
It was …
I hope …

d Read another student's note. What do they say thank you for?

UNIT PROGRESS TEST

CHECK YOUR PROGRESS

YOU CAN NOW DO THE UNIT PROGRESS TEST.

UNIT 8
Review

1 GRAMMAR

a Write simple past sentences and questions with *be* and the words and phrases.

> (?) where / you yesterday
Where were you yesterday?
1 (+) I / in a meeting.
2 (?) / you OK
3 (–) James / at work this morning.
4 (?) where / he
5 (+) Yasmin and Kylie / in New York two weeks ago.
6 (–) we / in Paris six years ago

b Complete the text with the simple past form of the verb in parentheses.

Last week my family and I [1]__________ (be) in Miami. We [2]__________ (arrive) on Wednesday morning. First, we [3]__________ (visit) my dad's family. My dad and his brothers [4]__________ (talk) for a long time. Then we [5]__________ (go) to a big museum in downtown Miami. We [6]__________ (see) a lot of interesting things there. In the evening, we [7]__________ (watch) a movie. We [8]__________ (stay) at the Dylan Hotel. The rooms [9]__________ (not / be) very big, but I [10]__________ (like) the bathroom and the food [11]__________ (be) great! Every morning I [12]__________ (have) toast, eggs, fruit, and coffee for breakfast.

2 VOCABULARY

a Check (✓) the correct answer.

Today is WEDNESDAY, OCTOBER 21.
It's 7:30 p.m.

1 Wednesday, October 7
a ☐ two weeks ago
b ☐ yesterday
2 2:30 p.m. on Wednesday, October 21
a ☐ last night
b ☐ this afternoon
3 August 21
a ☐ two months ago
b ☐ last month
4 Tuesday, October 20
a ☐ yesterday
b ☐ a few days ago
5 Saturday, October 17
a ☐ this morning
b ☐ last Saturday
6 Sunday, October 18
a ☐ six months ago
b ☐ on Sunday

b Ask and answer questions with *Where were you … ?* and a past time expression.

c Complete the chart with the words and phrases in the box.

a video game a soccer game (x2)
a magazine a pizza a podcast a shower

have	a drink, coffee, [1]__________
listen to	music, [2]__________
watch	[3]__________, a movie
read	a book, [4]__________, the newspaper
play	the guitar, [5]__________, soccer
go to	the movies, a party, [6]__________, a café
take	[7]__________

d Correct the sentences.

1 I was in Atlanta before two weeks ago.
2 We were in Quito last the weekend.
3 I had coffee with Lily at Friday.
4 We went a party yesterday.
5 I listened music last night.
6 We played the baseball this morning.

3 SOUND AND SPELLING

a 08.27 Look at the words in the box. Is the final sound /t/ or /d/? Complete the chart. Practice saying the words.

~~called~~ talked lived watched
listened played finished

/t/	/d/
	called

b 08.28 Listen to the sentences. Underline the word with the main stress.

1 That's a great idea.
2 It's a beautiful place.
3 It was good.
4 How was your weekend?

c Complete the conversation with the phrases from 3b. Then practice with a partner.

A Good morning! [1]__________
B [2]__________ I stayed at home and watched movies. What about you?
A On Saturday, I went to a new park in my city. [3]__________.
B [4]__________ Saturday was a beautiful day.
A Yes, it was.

REVIEW YOUR PROGRESS

How well did you do in this unit? Write 3, 2, or 1 for each objective.
3 = very well 2 = well 1 = not so well

I CAN …	
talk about past events	☐
describe events in the past	☐
make and respond to suggestions	☐

CAN DO OBJECTIVES

- Talk about travel and vacation experiences
- Talk about past vacations
- Make and respond to requests

UNIT 9

VACATIONS

GETTING STARTED

a Look at the picture and answer the questions.

1 What country do you think this is?
2 What transportation can you see?
3 What time of year is it?
4 What is the weather like in this place?

b Talk about the questions.

1 Where did you go on your last vacation?
2 What weather do you like while on vacation? Why?

c Ask your partner one question about their last vacation.

9A I DIDN'T STAY IN A HOTEL

Learn to talk about travel and vacation experiences

G Simple past: negative

V Transportation

BACKYARD CAMPING

Home | Find A Backyard | Reviews | Contact Us

How Does It Work?

Do you want a cheap vacation in a beautiful place? Why not camp in someone's backyard? It's cheap, and you can make new friends. We have more than 1,000 backyards in 70 countries, and you can camp in all of them!

Old house with a big backyard on a lake. 20 minutes from the Salt Lake City airport.

COST $15 a night

HOW TO GET THERE
Go to Stansbury Park by bus or tram. Then take a taxi or drive a car to the house (5 minutes).

ROBERT'S PLACE, STANSBURY PARK, UTAH, U.S.

42 big tents with beds and showers inside. 40 minutes from the city of Marrakesh.

COST $30 a night

HOW TO GET THERE
Fly to Marrakesh and then take a taxi or drive a car.

YOUSSEF'S PLACE, MARRAKESH, MOROCCO

1 READING

a Where do you usually stay on vacation? Here are some ideas:

- at a hotel
- at a hostel
- at a campsite
- with friends or family

b Read *How Does It Work?* on the *Backyard Camping* website. What do you think of the idea?

It's a great idea!

Hmm, interesting.

No, thanks!

c Read about three backyards on the *Backyard Camping* website. Which answers (a–d) are incorrect? Correct the wrong answers.

1 Robert's place:
  a old house
  b big backyard
  c in Salt Lake City
  d near the bus station

2 Youssef's place:
  a small tents
  b showers
  c not in Marrakesh
  d not very cheap

3 Guadalupe's place:
  a big backyard
  b pool
  c near some restaurants
  d expensive

2 VOCABULARY Transportation

a 09.01 Find words on the *Backyard Camping* website to match pictures 1–7. Listen and check.

b Find words on the *Backyard Camping* website to complete the charts.

go ______	bus plane tram

______	a bus a taxi

c Find verbs in the texts that mean:

a go by car
b go by plane

d Now go to Vocabulary Focus 9A on p. 151.

e How do you … ?

1 go to work or school
2 go to a big town or city nearby
3 go home late at night
4 go to a party
5 go on vacation

I usually take a bus to work.

House with a big backyard and swimming pool. Free bikes. Near restaurants, a river, and a zoo.

COST: $4 a night

HOW TO GET THERE: Go to Villavicencio by plane or bus. Then take a taxi or another bus to our house.

GUADALUPE'S PLACE, CUMARAL, COLOMBIA

Language Plus *go*

go *to the movies*   ***go*** *to work* NOT *to the ~~work~~*   ***go*** *home* NOT *to home*   ***go*** *on vacation*

f Sound and spelling the letter *a*

1 09.04 The letter *a* can have different sounds. Listen and practice the words.
1 /æ/ t**a**xi 2 /ɑ/ c**a**r 3 /eɪ/ pl**a**ne

2 09.05 Listen to these words. Are the letters in **bold** Sound 1, 2, or 3?

w**a**nt c**a**mp tr**a**in f**a**ther

3 09.06 Listen to these words. Which one in each group has a different *a* sound?

1 tr**a**m	w**a**nt	m**a**n
2 h**a**ve	l**a**ke	v**a**cation
3 p**a**rty	b**a**g	b**a**ckyard
4 pl**a**nt	gl**a**ss	w**a**nt

4 Practice saying the words.

3 GRAMMAR AND LISTENING
Simple past: negative

a Read the post from Julian's travel blog. Which place from the *Backyard Camping* website does he write about?

Julian

WEEK 3

Through the Country by Bus

We didn't go to big cities. We went by bus, and we stayed in small places in the country. In one place, we stayed with a family. We didn't stay in their house – we camped in their backyard. We bought food in the town, and we cooked meals in the house. And we went swimming every morning in their pool. It was very cheap, and the family was very friendly. We stayed for four days!

♡ 15 ◯ 7

b Read the blog post again. Check (✓) the correct sentences.

1 a ☐ They went to small places.
  b ☐ They didn't go to small places.
2 a ☐ They had a car.
  b ☐ They didn't have a car.
3 a ☐ They stayed in the house.
  b ☐ They didn't stay in the house.
4 a ☐ They used the kitchen.
  b ☐ They didn't use the kitchen.

c Look at the b sentences in 3b. Complete the rule.

Simple past negative (–):
I/you/he/she/it/we/they + ________ + verb

d Now go to Grammar Focus 9A on p. 130.

e 09.08 **Pronunciation** Listen to the sentences. Is *didn't* stressed or unstressed?

1 We didn't stay in their house.
2 We didn't have a car.

f 09.09 Listen to Julian. He says more things about his trip. What does he say about … ?

- emails
- money
- bikes
- photos

g What do you like about Julian's vacation? What don't you like?

h Think about your last vacation. Which sentences are true? If they aren't true, make them negative. Then write a true affirmative sentence.

1 I stayed in a hotel.
2 I visited museums.
3 I bought a lot of clothes.
4 I had my computer with me.
5 I went to bed early.
6 I cooked my own food.
7 I watched TV.
8 I read a lot of books.

1 I didn't stay in a hotel. I stayed in a hostel.

i Tell a partner your sentences in 3h.

I didn't visit museums.
I went to the zoo.

4 SPEAKING

Communication 9A Student A go to p. 114. Student B go to p. 110.

9B HOW DID YOU GET THERE?

Learn to talk about past vacations

G Simple past: questions

V The seasons; The weather

1 VOCABULARY The seasons

a 09.10 Match the words in the box with pictures a–d. Listen and check.

winter	summer	spring	autumn / fall

b Ask and answer the questions.

1 Do you have four seasons in your country?
2 Which seasons do you like? Which seasons don't you like?

a

b

c

d

2 READING

a Read about the Ortega family's vacation. What was different about this New Year's Eve and New Year's Day for them?

b Complete Michael's notes with the words in the box.

party	shopping	watched	cold

Notes Done

Thursday: 1 ____________ with family in Union Square

New Year's Eve: 2 ____________ in Times Square – great fireworks!

Friday: 3 ____________ and snowy weather; everyone stayed inside and 4 ____________ a movie.

The Ortega family from Puerto Rico went to New York City for New Year's Eve. Read Michael Ortega's blog post.

MY BLOG

MICHAEL ORTEGA

New Year's Fun in the BIG APPLE

Times Square ball drop

Thursday, December 31

We went shopping in Union Square – it has a lot of big stores, restaurants, and cafés. The weather is cold and windy in December, but we enjoyed it! We went to a big New Year's Eve party in Times Square in the evening and watched the ball drop. My sister and I loved the fireworks!

Friday, January 1

It's winter here, and it's very different to have our New Year's in the cold. I like the hot, sunny weather in Puerto Rico on New Year's Day, but in New York it was very cold and snowy. It didn't feel like New Year's Day. Everyone stayed inside and watched a movie!

3 VOCABULARY The weather

a 09.11 What does Michael say about the weather in New York City and Puerto Rico? Complete the sentences with *hot* or *cold*. Listen and check.

1 The weather is ______ and windy in December.

2 I like the ______, sunny weather in Puerto Rico on New Year's Day.

Language Plus *like*

*I **like** sunny weather.* = I think sunny weather is good.
*What's the weather **like**?* = How's the weather?

b Now go to Vocabulary Focus 9B on p. 152.

c **Sound and spelling** the letter *o*

1 09.14 The letter *o* can have different sounds. Listen and repeat the words.
1 /oʊ/ sn**ow** 2 /aʊ/ cl**ou**dy 3 /ɑ/ h**o**t

2 09.15 Listen to these words. Are the letters in **bold** Sound 1, 2, or 3?

sh**o**pping t**ow**n c**o**ld

3 09.16 Listen to these words. Which one in each group has a different *o* sound? Listen again and repeat.

1 g**o**t	j**o**b	g**o**
2 kn**ow**	n**o**t	sl**ow**
3 ph**o**ne	n**ow**	d**ow**n

d **Communication 9B** Student A go to p. 111. Student B go to p. 113.

4 LISTENING AND GRAMMAR Simple past: questions

a 09.17 Listen to Eric and Angie talk about summer vacations. Check (✓) the correct sentence.

1 ☐ They're on vacation now.
2 ☐ They talk about past and future vacations.
3 ☐ They only talk about past vacations.

b 09.17 Listen again. Match 1–3 with a–c.

1 Eric last year	a San Andrés Island
2 Angie last year	b Uruguay
3 Angie two years ago	c São Paulo

c 09.18 Listen to the end of the conversation. Choose one word from the box to complete the two questions.

do did

Eric How ______ you get there?
Angie By bus. And, you know, the weather was really warm.
Eric ______ you enjoy it there?
Angie Yes, I did. I had a great time, and I didn't want to leave!

d Now go to Grammar Focus 9B on p. 130.

e 09.21 Complete the two conversations about last weekend. Listen and check your answers.

Conversation 1
A go / movies last weekend?
B Yes, I did.
A What / see?
B The new James Bond movie.

Conversation 2
C go / restaurant last night?
D Yes, I did.
C Where / go?
D A new Thai restaurant.

f Tell a partner about last weekend. Use the conversations in 4e and your own ideas.

Did you see your friends last weekend?
Yes, I did.
Who did you see?
I saw Daniele.

g Work in new pairs. Tell your new partner about your first partner.

Jacob saw his friend Daniele last weekend.

5 SPEAKING

a Think about a past vacation. Write notes about the:

- place
- weather
- food
- things you did

b Write questions to ask about your partner's vacation.

1 When … the vacation? *When was the vacation?*
2 Where … go?
3 What … the weather like?
4 What … eat?
5 What … do?
6 (your idea for a question)

c Ask and answer the questions in 5b about your vacation.

When was the vacation?
It was last spring.
Where did you go?
We went to Lombok, in Indonesia.
What was the weather like?
It was hot and sunny.

9C EVERYDAY ENGLISH
Can you do something for me?

Learn to make and respond to requests

P Syllables

W An online post

1 LISTENING

a Talk about a place near your town or city with a partner. Ask and answer the questions.

1 Where's a nice place to visit for a day? Why?
2 What can you see and do there?
3 Do you go there often?

b 09.22 Look at pictures a and b and talk about the questions. Listen to Part 1 and check your answers.

1 Do you think Isabel and Sara like Mexico?
2 What is the first thing Sara buys at the market?

c 09.22 Listen to Part 1 again. Are the sentences true or false?

1 Isabel doesn't like the food.
2 Sara buys a hat, blankets, and bowls.
3 Sara's bag is heavy and difficult to carry.

d What do you buy when you visit another place?

2 PRONUNCIATION Syllables and spelling

a 09.23 Listen to the word in **bold** in the sentence. Do you hear all the letters?

It's very **different** from Baltimore.

09.23 Listen again and repeat the word in **bold**.

b 09.24 Listen to these words. Underline the letters you don't hear.

restaurant interesting favorite business
every family vegetable camera

c Practice saying the words in 2b.

3 LISTENING

a 09.25 Sara and Isabel are now at the hotel. Listen to Part 2 and check your answers.

1 What does Sara do on her phone?
2 Why can't they take the bus or the subway?

b 09.25 Listen to Part 2 again. Underline the correct answer.

1 Isabel wants to buy something at the *hotel* / *airport*.
2 Isabel puts Sara's new *blankets* / *bowls* in her suitcase.
3 Sara *asks* / *doesn't ask* Isabel for help with her bags.

c Who do you usually ask for help – a friend or someone in your family? Why?

4 USEFUL LANGUAGE Making and responding to requests

a 09.26 Listen to the questions. Underline the word you hear. Then answer the question below.

1 *Can / Could* you take it for a minute?
2 *Can / Could* you do something for me?
3 *Can / Could* you put these blankets in your suitcase?
4 *Can / Could* you help me with these bags, please?

Is it OK to use *can* and *could* in all the sentences?

b 09.27 Put the possible replies to the questions in 4a into the chart. Listen and check your answers.

Of course.	No, I can't.
I'm sorry, I can't.	Sure, no problem.

Yes	No

c 09.28 Complete mini-conversations 1 and 2 with the phrases in the box. Listen and check.

Oh, that's OK. I can do it.
Thanks, that's really nice of you.

1 **A** Could you help me with dinner?
B Sure, no problem.
A ______.

2 **C** Can you drive my sister to the train station?
D I'm sorry, I can't. I have a lot of work to finish.
C ______.

d Work in pairs. Take turns making requests and replying. Use the ideas below and *can/could*.

1 help me with my homework
2 give me your book
3 meet me after class
4 call me tonight

Could you meet me after class?

I'm sorry, I can't. I'm busy.

5 SPEAKING

a Work in pairs. You and your partner are on the phone. Look at the ideas below and think about what you want to say.

A	B
Say hello and who you are.	
	Say hello and ask how Student A is.
Answer. Ask for help with something.	
	Say yes.
Ask Student B to come shopping with you today.	
	Say no – you're busy today.
Ask about tomorrow.	
	Say yes.
Say thanks and goodbye.	
	Say goodbye.

b Have a phone conversation with your partner. Then switch roles.

6 WRITING

a Read about Sara's trip. What information about her trip to Mexico is new?

Last week I went to Mexico with Isabel. The last day was my favorite day. First, we went for a walk to the old part of the city. It was beautiful. Next, we had lunch at a small restaurant. The food was great! Then, we went shopping at a market, and I saw some beautiful things. I bought blankets, bowls, and a big hat. Isabel helped me with my bags because they were very heavy! Mexico is a great country – it's very different from Baltimore.

12 3

b Now go to Writing Plus 9C on p. 162 for Making the order clear.

c Write an online post about a trip to another place. Here are some ideas:

Last weekend, / month, / summer, I went to … with …
First, we … It was … Next, we … Then, we …
… is a nice / beautiful / great city / town / place.

d Read another student's online post. Do you like the activities he/she did?

UNIT PROGRESS TEST

CHECK YOUR PROGRESS

YOU CAN NOW DO THE UNIT PROGRESS TEST.

UNIT 9
Review

1 GRAMMAR

a Underline the correct answer.

1 We didn't *stay* / *stayed* in a hotel last year.
2 I didn't *take* / *took* any photos this morning.
3 She *doesn't* / *didn't* buy a book yesterday.
4 They didn't *have* / *had* fish for dinner last night.
5 We *don't watched* / *didn't watch* a movie last week.
6 He *didn't took* / *didn't take* a taxi to the airport.

b Look at the answers and complete the questions.

> "Did it rain yesterday?" "Yes, it did. It rained in the morning."
1 "__________ basketball last week?" "No, I didn't – but I played tennis!"
2 "What time __________ yesterday?" "I got up at six o'clock."
3 "__________ any photos on New Year's Eve?" "Yes, I did. I took some photos at the party."
4 "Where __________ yesterday?" "I went to the park."
5 "__________ your phone yesterday?" "Yes, of course! I use my phone every day!"
6 "What __________ for breakfast today?" "I had cereal and coffee."

c Work in pairs. Ask and answer the questions in 1b.

d Correct the simple past sentences.

> Where they did stay? *Where did they stay?*
1 Do you arrived last night?
2 Yes, I do arrived.
3 No, I not.
4 What did you bought?
5 I didn't watched TV.
6 What you cooked?
7 We don't visit Pedro yesterday.
8 Saw you the backyard?

2 VOCABULARY

a Write the words.

1 ritan __________
2 atix __________
3 bysauw __________
4 mart __________
5 elnap __________
6 pish __________

b Underline the correct answers.

A Was it [1] *cold* / *wet* / *warm*?
B Yes! It was –10°C! There was a lot of [2] *snow* / *snowy*.
A Wow! It never [3] *snows* / *snowy* in my country.

C Do I need an umbrella?
D I don't know. It's [4] *rainy* / *rain* – but it's very [5] *wind* / *windy*, too!

E Was it [6] *wet* / *hot*?
F Yes, very! It was about 35°C! But it was [7] *cloud* / *cloudy* all the time. We didn't see the sun.

3 SOUND AND SPELLING

a 09.29 Which of the letters in **bold** in each group has a different sound? Underline the word. Practice saying the words.

1 tr**ai**n c**ar** pl**a**ne r**ai**n
2 c**a**mp w**a**nt h**o**t n**o**t
3 g**o** b**oa**t sn**ow** t**o**wn
4 m**a**n c**a**mp t**a**ke tr**a**m
5 cl**ou**d h**o**me c**o**ld n**o**
6 cl**ou**d n**ow** dr**o**ve d**ow**n

b 09.30 Complete the chart with words in the box.

~~yesterday~~ beautiful ~~different~~ expensive interesting camera every difficult restaurant business favorite museum

We always say all the letters	We don't always say all the letters
yesterday	*different*

REVIEW YOUR PROGRESS

How well did you do in this unit? Write 3, 2, or 1 for each objective.
3 = very well 2 = well 1 = not so well

I CAN ...	
talk about travel and vacation experiences	☐
talk about past vacations	☐
make and respond to requests	☐

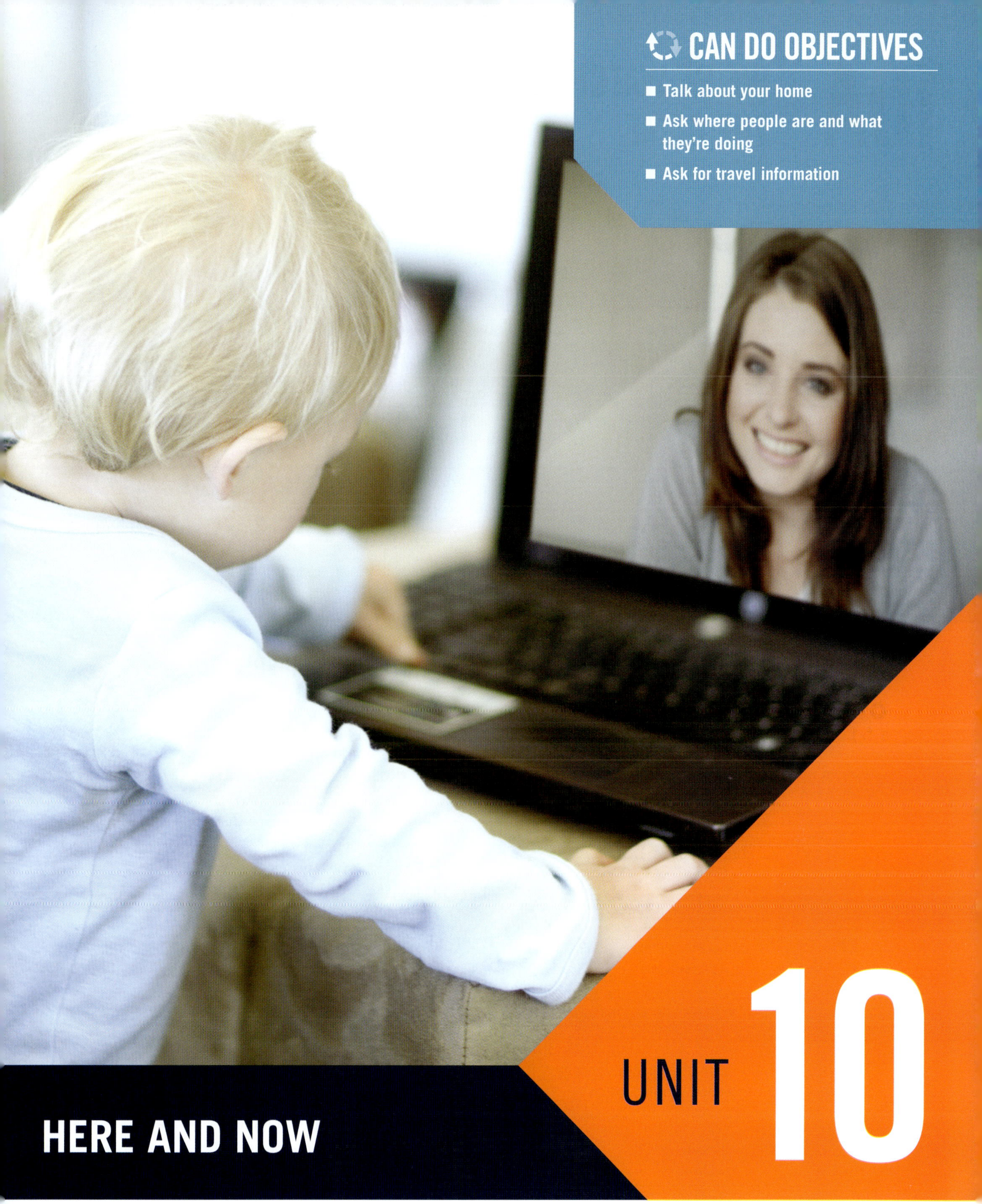

GETTING STARTED

a Look at the picture and answer the questions.

1 What is the boy doing?
2 Who is the woman? Where is she?
3 What do you think they're saying?
4 How often do you think they do this?
5 How do they feel? Why?

b Talk about the questions.

1 Do you speak to family and friends online? How often? Who do you speak to?
2 What programs or apps do you use to talk to people online?
3 What are the good things and bad things about using the Internet to speak to people?

10A WE'RE WATCHING THE GAME

Learn to talk about your home

G Present continuous: affirmative

V The home

a

b

c

d

e

f

1 VOCABULARY The home

a 10.01 Match the words in the box with pictures a–f. Listen and check.

bedroom yard living room
dining room kitchen bathroom

b Now go to Vocabulary Focus 10A on p. 153.

c Sound and spelling /tʃ/ and /θ/

1 10.03 Listen and practice these sounds.
1 /tʃ/ kit**ch**en 2 /θ/ ba**th**room

2 10.04 What sound do you hear in the words in the box, Sound 1 or Sound 2? Listen and add the words to the sound groups below.

cheese month birthday thanks change
both March question three watch

Sound 1 /tʃ/	Sound 2 /θ/
kit**ch**en	ba**th**room

3 Which letters usually spell /tʃ/ and which spell /θ/?

4 Practice saying the words.

d Ask and answer the questions with a partner.

1 How many bedrooms are there in your home?
2 Where do you eat your dinner?
3 Is there a TV in your home? Where?
4 Do you have a yard? If yes, is it big or small?
5 Which room is your favorite?

2 LISTENING AND SPEAKING

a 10.05 Listen to Grace talk about her apartment. Put pictures a–c on page 81 in the order Grace talks about them.

b 10.05 Listen again. Are the sentences true or false?

1 Grace's apartment isn't big.
2 The light in her apartment is good.
3 There isn't a TV in the living room.
4 There's a dining room in her apartment.
5 She uses her computer in her living room.

c Do you like Grace's apartment? Why / Why not?

Language Plus *in / on*

in + room	***on*** + floor, wall
*There's a desk **in** my bedroom.*	*The books are **on** the floor.*
*Put the cake **in** the kitchen.*	*There are pictures **on** the wall.*

d Think about your home and the rooms it has. Tell a partner about your home.

In my home, there are four bedrooms and a big bathroom.

e Choose a room in your home and write the names of some objects in that room. Then tell your partner about them.

In my bedroom, there's a bed, a chair, and a small desk.

3 READING

a Read the texts. Are they for people who are near or far away?

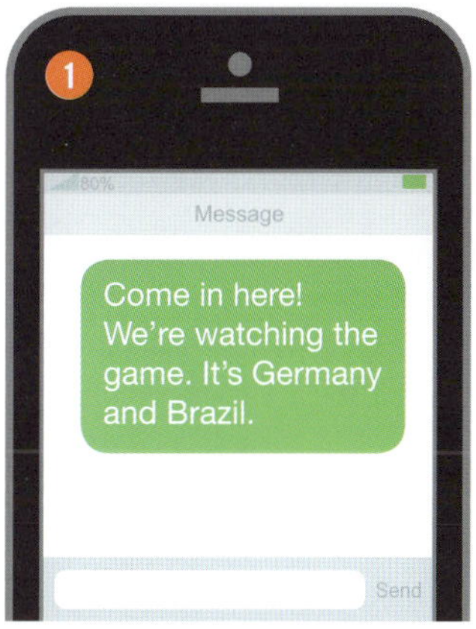

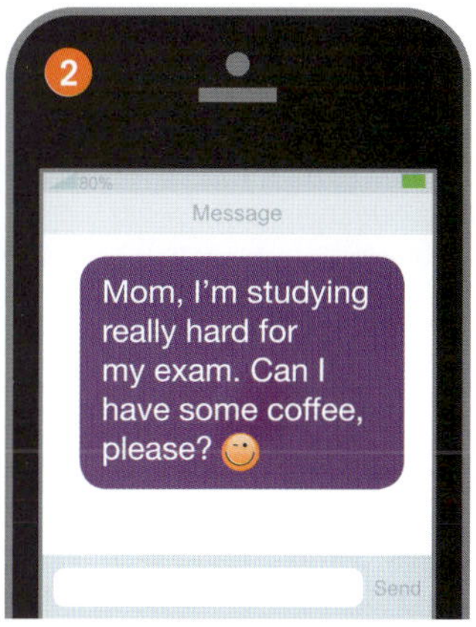

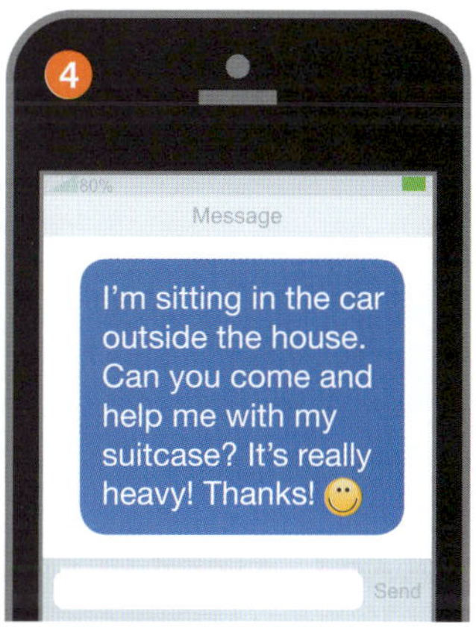

b Read the texts again. Where are the writers?

c Do you sometimes send a text to someone when you're in the same place? Why / Why not?

4 GRAMMAR
Present continuous: affirmative

a Look at the sentence from text 1. Does it mean *now* or *usually*?

We're watching the game.

b Complete the rule with *-ing* and *be*.

> Present continuous affirmative (+):
> *I/you/he/she/it/we/they* + ______ + verb + ______

c 10.06 **Pronunciation** Listen to the sentence in 4a. Underline the stressed words.

d Underline four more examples of the present continuous in texts 2–5 in 3a.

e Now go to Grammar Focus 10A on p. 130.

f It's 2 p.m. on Sunday. What are you doing? Write a text to a friend.

Hi!
I'm having lunch at a new restaurant downtown with my sister. It's really good! We're eating a lot of food.

g Read your text to the class. Listen to the other students. Is anyone doing the same thing?

5 SPEAKING

Communication 10A Student A go to p. 115. Student B go to p. 112.

10B ARE YOU WORKING?

Learn to ask where people are and what they're doing

G Present continuous: negative and questions

V Place phrases with prepositions

How much do you use your phone?

Some people always have their phone on, and they use it all the time — in a café, in the car, even in bed! Is this a good idea? Tell us what you think! And do you use your phone all the time?

RAOUL
My phone's always on, day and night, and I use it all the time – I talk on it, play games on it, send messages. When I wake up, I sit in bed, check my messages, and read the news on my phone. It's a great way to start the day!

YASMIN
I never talk on the phone when I'm with people in a restaurant. I have it on "silent" and put it in my bag – I don't want to talk while I'm eating. But I often take photos of the food with it. It's always by my bed at night, so I can wake up in the morning. I don't like talking on the phone much – I usually send text messages.

MIGUEL
I always have my phone with me – when I'm at home and when I'm at work, and I use it on the way to work to talk and check my emails. But I don't have it by the bed at night – I put it on "silent" and leave it in the kitchen. I want to sleep!

SAM
I use my phone all the time, but not at the movies, and not on a plane. I have it on at night by the bed. You never know – maybe someone needs to call you.

JENNY
My phone is usually off and I don't use it much. I use it to call people at the airport or on a bus – sometimes I need to say I'm late. But I don't like sending text messages.

a

b

1 READING

a Match the phrases in the box with pictures a–e.

at the movies in bed in the car
in a restaurant on a mountain

b Look at pictures a–e again. Answer the questions.

1 What object is in all the pictures?
2 Which are ... ?
- a good idea
- pretty normal
- a bad idea

c Read the message board comments and answer the questions.

1 You call the five people. They're in a restaurant. Who answers?
2 You call the five people at 3 a.m. Who answers?

d Which person do you think ... ?

a has good ideas
b has a problem

e Write a comment about you and your phone for the message board.

f Read your comment to your partner. Are you the same?

2 VOCABULARY Place phrases with prepositions

a Find phrases in the message board with *in*, *on*, or *at* and the nouns in the box. Add them to the chart.

~~café~~ airport car work bed plane
movies bus restaurant home

in	on	at
in a café ______	______	______ ______
______ ______	______	______ ______

b You're in a place in 2a and your partner calls you. Tell your partner what you're doing. Your partner guesses the place.

I'm going to work.

Are you in the car?

c Now go to Vocabulary Focus 10B on p. 147.

d **Sound and spelling /ə/**

1 10.09 Listen to the sound /ə/ in these words. Is it stressed or unstressed?
correct idea apartment station

2 10.10 Listen to these words. Underline the /ə/ sound in each word.

about banana woman television
problem breakfast company information

3 Practice saying the words.

3 LISTENING AND GRAMMAR Present continuous: negative and questions

a 10.11 Listen and match conversations 1–5 with pictures a–e.

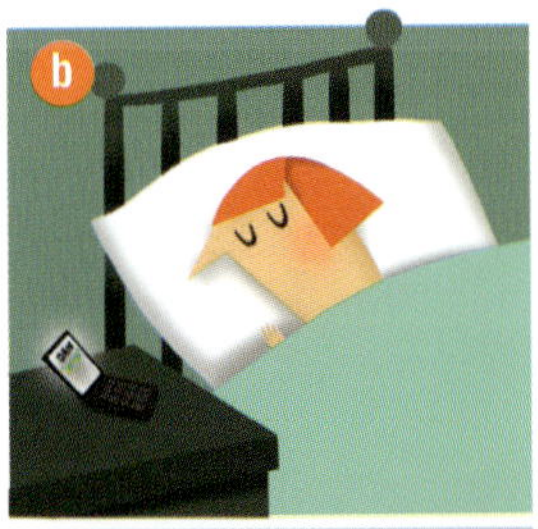

b Do you think … ?

1 Jack likes Ellie
2 Ellie likes Jack

How do you know?

c 10.12 Complete the chart. Listen and check.

+	–
I'm working.	I'm ______ ______.
I'm having dinner.	I'm ______ ______ dinner.

d 10.13 Complete Jack's questions. Listen and check.

1 **JACK** What ______ ______ doing?
ELLIE I'm at the bus stop. I'm going home.
2 **JACK** ______ ______ working?
ELLIE No, I'm not working.
3 **ELLIE** I'm watching a movie.
JACK Oh, what ______ ______ watching?

e 10.14 **Pronunciation** Listen to the questions in 3d again. Which word gets the most stress in each question?

f Now go to Grammar Focus 10B on p. 132.

g **Communication 10B** Student A go to p. 114. Student B go to p. 112.

4 SPEAKING

a You and a partner are in different places. You want to meet. Before you speak on the phone, write notes. Think about these questions:

- Where are you? (Choose a place from Vocabulary Focus 10B on page 147.)
- What are you doing? (Think of two or more activities.)
- When do you want to meet? (Think of a day, a time, and a place.)

b Call your partner and have a conversation.

- Ask where your partner is and what he/she is doing.
- Plan when and where to meet your partner.

Hi, Tom.
What are you doing?

I'm writing a report.

Are you free this evening? Do you want to go to Café Cabana?

10C EVERYDAY ENGLISH

What time's the train?

Learn to ask for travel information

- **P** Sound and spelling: /ɪə/ and /eə/
- **W** A text asking for information

1 LISTENING

a Look at pictures a and b and talk about the questions.

1 Where are Javier and Owen going?
2 Where do you think they go before?

b 10.18 Listen to Part 1. Check your ideas in 1a.

c 10.18 Listen to Part 1 again. Answer the questions.

1 What does Javier say about Jim?
2 Do they know what time the train leaves?

a

2 PRONUNCIATION Sound and spelling: /ɪə/ and /eə/

a 10.19 Listen to these words. Which word has a different sound?

here **yeah** **rea**lly

b 10.20 Listen and complete the chart with the words in the box.

chair care year dear hair
near there clear pair zero

Sound 1 /ɪə/	Sound 2 /eə/
here	*yeah*

c 10.20 Listen again and repeat.

3 LISTENING

a Look at picture b. What questions does Owen ask the ticket agent at the train station?

b 10.21 Listen to Part 2. Check your ideas in 3a.

c 10.21 Listen to Part 2 again. Complete the information.

1 Time of next train: ______
2 Time now: ______
3 Platform: ______

d In your country, what is an easy way to travel – train, bus, car?

b

4 USEFUL LANGUAGE Asking for travel information

a Who says these expressions – a passenger (P) or the ticket agent (TA)?

1 The next train is at 2:15.
2 Which platform is it?
3 Excuse me.
4 The train leaves in ten minutes.
5 No, you change at Penn Station.
6 Yes? How can I help you?
7 What time's the next train to Philadelphia?
8 Is it a direct train?
9 It's Platform 4.

b 10.22 Listen and check your answers in 4a. Then listen again and repeat.

c 10.23 Complete the sentences with *at* or *in*. Listen and check.

1 The next train leaves ______ half an hour.
2 The next train leaves ______ five o'clock.

d 10.24 Put the conversation in the correct order. Then listen and check.

A
- [ ] So, at 5:15. And is it a direct bus?
- [ ] Great! Thanks for your help.
- [ ] What time's the next bus to Dallas?
- [1] Excuse me.
- [ ] OK, and which bus stop is it?

B
- [ ] The next bus leaves in 20 minutes.
- [ ] It's stop 7, near the ticket office.
- [ ] No problem.
- [ ] Yes? How can I help you?
- [ ] No, you change at Austin.

e Practice the conversation in 4d with a partner. Take turns being the ticket agent and the passenger. Change the times, kind of transportation, and the platforms / bus stops.

5 SPEAKING

>>> Communication 10C

Student A go to p. 110.
Student B go to p. 112.

6 WRITING

a Owen helped his friend Anthony plan a vacation to Washington, D.C. Anthony sends Owen a message. Read it and answer the questions.

1 Where's Anthony now?
2 What two questions does he ask?

> Hi, Owen. I'm traveling to Washington, D.C. right now on the train. Sorry, I can't remember two things. First, where can I find a taxi at the train station? And how much is it from the station to the hotel?
> Thanks!
> Anthony

b >>> Now go to Writing Plus 10C on p. 162 for Word order in questions.

c Write a message to a friend. Ask two questions in your message. Here are some ideas:

Hi …
I'm going / doing / having …
Sorry, I can't remember …
Where / How / When … ?
Thanks …

d Read another student's message. Try to answer the questions.

UNIT PROGRESS TEST

CHECK YOUR PROGRESS

YOU CAN NOW DO THE UNIT PROGRESS TEST.

UNIT 10
Review

1 GRAMMAR

a Correct the present continuous sentences.

> Carmen be wearing a yellow T-shirt.
Carmen's wearing a yellow T-shirt.

1 You wearing my shoes!
2 They're geting a taxi.
3 I'm writeing to Kelly.
4 The class starting.
5 She's haveing lunch.
6 We waiting.

b Write present continuous questions with the words and phrases.

1 where / you / sit ?
2 you / wear / black shoes ?
3 it / rain ?
4 you / use / a computer ?
5 why / you / study / English ?
6 what / your friends / do ?

c Ask and answer the questions in 1b.

d Complete the phone conversation with the verbs in parentheses.

GABY Hi, it's me.
JUAN Oh, hi. What [1]______ (you / do)?
GABY I [2]______ (talk) to you, of course. I'm on the train.
JUAN Oh, very funny. Well, I [3]______ (cook) dinner. So, [4]______ (you / listen to) music?
GABY Mm, no. I [5]______ (read) a book.
JUAN Oh, great. What's the weather like there?
GABY Not good. It [6]______ (rain) outside.
JUAN Well, it [7]______ (not / rain) here – it [8]______ (snow)! But Gwen and Carla are in the yard.
GABY The yard? Why? What [9]______ (they / do)?
JUAN They [10]______ (make) a snowman!

2 VOCABULARY

a Write the rooms.

b Complete the questions with *in*, *on*, or *at*.

1 Do you listen to music ______ the car?
2 Do you sleep ______ trains / buses / planes?
3 Do you read ______ bed?
4 Do you eat ______ the movies?
5 Were you ______ home yesterday for lunch?
6 Did you play volleyball ______ school?
7 What's ______ the floor in this room?
8 Are there any pictures ______ the walls?

c Ask and answer the questions in 2b.

3 SOUND AND SPELLING

a Notice the two sounds and the letters in **bold**.

1 /tʃ/ **ch**oose
2 /θ/ **th**ree

b 10.25 Complete the chart with the words in the box. Practice saying the words.

ba**th**room bir**th**day **ch**ange ~~**ch**oose~~ kit**ch**en ques**t**ion **th**anks ~~**th**ree~~

/tʃ/	/θ/
choose	*three*

c 10.26 Are the two sounds in **bold** in each sentence the same (S) or different (D)? Practice saying the sentences.

1 The m**ea**l is h**ere**.
2 W**ear** a p**air** of shoes.
3 Th**eir** house is n**ear**.
4 It's r**eal** h**air**.
5 Y**eah**, it's th**ere**.
6 Wh**ere**'s the ch**air**?

REVIEW YOUR PROGRESS

How well did you do in this unit? Write 3, 2, or 1 for each objective.
3 = very well 2 = well 1 = not so well

I CAN ...	
talk about my home	☐
ask where people are and what they're doing	☐
ask for travel information	☐

CAN DO OBJECTIVES

- Talk about people's lives
- Talk about things you know how to do
- Talk about opinions

UNIT 11

ACHIEVERS

GETTING STARTED

a Look at the picture and answer the questions.

1 What did this man do before he went into his tent? What are his plans tomorrow?

2 Check (✓) the things the man can do in his tent tonight. Why can't he do some things?

☐ listen to music ☐ cook dinner
☐ read a magazine ☐ do yoga
☐ play the guitar ☐ sleep well

3 What do you think he is writing in his book?

4 What questions do you want to ask him? Write down three.

b Would you like to be where this man is? Why / Why not?

11A SHE WENT AROUND THE EARTH

Learn to talk about people's lives

G Object pronouns

V Life events

1 READING

a Think of two famous people from your country (present or past). Ask and answer the questions with a partner.

1 Why are / were they famous?
2 What do you know about them?
3 Do you think people from other countries know about them? Why / Why not?

b Read *They Were the First!* Who … ?

1 died over 15 years ago
2 had new ideas for computers
3 studied and worked at the same time
4 came from a poor family
5 lived in a few different places
6 had one child

c Read *They Were the First!* again. Choose one thing about each person you think is interesting and say why.

THEY WERE THE FIRST!

#1 THE FIRST WOMAN IN SPACE

Valentina Tereshkova (born 1937)

Who is she?

A Russian cosmonaut

What did she do?

In 1963, she flew in *Vostok 6*. She went around the Earth 48 times, and she was in space for almost three days.

Her life

She was born in 1937 in a small town in Russia. Her father was a tractor driver, and her mother worked in a factory. She finished school at 16 and started work in a factory. In her free time, she studied and she also went parachute jumping.

In 1963, she got married, and the next year she had a daughter, Elena. After that, Valentina never flew into space again.

2 VOCABULARY Life events

a 11.01 Look at these events in a person's life. Match events 1–6 with pictures a–f. Listen and check.

1 die
2 grow up
3 finish college
4 get married
5 go to school
6 be born

b Write the events in three lists.

1 everyone does this
2 most people do this
3 only some people do this

c Compare your lists with other students. Are they the same?

d Read *They Were the First!* again. Write simple past sentences about the years below.

Valentina Tereshkova
• 1937 • 1953 • 1963 • 1964

1937 – Valentina was born.

William Higinbotham
• 1910 • 1928 • 1932 • 1949

Language Plus Years

To say a year, we usually say the numbers in pairs:

1937 → 19 37 *nineteen thirty-seven* 2021 → 20 21 *twenty twenty-one*

We sometimes say the complete number for years after 2000:

2019 = *two thousand nineteen* 2021 = *two thousand twenty-one*

Note: 1900 = *nineteen hundred* 2000 = *two thousand*

2005 = *two thousand five*

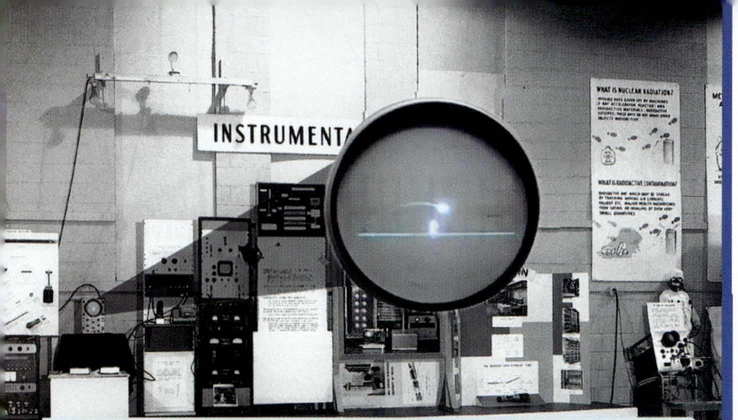

#2 THE GRANDFATHER OF VIDEO GAMES

William Higinbotham (1910–1994)

Who was he?

An American scientist

What did he do?

In 1958, he made a video game called "Tennis for Two." It was the first video game in the world, and people waited in line all day to play it.

His life

He was born in 1910, and he grew up in Caledonia, New York. When he was 18, he went to college, and four years later he studied at Cornell University.

When he was 39, he got married and moved to Bellport, New York, where he worked at a science lab. William wanted to make a fun game for people to play at his science lab, so he made "Tennis for Two," and he showed it during Visitor Day. It was a big success – but he didn't make any money from it!

e Sound and spelling Numbers

1 11.02 Listen to the words.
thirty thirteen
In each word ...
a <u>Underline</u> the main stress. Is it in the first part of the word or the second part?
b Does the letter *t* sound like /t/ or more like /d/?

2 11.03 Listen to eight numbers. Write the number you hear.

3 Work with a partner.
Student A: Say one of the numbers in the box.
Student B: Point to the number.
Then switch roles.

14 40 18 80 16 60 15 50 13 30

f Now go to Vocabulary Focus 11A on p. 154.

3 LISTENING AND GRAMMAR
Object pronouns

a 11.06 Listen to two friends talking about Valentina Tereshkova. Check (✓) the questions you can answer after listening to their conversation.

1 ☐ Where did she go to school?
2 ☐ Why did she get the job?
3 ☐ How did she meet her husband?
4 ☐ Where does she live now?
5 ☐ What does she want to do in the future?

b 11.06 Listen again and answer the questions you checked in 3a.

c 11.07 Complete the sentences from the conversation with the words in the box. Listen and check.

he him she her

1 ______'s a Russian cosmonaut. Do you know about ______?
2 She married a cosmonaut. She met ______ in 1963. ______ was in the same space program.

d <u>Underline</u> the correct words to complete the rules.

1 We use **he** and **she** *before* / *after* a verb.
2 We use **him** and **her** *before* / *after* a verb or preposition.

e Now go to Grammar Focus 11A on p. 132.

4 SPEAKING

a Write four or five events in your life and the years.
2005–2019 – I lived in Panama City.
2019 – I started college.

b Work in pairs. Read your partner's sentences and ask some questions.

Where did you ...?
When did you ...?
Why did you ...?

c Tell the class two things about your partner's life.

11B SHE CAN PULL A PLANE

Learn to talk about things you know how to do

G *can* for ability
V Abilities

1 READING

a Look at 1–3 below.
What's difficult for you to do?
Why / Why not?

1 be cold for a long time
2 swim underwater
3 pull or carry big objects

b Read *Amazing Humans*. Are the amazing humans real or not?

c Read *Amazing Humans* again. Answer the questions.

1 How long can Wim Hof stay in a cold bath?
2 How long can the Bajau Laut people stay underwater?
3 How does Seema Bhadoria pull things?

d Which real person/people in *Amazing Humans* can do something useful?

2 GRAMMAR *can*: affirmative and negative

a Complete the chart. Check your answers in the text.

Affirmative			
I **can** You **can** He/She ______	swim underwater.	We **can** They ______	swim underwater.
Negative			
I **can't** You **can't** He/She ______	make ice.	We **can't** They ______	make ice.

b Underline examples of *can*/*can't* in *Amazing Humans*. What is after *can*/*can't*, a noun or a verb?

c Now go to Grammar Focus 11B Part 1 on p. 134.

AMAZING HUMANS

Do you sometimes do things that are different and interesting? Do you make videos of these things? Maybe you're not Superman or Superwoman, but you can do something amazing. Here are some stories about people who can do amazing things!

THE ICEMAN

Wim Hof is from the Netherlands, and he's often called "The Iceman." He can't make ice, but he can sit in a bath of ice for one hour, 52 minutes, and two seconds. He doesn't feel cold. In 2009, he ran more than 40 kilometers in –20°C wearing only shorts!

THE FISHMEN

The Bajau Laut people in Southeast Asia can swim underwater for a long time. Sometimes they can go underwater for more than five minutes. They can also see very well in the water – it helps them to see the fish!

THE STRONG WOMAN

Seema Bhadoria is an amazing young woman from India – she can pull really big objects with only her teeth. When she was only 18 years old, she pulled a plane with her teeth! She can also pull a ship or a big truck.

3 VOCABULARY Abilities

a Match the verbs in the box with pictures a–d.

cook sing swim paint

a

b

c

d

b Now go to Vocabulary Focus 11B on p. 155.

Language Plus (*very / pretty*) *well*

I can swim ***very well***. = I'm very good.
I can swim ***well***. = I'm good.
I can swim ***pretty well***. = I'm OK.
*I can**'t** swim* ***at all***. = It's impossible for me.

c Talk about people you know and what they can or can't do.

My brother can't dance very well.

4 LISTENING

a Read the job description. Does the school want someone who can do one thing or a lot of things?

JOB ALERT CLOSE ⊗

We need people to work at our summer school in Chapel Hill.

We want people who can do a lot of different things – sing, dance, play the guitar, draw, ride a horse, but we also want good teachers!

If you're interested, please send us an email or give us a call …

b 11.12 Listen to Claire, the principal at the school, talk to Andy. Is he a good person for the job?

c 11.12 Listen again. What can Andy do? Complete sentences 1–4 with the words and phrases in the box.

teach ride a horse play the guitar sing dance

1 He can ______ and ______ pretty well.
2 He can ______ very well.
3 He can't ______ very well.
4 He can't ______ at all.

5 GRAMMAR *can*: questions

a 11.13 Complete the conversations. Listen and check your answers.

1 **CLAIRE** And ______ ______ sing?
ANDY Yes, ______ ______.
2 **CLAIRE** ______ ______ dance well?
ANDY No, ______ ______.

b Now go to Grammar Focus 11B Part 2 on p. 134.

c 11.15 **Pronunciation** Listen to the sentences. Check (✓) when *can*/*can't* is stressed.

1 ☐ I can sing pretty well.
2 ☐ I can't dance very well.
3 ☐ Can you sing?
4 ☐ Yes, I can.

d Practice saying the sentences. Underline the correct words to complete the rules.

Can *is / isn't* stressed in affirmative sentences and questions.
Can *is / isn't* stressed in negative sentences and short answers.

e 11.16 Complete the conversation with the correct form of *can*. Listen and check.

A ______ Andy play the guitar?
B Yes, he ______.
A And ______ he ride a horse?
B Yes, he ______ ride a horse very well.
A ______ he teach?
B No, he ______ teach at all.

f Practice the conversation in 5e with a partner.

6 SPEAKING

a Work in pairs. Write one question with *can* for each topic.

- sports — *Can you play tennis?*
- food — *Can you make a cake?*
- language
- music / art

b Work with a new partner. Ask and answer your questions in 6a.

Can you play tennis?

No, I can't play tennis at all.

c Work with your first partner again. Tell them about your second partner.

Lola can speak Portuguese pretty well, but she can't speak Italian.

11C EVERYDAY ENGLISH

What do you think?

Learn to talk about opinions

P Consonant clusters

W An email to a friend

1 LISTENING

a Ask and answer the questions.

1 What's your favorite restaurant in your town or city?
2 What food do you usually eat there?

b Look at pictures a–c. What do you think happens in the story, idea 1 or 2?

1 Leah and Carter are brother and sister. They're at a restaurant. Their mom calls and invites them for dinner. They leave the restaurant and go to her house.
2 Carter and Leah are brother and sister. They're at a restaurant. They talk about what restaurants their mom would like. They can't decide what restaurant to take her to.

c 11.17 Listen. Check your answer in 1b.

d 11.17 Listen again. Read the sentences. Write Leah (L), Carter (C), or both (B). Who … ?

1 loves Indian food
2 talked to their mom on the phone
3 wants to visit their mom next weekend
4 wants to take their mom to an Indian restaurant
5 doesn't think an Italian restaurant is a good idea for their mom
6 is hungry

e Are there any interesting places to visit in/near your town or city?

2 USEFUL LANGUAGE Talking about opinions

a Look at the expressions. Do we use them to … ?

a ask for an opinion
b give an opinion
c have the same opinion
d have a different opinion

1 Where's a good place to take Mom?
2 No, that's not my favorite.
3 Maybe you're right.
4 I don't think the Italian place is a good idea.
5 It looks good.
6 How about that new restaurant near here?
7 I think you're right.
8 What do you think?

11.18 Listen and check your answers.

b 11.18 **Pronunciation** Listen to sentences 1–8 in 2a again. Underline the words with the most stress. Listen again and repeat.

c 11.19 Look at expressions 1–4. Are they in group a, b, c, or d in 2a? Listen and check.

1 Me, too.
2 What's good here?
3 What about the Italian restaurant near you?
4 I'm not so sure.

d 11.20 Put the words in the correct order to make expressions. Listen and check.

1 visit her / we can go / next weekend .
2 you think / what do / new restaurant / of the ?
3 you're / I think / right .
4 so / think / I don't .
5 idea / good / that's / a .

e Complete the conversation with your ideas.

A What do you think of English?
YOU ______________________
A Yes, maybe you're right. What about the grammar?
YOU ______________________
A Really? I don't think so. I think your language is very hard.
YOU ______________________
A Well, all languages are a little hard.
YOU ______________________

f Practice the conversation in 2e with a partner. Take turns being A.

C

3 PRONUNCIATION Consonant clusters

a 11.21 Listen to the words. Notice how the letters in **bold** are pronounced. Listen again and repeat.

1 /t/ righ**t** 2 /ŋk/ thi**nk** 3 /st/ touri**st**

b 11.22 Listen and match the letters in **bold** in 1–6 with a–f.

1 a**sk** 3 fi**nd** 5 restaura**nt**
2 da**nce** 4 difficu**lt** 6 si**x**

a /nt/ c /sk/ e /nd/
b /lt/ d /ks/ f /ns/

c Practice saying the words.

4 SPEAKING

Communication 11C

Student A go to p. 113.
Student B go to p. 114.

5 WRITING

a Read Leah's email to an old friend. What does she like about her life in Ann Arbor?

Ann Arbor

Hi Hailey,

Thanks for your email – it was really good to hear from you.

Things here at school are going well. Ann Arbor is a great city, and there are a lot of things I can do. I'm making some new friends in my classes. I study with a girl named Megan. She's from Ann Arbor, and she's really nice. She and her boyfriend, Chris, helped me a lot when I arrived. I often see them at the library. I also know my brother, of course! He's really busy with school and work, but we sometimes meet for coffee or dinner. It's good to have him in the same city.

My apartment is pretty small, but it's comfortable. I live with three other girls, but we have a good time. It's near my classes, so I can walk to class every day. I like that!

I miss my friends from home. How are things at school for you?

Write again soon.

Love,

Leah

b Now go to Writing Plus 11C on p. 163 for Pronouns.

c Write an email to a friend. Tell them about your life now. Here are some ideas:

- Say hi and thank the person for his/her email. (*Hi … Thanks …*)
- Write about your life – your job or studies. (*I'm working/studying …*)
- Write about family and/or friends. (*My parents are well … I see my friend Luisa every …*)
- Say goodbye and ask the person to write to you. (*Goodbye for now … Love / See you soon …*)

d Read another student's email. What's interesting about their life?

UNIT PROGRESS TEST

CHECK YOUR PROGRESS

YOU CAN NOW DO THE UNIT PROGRESS TEST.

UNIT 11
Review

1 GRAMMAR

a Complete the sentences with the correct pronoun.

1 I like Rob, but I don't think he likes ______.
2 Those shoes are beautiful. Can I buy ______, please?
3 Sarah's a good friend. I met ______ at college.
4 My husband and I live in the city, but my parents live in a small town. They sometimes visit ______ on weekends.
5 They had a baby boy, and they named ______ Antonio.
6 Happy birthday! I got ______ a present!
7 Your car is dirty. You need to clean ______.

b Look at the chart. Then complete the conversation with the words and phrases in the box.

	dance	play tennis	ride a horse
Beto	✗	✓✓	✓
Melanie	✓	✗	✓✓

can (x4) can't can she can you
he can't I can she can

A 1______ Beto dance?
B No, 2______ . But he 3______ play tennis very well, and he 4______ ride a horse.
A What about Melanie? 5______ ride a horse?
B Yes, 6______. She can ride a horse very well, and she 7______ dance, but she 8______ play tennis.
A What about you? 9______ play tennis?
B Yes, 10______ .

c Ask a partner about the activities in 1b. Use *Can you … ?*

2 VOCABULARY

a Complete the text with the correct form of the verb phrases in the box.

have a baby boy finish school be born
go to college die grow up get married

My parents met in London, and I 1______ in England, but my family came here to Michigan when I was three. I 2______ here, and I don't remember anything about England. I 3______ when I was eighteen. I got a job at a hotel, but it wasn't very interesting.
Then I 4______ in Atlanta. I studied engineering, and I met Daniela – she's now my wife!
Daniela and I 5______ five years ago. We both got good jobs in Atlanta, but then my father 6______, so we came back here to Michigan to be near my mom.
We 7______ last year. Life is good!

b Complete the verb phrases with the words in the box.

dinner basketball a motorcycle songs to work walls

play	cards, 1__________, volleyball
sing	2__________
paint	a picture, 3__________
ride	a horse, 4__________, a bike
drive	a car, 5__________
cook	6__________

c Which of the things in 2b do you do every day? Which do you sometimes do? Which do you never do?

3 SOUND AND SPELLING

a 11.23 Underline the main stress in these words. Practice saying the words.

thirteen nineteen
fifteen twenty
sixty fourteen
forty seventy
ninety thirty
eighteen eighty

b 11.24 Are the sounds in **bold** the same (S) or different (D)? Practice saying the words.

1 si**x** – than**ks**
2 da**nc**e – a**nsw**er
3 ri**ght** – whi**te**
4 touri**st** – dan**ced**
5 a**sk** – **sch**ool
6 si**ng** – sa**ng**

REVIEW YOUR PROGRESS

How well did you do in this unit? Write 3, 2, or 1 for each objective.
3 = very well 2 = well 1 = not so well

I CAN …	
talk about people's lives	☐
talk about things I know how to do	☐
talk about opinions	☐

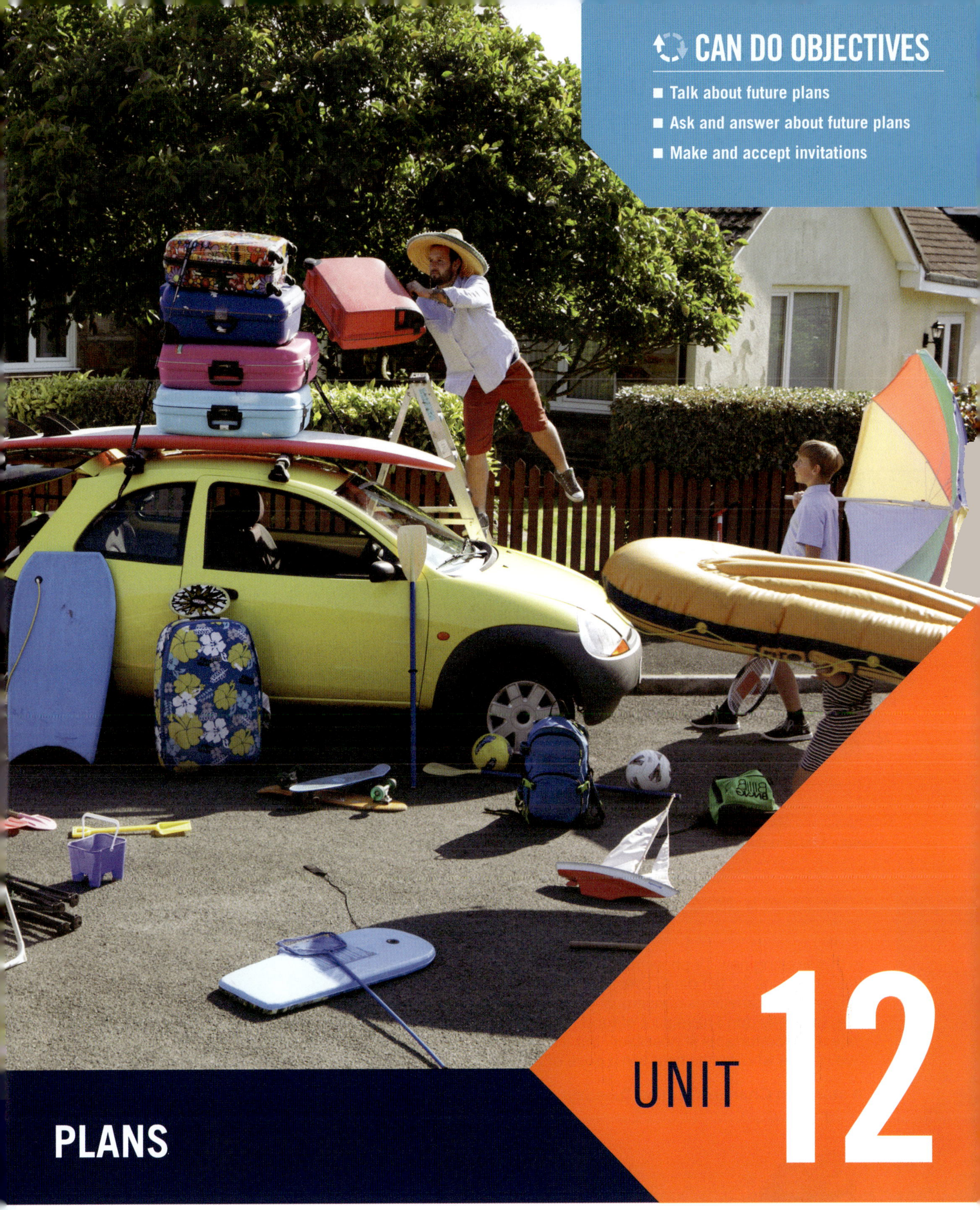

CAN DO OBJECTIVES

- Talk about future plans
- Ask and answer about future plans
- Make and accept invitations

UNIT 12
PLANS

GETTING STARTED

a Look at the picture and answer the questions.

1 Do you think this family is going to … ?
- go on a long or short vacation
- go somewhere near or far
- go somewhere hot or cold
- go by car or drive to the airport

Why?

2 What did the man do … ?
- the day before the trip
- the morning of the trip
- a month before the trip

3 What do you think this family is going to do on the trip? Why?

b Talk about the questions.

1 When you go on vacation, do you pack too much or not enough?
2 What do you sometimes forget to take when you go on vacation?

12A I'M GOING TO TAKE A LONG HOT BATH

Learn to talk about future plans

- **G** *be going to*: affirmative and negative
- **V** Months and future time expressions; Ordinal numbers

1 READING

a Talk about everyday objects and activities that are important to you. Think about:

- food and drink (*my morning coffee* …)
- your things (*my sofa* …)
- things you do (*listen to music* …)

> Every day I play video games – I really like them.

b Read about *Danger Zone*. Is it about … ?

1 a fun vacation
2 a dangerous competition

c Read about the TV show again. Answer the questions.

1 Where do people on the TV show go?
2 Do they have an easy time? Why / Why not?
3 What do the two best people get?

d Read the people's ideas for after the TV show. Which is the best idea? Tell a partner.

2 GRAMMAR *be going to*: affirmative

a 12.01 Complete Mason's sentences with the words in the box. Listen and check.

to	are	going

1 I'm ________ to sleep for a long time.
2 Abby's going ________ take a long hot bath.
3 Santiago and Manuela ________ going to have their favorite food and drink.

b Underline the correct answer in the rule.

> We use *be* + *going to* to talk about *now* / *the future*.

c 12.01 **Pronunciation** Listen to the sentences in 2a again. Notice the sentence stress and the pronunciation of *going to*. Answer the questions.

1 Do we stress *going*, the main verb, or both?
2 Can we hear the words *going to* clearly?

Practice saying the sentences.

d Now go to Grammar Focus 12A Part 1 on p. 134.

e Write three sentences about something you're going to do after class.

After class, I'm going to meet my friend Diego.

f Tell other students your sentences in 2e.

> I'm going to study in the Learning Center. What about you?

> I'm going to get some coffee.

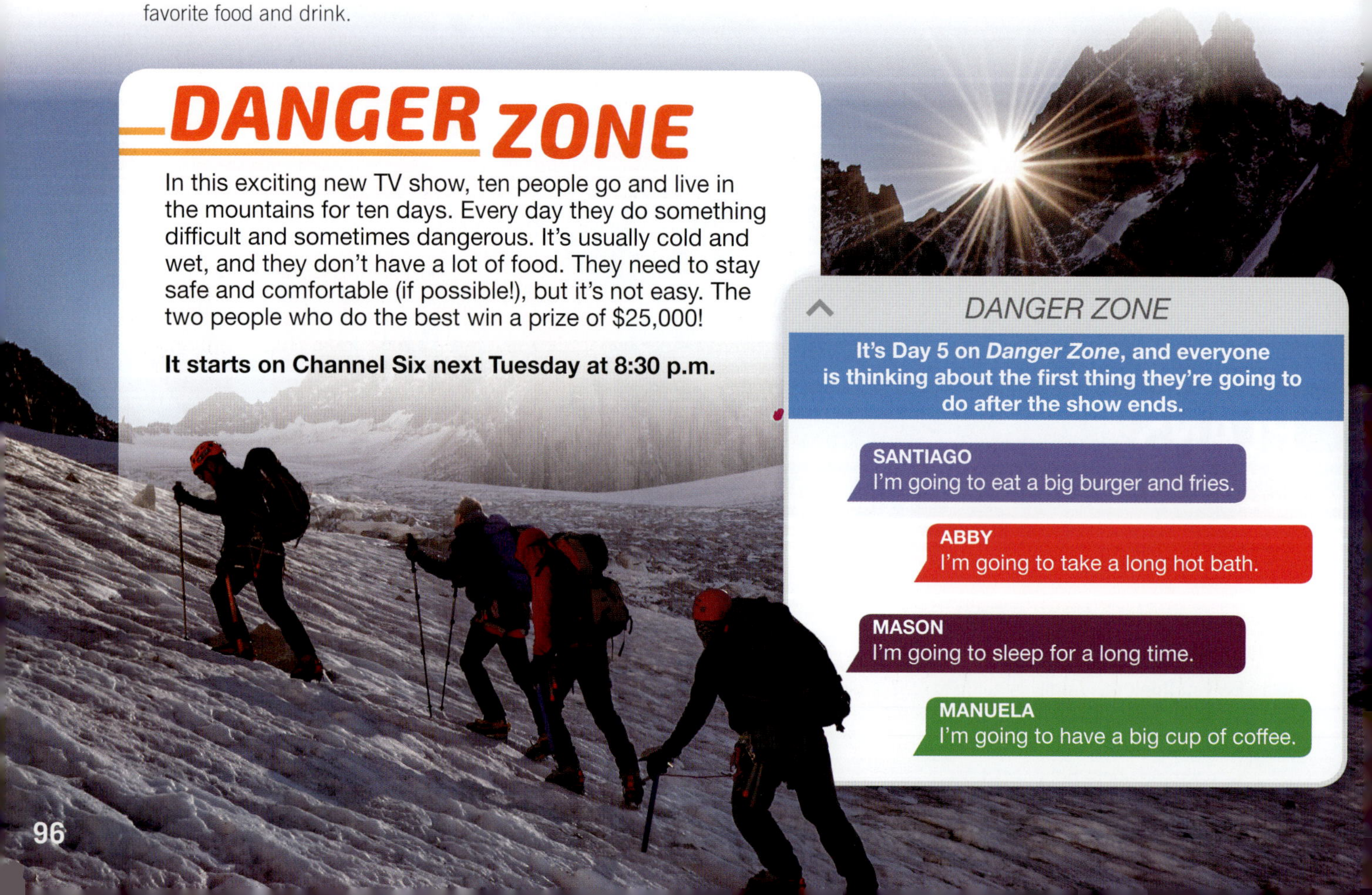

DANGER ZONE

In this exciting new TV show, ten people go and live in the mountains for ten days. Every day they do something difficult and sometimes dangerous. It's usually cold and wet, and they don't have a lot of food. They need to stay safe and comfortable (if possible!), but it's not easy. The two people who do the best win a prize of $25,000!

It starts on Channel Six next Tuesday at 8:30 p.m.

DANGER ZONE

It's Day 5 on *Danger Zone*, and everyone is thinking about the first thing they're going to do after the show ends.

SANTIAGO
I'm going to eat a big burger and fries.

ABBY
I'm going to take a long hot bath.

MASON
I'm going to sleep for a long time.

MANUELA
I'm going to have a big cup of coffee.

3 VOCABULARY Months and future time expressions; Ordinal numbers

a It's Monday morning. Put time expressions 1–6 in the correct place on the timeline.

1 tonight   2 tomorrow   3 this Wednesday   4 on Friday   5 on the weekend   6 next Monday

MONDAY		TUESDAY		WEDNESDAY		THURSDAY		FRIDAY		SATURDAY		SUNDAY		MONDAY	
a.m.	p.m.	a.m.	p.m.	a.m.	p.m.	a.m.	p.m.	a.m.	p.m.	a.m.	p.m.	a.m.	p.m.	a.m.	p.m.

Language Plus The date

What's the date today? It's ***August fifth****.*
When's your birthday? It's ***on March twentieth****.*
Note: With dates we use ordinal numbers:
first, second, third, fourth …

b Now go to Vocabulary Focus 12A on p. 156.

c Ask and answer the questions with a partner. Use time expressions in your answers.

1 When's your next English class?
2 When's your next English test?
3 When's your birthday?

It's on November fifteenth.

4 LISTENING

a 12.06 Listen to Paola (P), Azra (A), and Gabe (G) talk about their vacation plans this summer. Match them with pictures a–c.

b 12.06 Listen again. Are the sentences true or false?

1 Paola often goes to a cooking school for vacation.
2 The trip to Italy is a different kind of vacation for Azra.
3 Gabe doesn't want to make money on the farm.

c Which vacation plan do you like? Which don't you like? Why?

a

b

c

5 GRAMMAR *be going to*: negative

a 12.07 Listen and complete the sentences.

1 **PAOLA** I ______ going ______ have a normal vacation.
2 **AZRA** We ______ going ______ do that this year.

b Now go to Grammar Focus 12A Part 2 on p. 134.

c 12.09 Complete the conversations. Listen and check.

1 **A** After class, I'______ not ______ to do my homework.
B Why not?
A I'm tired. I'm going ______ do it tomorrow.
2 **C** After class, I'______ not ______ to go home.
D Why not?
C I'm going ______ meet friends at a café.

d Practice the conversations in 5c. Use your own ideas to have similar conversations.

6 SPEAKING

a Write two things you're going to do on your next vacation. Think about:

- places
- things to buy
- activities
- sports
- places to stay
- people

b Write two things from your everyday life you aren't going to do on your vacation.

- things you do at school / work
- things you do at home

c Talk to other students about your ideas in 6a and 6b. Do you all have the same ideas?

I'm going to go to the beach.

I'm not going to read work emails.

12B WHAT ARE YOU GOING TO DO THIS WEEKEND?

Learn to ask and answer about future plans

G *be going to:* questions

V Common verbs and collocations

ONLY 4,000 WEEKENDS IN YOUR LIFE!
So, What Are You Going To Do With Them?

d

What's your answer to this question? Perhaps it's "I don't know" or "Not a lot." In her new book, *What the Most Successful People Do on the Weekend*, Laura Vanderkam says these are bad answers. She says the weekend is a time to relax, but also a time to do interesting things. With only 4,000 weekends in our life, each one is important. So don't just sit on the sofa and watch TV. It's a good idea to plan the weekend – then you can use the time well. Here are some of her ideas:

1 Plan three to five activities to do on the weekend and write them down. Be sure you do these things.

2 Plan to read a book. Buy a book for the weekend and then plan a time to read it.

3 Write a list of 100 "big" things you'd like to do in your life. Choose one to do this weekend.

4 Get up early. Between 6:00 and 8:00 in the morning is the best time to do things. Plan to wake up early and do something before breakfast!

5 Turn off your phone and don't use your computer. You can read your emails on Monday. On Sunday evening, go for a run, play some music, or do yoga so you relax and don't think about work.

6 Don't clean your house or apartment on the weekend. It's a time to do things you like!

e

a

b

c

1 READING

a Talk about sentences 1–3 in small groups. Which are true for you?

1 Weekends are too short, and we don't have many of them.
2 It's not a good idea to do a lot on the weekend.
3 It's important to use the time well on the weekend.

b Read about Laura Vanderkam's new book. Which sentence in 1a is her main idea?

c Look at pictures a–e. Which does Laura say are good things to do on the weekend? Which aren't good?

d Look at Wendy's, David's, and Rachel's plans for the weekend. Match them with ideas 1–3 in the text.

e What do you think of Laura's ideas? Which do you like? Which don't you like? Why / Why not?

Great ideas! I'd like to try them.

Interesting ideas, but …

That's not my idea of a good weekend.

Wendy's big ideas

I'd like to …
- make a cheesecake
- visit Paris
- paint my room
- learn Chinese
- read a book by Stephen King
- start a blog
- go skydiving

DAVID'S SCHEDULE

	SUNDAY
10:00	
11:00	
12:00	Sit in the park and read my new book.
1:00	
2:00	Play basketball with friends.

Rachel's weekend to-do list

This weekend I'm going to:
1 go for a long run (10 km or more!).
2 invite some friends for dinner.
3 take my first tennis lesson.

2 VOCABULARY Common verbs and collocations

a 12.10 Match the verbs in the box with the words and phrases in 1–8. Listen and check.

paint clean use make invite visit go do play

1 ________ laundry / your homework
2 ________ someone to a party
3 ________ a friend
4 ________ a list / lunch
5 ________ a picture / a wall
6 ________ your apartment / your windows
7 ________ your phone / the Internet
8 ________ for a walk / shopping / to a museum
9 ________ sports

b Find examples of each verb on page 98. Add them to 1–9 in 2a.

c Tell a partner which activities in 2a and 2b you do on the weekend.

I always … I often …
I sometimes … I never …

d Now go to Vocabulary Focus 12B on p. 157.

e **Sound and spelling** /v/ and /w/

1 12.12 Listen and practice these sounds.
1 /v/ **v**isit 2 /w/ **w**eekend

2 12.13 Listen to these words and practice saying them.

invite verb watch with evening well never

3 LISTENING AND GRAMMAR *be going to*: questions

a 12.14 Listen to Lee and Marcus talk to a friend about their weekend plans. Write their names on the line.

NO PLAN ⟷ CLEAR PLAN

b 12.14 Listen again. Check (✓) the things you know after listening to the conversations.

1 ☐ the name of the movie Lee's going to see
2 ☐ Lee's plans for Sunday
3 ☐ Marcus's shopping plans
4 ☐ the name of the restaurant Marcus is going to go to
5 ☐ Marcus's plans for Sunday

c 12.15 Check (✓) the correct questions in 1–2. Listen and check.

1 a ☐ What are you going to do on Saturday?
  b ☐ What you are going to do on Saturday?
2 a ☐ You going to go shopping?
  b ☐ Are you going to go shopping?

d Now go to Grammar Focus 12B on p. 134.

e 12.18 Put the words in the correct order to make questions. Listen and check.

1 what / you / this weekend / do / going to / are ?
2 go out / you / are / going to ?
3 what / going to / movie / see / are / you ?
4 you / are / buy / going to / what ?
5 go / going to / where / you / are ?

f Have two conversations with a partner.

1 Student A: You're Lee.
  Student B: Ask questions 1, 2, and 3 in 3e.
2 Student B: You're Marcus.
  Student A: Ask questions 1, 4, and 5 in 3e.

4 SPEAKING

a Write questions to ask your partner about their plans. Use the ideas below and *be going to*.

- this evening
- the weekend
- on your next birthday

b Ask your partner your questions in 4a. Listen to the answers and write your partner's name on the line in 3a.

c Compare your line with other students. Who has clear plans for the future?

12C EVERYDAY ENGLISH

Do you want to watch the game?

Learn to make and accept invitations

- P Sound and spelling: *oo*
- W An invitation

1 LISTENING

a You invite friends to your house. Which of these things do you do? Write *Yes*, *No*, or *Sometimes*.

- make special food
- do homework
- play video games
- cook with your friends
- listen to music
- watch a show or movie

b Talk about your ideas in 1a with a partner.

c Look at pictures a and b. What do you think Ryan invites Carlos to do?

d 12.19 Listen to Part 1. Check your answer in 1c.

e 12.19 Listen to Part 1 again. Underline the correct answer.

1. Carlos invites Ryan to *the movies* / *watch a football game*.
2. Ryan *has* / *doesn't have* plans for tonight.
3. Carlos *accepts* / *doesn't accept* Ryan's invitation.

a

b

2 USEFUL LANGUAGE Making and accepting invitations

a Look at the expressions. Do we use them to ... ?

a make an invitation
b accept an invitation
c say no to an invitation

1. Do you want to go see a movie?
2. I'd like to, but ...
3. OK, sure. That sounds like fun.
4. Are you free tonight?
5. Sorry. Next time!
6. Great. See you then!

12.20 Listen and check your answers.

b 12.21 Complete the conversation with the words in the box. Listen and check.

sorry thank love want OK free busy

A Do you [1]_______ to go to dinner?
B Yes, I'd [2]_______ to. [3]_______ you.
A Are you [4]_______ on Saturday?
B No, [5]_______, I'm [6]_______ on Saturday. But Sunday's [7]_______.
A OK, we can go on Sunday.

c Practice the conversation in 2b with a partner.

3 LISTENING

a Do you often meet people from other countries? Where do you meet them?

b 12.22 Listen to Part 2. Answer the questions.

1. Where do they watch the game?
2. When did Carlos move there?

c 12.22 Listen to Part 2 again. Check (✓) the correct answers.

1. ☐ Carlos meets Ryan's friends for the first time.
2. ☐ Carlos knows Ryan's friends from before.
3. ☐ The football game is going to start soon.
4. ☐ The football game started before Carlos arrived.
5. ☐ Carlos doesn't understand football.
6. ☐ Carlos understands football.

d Why was Carlos confused about the football game?

4 PRONUNCIATION Sound and spelling: *oo*

a ▶ 12.23 Listen to these sentences. Notice the different *oo* sounds.

1 G**oo**d – now you're both here.
2 I'll bring the f**oo**d.

b ▶ 12.24 Listen to these words. Put them in the correct place in the chart.

cool cook spoon look
book soon football

Sound 1 /ʊ/	Sound 2 /u/
good	*food*

c Practice saying the words in 2b with a partner.

5 SPEAKING

Communication 12C

Student A go to p. 110.
Student B go to p. 115.

6 WRITING

a Carlos wrote invitations to his new friends. Read the invitations and the replies. Do they say yes or no? Why?

Birthday on Saturday

Hi guys,

It's my birthday on Saturday. Do you want to come to my party?

It's at my apartment at 2:00. We're going to watch my favorite soccer team play on TV at 3:00.

I hope to see you then!

Carlos

RE: Birthday on Saturday

Hi Carlos,

Thanks for the invitation!

Sorry, but I'm working until 4:00 on Saturday. I can come late at 4:30. Is that OK with you? Maybe I can still see part of the soccer game!

Ryan

RE: Birthday on Saturday

Hi Carlos,

I'd love to come, but I'm at my parents' house until Sunday.

Do you want to watch a game next week? I'm free after 2:00. Soccer or football sounds good to me!

Hope you have a great time!

Steve

RE: Birthday on Saturday

Hi Carlos,

Thanks for the invitation. Adriana and I can come! What can we bring? We can make some cookies if you'd like!

See you Saturday!

Hayley

b Now go to Writing Plus 12C on p. 163 for Paragraphs.

c You want to meet a friend. Think of a place and time. Write an invitation. Here are some ideas:

Do you want to … ?
I'm free at …
See you …
We could …
Is that OK with you?

d Read another student's invitation. Write a reply.

UNIT PROGRESS TEST

CHECK YOUR PROGRESS

YOU CAN NOW DO THE UNIT PROGRESS TEST.

UNIT 12
Review

1 GRAMMAR

a Complete Emily's email with *be going to* and the verbs in parentheses.

Hi Mia,

I have so many plans for this week! This afternoon I [1]__________ (study), and then I [2]__________ (work) from Tuesday to Thursday. On Wednesday evening, I [3]__________ (cook) for my parents, and then on Thursday evening, Marco [4]__________ (cook) dinner for me!

I [5]__________ (not / work) on Friday morning because you [6]__________ (arrive) at lunchtime! James [7]__________ (have) a party on Friday evening. Do you want to go? He [8]__________ (not / invite) a lot of people.

It's a busy week for me! So I [9]__________ (not / do) any work or housework this weekend, and we [10]__________ (not / go) to a lot of different places! I hope that's OK.

See you on Friday!

Emily

b Correct the sentences.

> "Is your friend going to have lunch with us?" "No, she not."
No, she's not.
1 "You are going to watch TV this evening?" "No, I'm not."
2 Are your mom going to cook your dinner this evening?
3 "Are you going to clean your bedroom?" "Yes, I'm going."
4 What do you going to wear tomorrow?
5 "Are your friends going to visit you today?" "Yes, they're."
6 What you going to do next summer?

c Ask and answer the questions in 1b. Use *be going to*.

2 VOCABULARY

a ~~Cross out~~ the answers that are NOT possible.

1 *tomorrow* / *on tomorrow*
2 *this* / *in* / *next* / *on* Friday
3 *on* / *in* the weekend
4 *on* / *this* / *in* / *next June*
5 *next* / *at* weekend
6 *on* / *in* Sunday
7 *in* / *on* three weeks
8 *this* / *at* afternoon

b Complete the ordinal numbers.

> 6th s *i* *x* *t* h
1 2nd s _ _ _ _ d
2 30th t _ _ _ _ _ _ _ _ h
3 21st t _ _ _ _ y-f _ _ _ t
4 3rd t _ _ _ d
5 15th f _ _ _ _ _ _ _ _ h
6 9th n _ _ _ h

c Complete the questions with the words in the box.

clean play invite make use go

1 Do you often ______ to museums?
2 Are you going to ______ a cake this weekend?
3 Did you ______ any sports yesterday?
4 Are you going to ______ your bedroom today?
5 Do you ______ your computer every day?
6 Are you going to ______ someone for lunch next week?

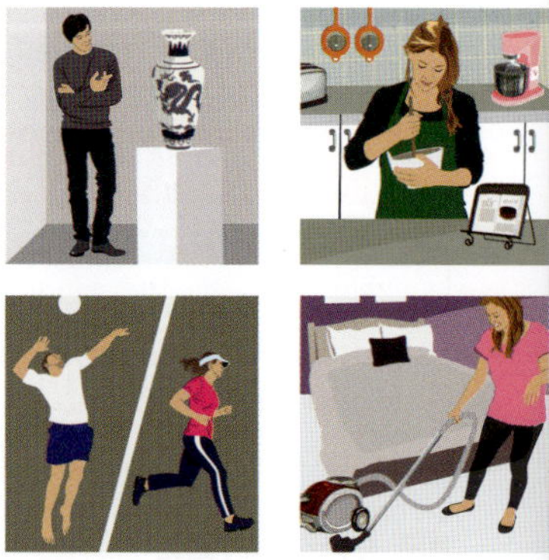

d Ask and answer the questions in 2c.

3 SOUND AND SPELLING

a 12.25 Circle the /v/ sounds in the phrases and underline the /w/ sounds. Practice saying the phrases and sentences.

1 visit in the evening
2 We never invite Wendy.
3 I love weekends in the winter.
4 win video games every week
5 watch TV with Valeria and William
6 on Wednesday, November twelfth

b 12.26 Complete the chart with the words in the box. Practice saying the words.

good book football boots
cool look school soon

/ʊ/	/u/
cooking	*spoon*

REVIEW YOUR PROGRESS

How well did you do in this unit? Write 3, 2, or 1 for each objective.
3 = very well 2 = well 1 = not so well

I CAN ...	
talk about future plans	☐
ask and answer about future plans	☐
make and accept invitations	☐

Phonemic symbols

Vowel sounds

/ə/	/æ/	/ʊ/	/ɑ/	/ɪ/	/i/	/e/	/ʌ/	/ɜ/	/u/	/ɔ/
breakfast	man	put	got	chip	happy	men	up	shirt	who	walk

Diphthongs (two vowel sounds)

/eə/	/ɪə/	/ɔɪ/	/ɑɪ/	/eɪ/	/oʊ/	/ɑʊ/
hair	near	boy	nine	eight	window	now

Consonants

/p/ picnic	/b/ book	/f/ face	/v/ very	/t/ time	/d/ dog	/k/ cold	/g/ go
/θ/ think	/ð/ the	/tʃ/ chair	/dʒ/ job	/s/ sea	/z/ zoo	/ʃ/ shoe	/ʒ/ television
/m/ me	/n/ now	/ŋ/ sing	/h/ hot	/l/ late	/r/ red	/w/ went	/j/ yes

Irregular verbs

Infinitive	Simple past
be	was
begin	began
buy	bought
catch	caught
choose	chose
come	came
do	did
drink	drank
drive	drove
eat	ate
feel	felt
find	found
fly	flew
forget	forgot
get	got
give	gave
go	went
grow up	grew up
have	had
hear	heard
know	knew
leave	left
lose	lost

Infinitive	Simple past
meet	met
pay	paid
put	put
read	read
ride	rode
run	ran
say	said
see	saw
sell	sold
send	sent
sing	sang
sit	sat
sleep	slept
speak	spoke
swim	swam
take	took
teach	taught
tell	told
think	thought
understand	understood
wake up	woke up
wear	wore
write	wrote

1A STUDENT A

a You're Yoshi from Japan. You're a student. Complete the conversation.

A Hello, I'm ________.
B Hi, I'm Bella. Nice to meet you.
A Are you from the U.K.?
B No, I'm not. I'm from the U.S. And you?
A I'm from ________.
B Are you a teacher?
A No, I'm a ________. And you?
B I'm a teacher.

b Have a conversation with Student B.

c Choose a name and a country and have another conversation.

1B STUDENT A

Jenna = British   Diego = Ecuadorian   Sandra = Italian

a Look at the picture and the information box. Then cover the box.

b Tell Student B the names of the people and answer Student B's questions.

This is …

c Listen to Student B talk about the people in the picture. Then ask Student B about the nationalities of the people.

Are they Spanish?

No, they're not. They're Brazilian.

2A STUDENT A

a Read the information about Kate.

Name: Kate
Town/city: Beaverton – small city near Portland, Oregon, in the U.S.
Home: beautiful, old house

b Tell Students B and C about Kate.

Her name's …

She's from …

Her home is …

c Listen to Students B and C talk about two people. What information is the same about all three people?

2B STUDENT A

a Look at the picture. Student B has a similar picture. Ask and answer questions to find seven differences.

Do you have a phone in your picture?

I have two phones.

b Now go back to p. 19.

4C STUDENT A

a Look at the pictures. The two people are your friends. You want to show the pictures to Student B. Think about what you want to say.

Rob, teacher, interesting

Carla, hotel manager, happy

b Cover the information under the pictures. Show them to Student B and talk about your friends.

These are my friends Rob and Carla.

c Ask Student B about his/her two friends.

Do you have photos of your friends?

d Now go back to p. 37.

4A STUDENT A

a Read the information.

- You live in Montreal, Canada, but you work three days a week in Essex, Vermont, in the U.S.
- You work two days a week from home.
- You study French and you go to class on Friday.

b Start a conversation with Student B about their life. Use the questions below to help you.

Where do you live?

Do you work in …?

Do you speak …?

c Listen to Student B and reply.

I live in …

I speak a little …

2C STUDENT A

a Ask Student B about his/her:

- last name
- address
- phone number
- email address

What's your last name?

b Read the information on your card. Answer Student B's questions.

Last name: Ramirez
Address: 5 High Street
Phone number: (714) 555-4321
Email address: toniramirez@travelmail.com

c Now go back to p. 20.

3B STUDENT A

a Ask Student B the time in these cities:

- Paris
- Rio de Janeiro
- Beijing
- Los Angeles

b Answer Student B's questions about the time in these cities.

Tokyo New York Mexico City Berlin

c Now go back to p. 27.

4B STUDENT A

a Read the information about Omar on your card.

"I'm a student. I'm 19, and I study English at Cairo University, in Egypt. I live at home with my parents. My mother is a teacher, and my father works at the Bank of Cairo. He's a bank manager. I have one brother. He's married, and he lives in Dubai. He works at Dubai Airport."

b Tell Student B about Omar.

He's a student. He studies English …

c Listen to Student B talk about Monica. Find six things that are the same about Omar and Monica.

1 They're both students.

d Now go back to p. 35.

1A STUDENT B

a You're Bella from the U.S. You're a teacher. Complete the conversation.

A Hello, I'm Yoshi.
B Hi, I'm ____________. Nice to meet you.
A Are you from England?
B No, I'm not. I'm from ____________. And you?
A I'm from Japan.
B Are you a ____________?
A No, I'm a student. And you?
B I'm a ____________.

b Have a conversation with Student A.

c Choose a name and a country and have another conversation.

1B STUDENT B

Sara = Spanish Luis and Marta = Brazilian Tony = American

a Look at the picture and the information in the box. Then cover the box.

b Listen to Student A talk about the people in the picture. Then ask Student A about the nationalities of the people.

Is he British?

No, he's not. He's American.

c Tell Student A the names of the people and answer Student A's questions.

This is ...

2A STUDENT B

a Read the information about Carla.

Name: Carla
Town/city: Hamilton – small city near Toronto, in Canada
Home: nice, new apartment

b Listen to Student A.

c Tell Students A and C about Carla.

Her name's ...

She's from ...

Her home is ...

d Listen to Student C talk. What information is the same about all three people?

2B STUDENT B

a Look at the picture. Student A has a similar picture. Ask and answer questions to find seven differences.

Do you have keys in your picture?

I have one key.

b Now go back to p. 19.

5C STUDENT B

a **Conversation 1.** You're on a street you know. Use the information to answer Student A's questions.

a hotel: not near here – near the train station
cafés: Black Cat Café on this street

b **Conversation 2.** Now you're on a street you don't know. Ask Student A about:

- a bank
- stores

c Now go back to p. 45.

5B STUDENT B

a Read the information about a hotel on your card.

> **Hotel Helena**
> - Rooms with showers and TVs
> - Restaurant
> - Swimming pool
> - Parking
>
> ***Note:*** *There isn't free Wi-Fi in the hotel. You pay for it.*

b Student A has information about a hostel. Ask and answer questions to find what things are the same and what things are different in the hotel and the hostel.

Is there free Wi-Fi in the hostel?

Yes, there is.

6A STUDENT B

a Look at the information about Sarah and Hassan. Make affirmative (+) and negative (–) sentences.

+ meet a lot of people
+ work in a restaurant
→ a server

– work in the morning
– sit a lot

+ meet a lot of people
+ like his job
→ a taxi driver

– work during the day
– work very hard

b Ask Student A about Rosa and Franco.
Say: *Tell me about … .*
Can you guess their jobs?

c Tell Student A about Sarah and Hassan. Don't say their jobs.

Sarah meets a lot of people.

3B STUDENT B

a Answer Student A's questions about the time in these cities.

Paris Rio de Janeiro Beijing Los Angeles

b Ask Student A the time in these cities:

- Tokyo
- New York
- Mexico City
- Berlin

c Now go back to p. 27.

6B STUDENT B

a Peter and Gamal live in the same apartment. Read about Peter's daily routine.

Peter works at a bank. He always wakes up at 6:30. He gets up at 7:00, has coffee, and goes to work. He starts work at 8:30, and he finishes at 5:30. He gets home at 6:00, has dinner, and watches TV. Sometimes he goes out, but he always goes to bed at 10:30.

b Answer Student A's questions about Peter.

c Ask Student A questions about Gamal. Then write the answers.

When does he go to class?

What does he do in the afternoon?

- When / get up? *9:00*
- When / go to class?
- What / do in the afternoon?
- When / get home?
- What / do in the evening?
- When / start work?
- When / finish work?
- When / go to bed?

d When does Peter see Gamal?

4A STUDENT B

a Read the information.

- You live in Monterrey, Mexico, but you work four days a week in Austin, Texas, in the U.S.
- You work one day a week from home.
- You study Spanish and you go to class on Saturday.

b Listen to Student A and reply.

I live in …

I speak a little …

c Start a conversation with Student A about their life. Use the questions below to help you.

Where do you live?

Do you work in …?

Do you speak …?

4C STUDENT B

a Look at the pictures. The two people are your friends. You want to show the pictures to Student A. Think about what you want to say.

Haley, student, kind

Will, bank manager, funny

b Ask Student A about his/her two friends.

Do you have photos of your friends?

c Cover the information under the pictures. Show them to Student A and talk about your friends.

These are my friends Haley and Will.

d Now go back to p. 37.

2A STUDENT C

a Read the information about Dave.

Name: Dave
Town/city: Newcastle – small city near Sydney, in Australia
Home: big, new apartment

b Listen to Students A and B talk about two people.

c Tell Students A and B about Dave. What information is the same about all three people?

His name's …

He's from …

His home is …

2C STUDENT B

a Read the information on your card. Answer Student A's questions.

Last name: Adams
Address: 8 Park Road
Phone number: (714) 555-9876
Email address: alexadams@travelmail.com

b Ask Student A about his/her:

- last name
- address
- phone number
- email address

What's your last name?

c Now go back to p. 20.

4B STUDENT B

a Read the information about Monica on your card.

"I'm Peruvian. I'm 20. I live in Lima, and I study English in college. I live at home with my parents. I have a brother and two sisters. My brother works at the airport. He's married and he has two children."

b Listen to Student A talk about Omar.

c Tell Student A about Monica. Find six things that are the same about Omar and Monica.

She's a student.
She studies English …

1 *They're both students.*

d Now go back to p. 35.

5B STUDENT A

a Read the information about a hostel on your card.

HARRY'S HOSTEL

- Big rooms with no shower
- Small rooms with a shower
- Free Wi-Fi
- A small café

Note: *There isn't a swimming pool or parking.*

b Student B has information about a hotel. Ask and answer questions to find what things are the same and what things are different in the hotel and the hostel.

Is there a swimming pool in the hotel?

Yes, there is.

6B STUDENT A

a Gamal and Peter live in the same apartment. Read about Gamal's daily routine.

Gamal is a student. He usually gets up at 9:00 and has breakfast. Then he goes to class at 10:00. In the afternoon, he studies in the library, and he gets home at 5:00. In the evening, he works in a café near their apartment. He starts work at 7:00 and finishes at 11:00. He goes to bed at 12:00.

b Ask Student B questions about Peter. Then write the answers.

When does he get up?

What does he do then?

- When / wake up? *6:30*
- When / get up?
- What / do then?
- When / start work?
- When / finish work?
- When / get home?
- What / do in the evening?
- When / go to bed?

c Answer Student B's questions about Gamal.

d When does Gamal see Peter?

6A STUDENT A

a Look at the information about Rosa and Franco. Make affirmative (+) and negative (–) sentences.

+ work very hard
+ work at a hospital
→ a doctor

– have a lot of free time
– sit a lot

+ work long hours
+ like his job
→ a teacher

– sit a lot
– work in the summer

b Tell Student B about Rosa and Franco. Don't say their jobs.

Rosa works very hard.

c Ask Student B about Sarah and Hassan. Say: *Tell me about …* . Can you guess their jobs?

7B STUDENT A

a Look at picture 1. Write notes about their clothes.

b Tell Student B about the clothes the people in picture 1 are wearing. Find out their names and write them under each picture.

> This person has a blouse and a skirt. What's this person's name?

c Listen to Student B talk about the clothes in picture 2. Tell him/her the people's names.

d Now go back to p. 58.

9A STUDENT B

a Read notes about your trip to Dubai, in the UAE. Make sentences from the notes. Use the simple past.

- in the north of the UAE
- plane to Dubai …
- didn't stay in a hotel …
- … my brother's apartment (he lives in Dubai)
- … then taxi around the city
- a lot of photos
- shopping – a lot of clothes
- restaurants – very good food

b Listen to Student A talk about a trip to Seville.

c Tell Student A about your trip. Find four things you both did on your trips.

12C STUDENT A

a You want to invite Student B to:

1 go for a walk this weekend.
2 meet for coffee.

Think about what you want to say. Start the conversation with Student B. Try to find times when you're both free.

> Do you want to go for a walk this weekend?

YOUR SCHEDULE

SUN	visiting parents 12:00–5:00	THURS	work 8:00–6:00
MON	work 8:00–6:00	FRI	work 8:00–6:00 yoga 7:00–8:30
TUES	work 8:00–6:00	SAT	concert 7:00 p.m.
WED			

b Now go back to p. 101.

10C STUDENT A

a **Conversation 1.** Read your first card. Think about what you want to say. Then start the conversation with Student B with *Excuse me.*

1 You want to go to Chicago.
- Time now: 11:15 a.m.
- Ask about the next train.
- Ask about the platform.
- You have a big suitcase – it's difficult to run.

b **Conversation 2.** Now read your second card. Think about what you want to say. Listen to Student B and reply.

2 You're a ticket agent at a bus station.
- Time now: 2:45 p.m.

	Time	Bus stop	Price
Phoenix	3:00 p.m.	4	$16
Phoenix	4:00 p.m.	3	$11

c Now go back to p. 85.

7A STUDENT B

a You have a stall at a flea market. You sell the objects in the box.

pictures clocks lamps chairs old books

Write a price for each object.

b At Student A's stall, you see three things you like:

- some beautiful plates
- an interesting plant
- a good knife for your kitchen

Try to buy them for a good price.

They're expensive. Is $2 OK?

c Try to sell things to Student A.

They're $10 each. They're very old.

It's only $5 – it's very cheap.

8A STUDENT B

a Answer Student A's questions about Morgan.

1 year ago	**last weekend**	**on Monday**
in Atlanta, Georgia	at a party at her home	in class

Morgan

b Ask Student C about Marcella.

Where was she a year ago?

Where was she last weekend?

Was she at work on Monday?

c Listen to Students A and C talk about Jaime.

d What is the same for all three people?

7C STUDENT A

a **Conversation 1.** You're a sales assistant at a store. Student B is your customer. You have six glasses, and they are $2.00 each. Your customer can pay by card. Start a conversation with *Hello, can I help you?*

b **Conversation 2.** You're a customer at a store. Student B is a sales assistant. You want to buy four plates. Ask how much they are.

c Now go back to p. 61.

8B STUDENT B

a Look at the pictures of Charlotte's day yesterday. Write notes about what she did.

b Listen to Student A talk about what Leo did yesterday.

c Tell Student A what Charlotte did yesterday. What activities are the same?

9B STUDENT A

a Read the information about the weather in Mumbai, in India. Listen to Student B and reply.

Weather in Mumbai	
Yesterday	hot, sunny
Today	cloudy, warm
Summer	a lot of rain, hot

b Ask Student B these questions about the weather in Berlin, in Germany.

What was the weather like yesterday?

What's the weather like today?

What's the weather like in winter?

c Now go back to p. 75.

10A STUDENT B

a Listen to Student A. Are they talking about picture 1, 2, or 3?

b Carlos is in picture 6. Tell Student A:

- where he is (*He's sitting in …*)
- what's in the next room (*There's a … next door.*)
- what he's doing (*He's …*)

c Listen to Student A again. Which picture are they talking about now?

d Choose picture 1 or 3. Describe it to Student A.

7C STUDENT B

a **Conversation 1.** You're a customer at a store. Student A is a sales assistant. You want to buy four glasses. Ask how much they are. You'd like to pay by card.

b **Conversation 2.** You're a sales assistant at a store. Student A is your customer. You have four plates, and they are $3 each. Your customer can pay by card. Start a conversation with *Hello, can I help you?*

c Now go back to p. 61.

10C STUDENT B

a **Conversation 1.** Read your first card. Think about what you want to say. Listen to Student A and reply.

1 You're a ticket agent at a train station.

- Time now: 11:15 a.m.
- Platform 6 is a two-minute walk.

	Time	Platform
Chicago	11:17 a.m.	6
Chicago	11:35 a.m.	6

b **Conversation 2.** Now read your second card. Think about what you want to say. Then start the conversation with Student A with *Excuse me.*

2 You want to go to Phoenix.

- Time now: 2:45 p.m.
- Ask about the next bus.
- Ask about the bus stop.
- Ask about the price. (You only have $15 with you.)

c Now go back to p. 85.

10B STUDENT B

a Look at the picture. What are the people doing? Write notes.

b Student A has a similar picture. Ask and answer questions to find five differences. Student A starts.

Is Ali in the kitchen?

Yes, he is.

Is he eating?

No, he's not. He's …

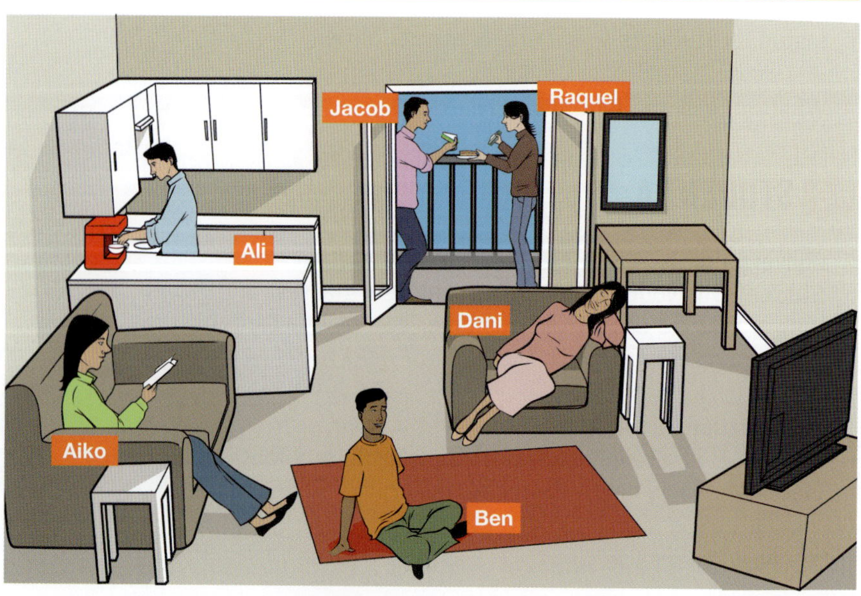

c Now go back to p. 83.

7A STUDENT A

a You have a stall at a flea market. You sell the objects in the box.

cups glasses plates plants knives

Write a price for each object.

b Try to sell things to Student B.

It's only $5 – it's very cheap.

They're $3 each. They're very beautiful.

c At Student B's stall, you see three things you like:

- a beautiful old picture
- a lamp
- some interesting old books

Try to buy them for a good price.

It's very expensive. Is $10 OK?

8A STUDENT A

a Ask Student B about Morgan.

Where was she a year ago?

Where was she last weekend?

Was she at work on Monday?

b Listen to Students B and C talk about Marcella.

c Answer Student C's questions about Jaime.

1 year ago	last weekend	on Monday
in Chile	at a party in Medellín	at work in Bogotá

d What is the same for all three people?

11C STUDENT A

a You and Student B live in the same city. Talk about good places for tourists to visit. This is what you think of the four main places to visit:

the Museum of History – very interesting
Central Park – OK, nice
Old Town – a little boring
Mega Department Store – very expensive

What do you think of Central Park?

I think Central Park is OK.

Really? I don't think so.

b Now go back to p. 93.

9B STUDENT B

a Ask Student A these questions about the weather in Mumbai, in India.

What was the weather like yesterday?

What's the weather like today?

What's the weather like in summer?

b Read the information about the weather in Berlin, in Germany. Listen to Student A and reply.

Weather in Berlin	
Yesterday	wet, windy
Today	sunny, cold
Winter	snows, cold

c Now go back to p. 75.

8B STUDENT A

a Look at the pictures of Leo's day yesterday. Write notes about what he did.

b Tell Student B what Leo did yesterday.

c Listen to Student B talk about what Charlotte did yesterday. What activities are the same?

7B STUDENT B

a Look at picture 2. Write notes about their clothes.

b Listen to Student A talk about the clothes in picture 1. Tell him/her the people's names.

c Tell Student A about the clothes the people in picture 2 are wearing. Find out their names and write them under each picture.

> This person has a coat and pants. What's the person's name?

d Now go back to p. 58.

10B STUDENT A

a Look at the picture. What are the people doing? Write notes.

b Student B has a similar picture. Ask and answer questions to find five differences. You start. Ask about Ali.

> Is Ali in the kitchen?
>
> Yes, he is.
>
> Is he eating?
>
> No, he's not. He's …

c Now go back to p. 83.

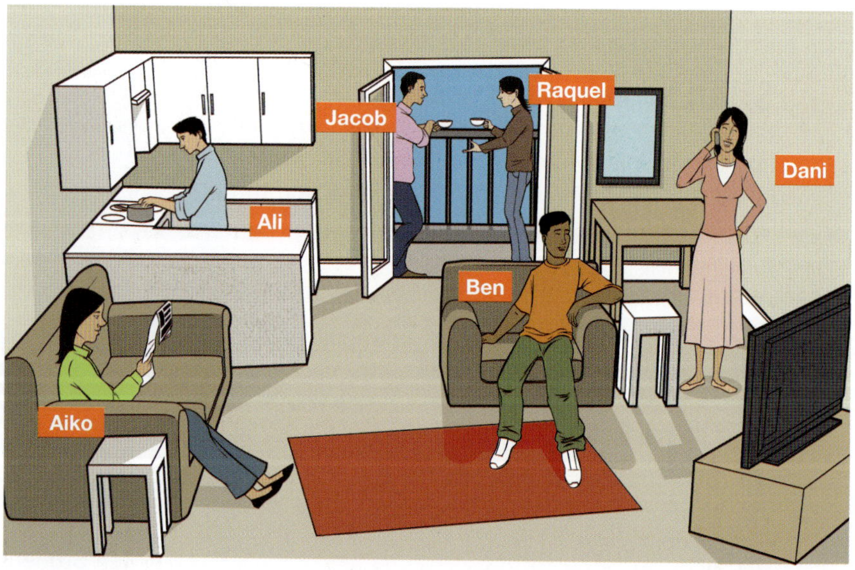

9A STUDENT A

a Read notes about your trip to Seville, in Spain. Make sentences from the notes. Use the simple past.

- in the south of Spain
- plane to Madrid …
- … then train to Seville
- small hotel – downtown
- a lot of photos
- shopping – didn't buy anything
- restaurants – very good food
- a concert – you liked it!

b Tell Student B about your trip.

c Listen to Student B talk about a trip to Dubai. Find four things you both did on your trips.

11C STUDENT B

a You and Student A live in the same city. Talk about good places for tourists to visit. This is what you think of the four main places to visit:

the Museum of History – OK
Central Park – boring
Old Town – beautiful
Mega Department Store – a lot of fun

> What do you think of the Museum of History?
>
> I think the museum is OK.
>
> Really? I don't think so.

b Now go back to p. 93.

8A STUDENT C

a Listen to Students A and B talk about Morgan.

b Answer Student B's questions about Marcella.

1 year ago	last weekend	on Monday
in Canada	at a party in Orlando	in a meeting at work

Marcella

c Ask Student A about Jaime.

Where was he a year ago?

Where was he last weekend?

Was he at work on Monday?

d What is the same for all three people?

12C STUDENT B

a You want to invite Student A to:

1 go out for dinner one evening.
2 go shopping for clothes.

Think about what you want to say. Listen to Student A and reply. Try to find times when you're both free.

Do you want to go out for dinner?

YOUR SCHEDULE	
SUN	
MON	work 8:00–6:00 theater 8:00 p.m.
TUES	
WED	work 8:00–6:00 Spanish class 7:00–8:30
THURS	on vacation – not here
FRI	on vacation – not here
SAT	soccer 9:00–2:00

b Now go back to p. 101.

10A STUDENT A

a Carlos is in picture 2. Tell Student B:

- where he is (*He's sitting in …*)
- what's in the next room (*There's a … next door.*)
- what he's doing (*He's …*)

b Listen to Student B. Are they talking about picture 4, 5, or 6?

c Choose picture 4 or 5. Describe it to Student B.

d Listen to Student B again. Which picture are they talking about now?

GRAMMAR FOCUS

1A *be: I / you / we*

Part 1: Affirmative and questions

▶ 01.03

	Affirmative (+)
I	*I'm fine.*
you	*You**'re** right.*
we	*We**'re** from the U.S.*
you	*You**'re** John and Hannah.*

Tip
I **am** → I'**m**
You **are** → You'**re**
We **are** → We'**re**

▶ 01.05

	Wh- questions (?)
I	*Where **am** I?*
you	*How **are** you?*
we	*Where **are** we?*
you	*Where **are** you?*

▶ 01.04

Yes/No questions (?)		Short answers	
***Am** I*	*at home?*	*Yes, you **are**.*	*No, you**'re not**.*
***Are** you*	*OK?*	*Yes, I **am**.*	*No, I**'m not**.*
***Are** we*	*in Los Angeles?*	*Yes, you **are**.*	*No, you**'re not**.*
***Are** you*	*students?*	*Yes, we **are**.*	*No, we**'re not**.*

***Are you** from Spain?* NOT ~~*You are from Spain?*~~
*Yes, **I am**.* NOT ~~*Yes, I'm.*~~

Part 2: Negative

▶ 01.08

	Negative (–)
I	*I**'m not** from Italy.*
you	*You**'re not** a teacher.*
we	*We**'re not** from the U.S.*
you	*You**'re not** teachers.*

Tip
I **am not** → I'**m not**
You **are not** → You'**re not** / You **aren't**
We **are not** → We'**re not** / We **aren't**

*I**'m not** from Brazil.* NOT ~~*I amn't from Brazil*~~.

1B *be: he / she / they*

Part 1: Affirmative

▶ 01.16

	+
he	*He**'s** Japanese.*
she	*She**'s** Mexican.*
they	*They**'re** American.*

Tip
He **is** → He'**s**
She **is** → She'**s**
They **are** → They'**re**

He's Japanese.

She's Mexican.

They're American.

Part 2: Negative and questions

▶ 01.18

	–
he	*He**'s not** Japanese.*
she	*She's **not** Mexican.*
they	*They**'re not** American.*

Tip
He **is not** → He'**s not** / He **isn't**
She **is not** → She'**s not** / She **isn't**
They **are not** → They'**re not** / They **aren't**

▶ 01.19

Yes/No questions (?)		Short answers	
he	***Is** he Japanese?*	*Yes, he **is**.*	*No, he**'s not**.*
she	***Is** she Mexican?*	*Yes, she **is**.*	*No, she**'s not**.*
they	***Are** they American?*	*Yes, they **are**.*	*No, they**'re not**.*

▶ 01.20

	Wh- questions (?)
he/she	*Where**'s** he/she from?* *Who**'s** he/she?*
they	*Where **are** they from?* *Who **are** they?*

***Is he** Japanese?* NOT ~~*Is Japanese?*~~ OR ~~*He is Japanese?*~~
***Are they** American?* NOT ~~*Are American?*~~ OR ~~*They are American?*~~
*Yes, **he is**.* NOT ~~*Yes, he's.*~~

Tip
*Where **is** he from?* → *Where**'s** he from?*
*Who **is** she?* → *Who**'s** she?*

1A *be*: *I* / *you* / *we*

Part 1: Affirmative and questions

a Write sentences with *'re* or *'m*.

1 I am from New York. *I'm from New York.*
2 We are students.
3 You are Roberto.
4 I am fine, thanks.
5 We are from Mexico.

b Put the words in the correct order to make questions.

1 you / are / how ? *How are you?*
2 are / from / the U.S. / you ?
3 we / in / Ecuador / are ?
4 OK / I / am ?
5 name / your / what's ?

c Now go back to p. 8.

Part 2: Negative

a Write one affirmative (+) and one negative (–) sentence for 1–5.

1 We / from Brazil
We're from Brazil. We're not from Brazil.
2 You / Rebecca
3 I / a teacher
4 We / in Paris
5 I / OK

b Write short answers.

1 **A** Are you from the U.S.?
B No, *I'm not*.
2 **A** Are you Eric?
B Yes, ______.
3 **A** Are we in Spain?
B No, ______.
4 **A** Are you students?
B Yes, ______.

c Now go back to p. 9.

1B *be*: *he* / *she* / *they*

Part 1: Affirmative

a Complete the sentences with *he's*, *she's*, or *they're*.

1 ______ Italian.

2 ______ Chinese.

3 ______ Brazilian.

4 ______ Mexican.

5 ______ Spanish.

6 ______ British.

b Now go back to p. 11.

Part 2: Negative and questions

a Complete the sentences with *'s not* or *'re not*.

1 She ______ Italian. She's Brazilian.
2 They ______ American. They're English.
3 He ______ Chinese. He's American.
4 They ______ Colombian. They're English.
5 He ______ Spanish. He's Italian.
6 She ______ Brazilian. She's Ecuadorian.

b Check (✓) the correct questions. Correct the wrong questions.

1 ☐ He is Colombian?
2 ☐ Is she Brazilian?
3 ☐ Are English they?
4 ☐ Are he Italian?
5 ☐ She is Chinese?
6 ☐ Are they Japanese?

c Complete the conversations with *is*, *'s not*, *'s*, *are*, *'re not*, or *'re*.

A Who is this?
B He [1] ______ my friend Lee.
A [2] ______ he Chinese?
B No, he [3] ______. He [4] ______ from the U.S.

A Who are they?
B They [5] ______ my friends Nick and Anna.
A [6] ______ they from England?
B No, they [7] ______. They [8] ______ Brazilian.

d Now go back to p. 11.

2A *be*: *it's / it's not*; Possessive adjectives

Part 1: *it's / it's not*

it = a place/thing

they = 2+ places/things

02.04

	+	–
it	*It's an old hotel.*	*It's **not** a new hotel.*
they	*They**'re** small houses.*	*They**'re not** big houses.*

02.05

	Yes/No questions	Short answers	
it	***Is** it a big hotel?*	*Yes, it **is**.*	*No, it**'s not**.*
they	***Are** they new houses?*	*Yes, they **are**.*	*No, they**'re not**.*

***Is it** in Japan?* NOT ~~*Is in Japan?*~~ OR ~~*It is in Japan?*~~
*Yes, **it is**.* NOT ~~*Yes, it's.*~~

> **Tip**
> *It **is** in Ecuador.* ➔ *It**'s** in Ecuador.*
> *It **is not** in Italy.* ➔ *It**'s not** in Italy. / It **isn't** in Italy.*

Part 2: Possessive adjectives

Pronoun	Possessive adjective	02.10
I	**my**	***My** apartment is small.*
you	**your**	*Is this **your** book?*
he	**his**	***His** home is old and beautiful.*
she	**her**	*She's here with **her** friend.*
we	**our**	*This is **our** home in Quito.*
they	**their**	*Is that **their** home?*

***your** bag* NOT ~~*you're bag*~~
***their** house* NOT ~~*they're house*~~

2B Plural nouns

SPELLING: Plural nouns

most words ➔ add *-s*	*book* ➔ *book**s*** *boy* ➔ *boy**s*** *house* ➔ *house**s***
consonant + *-y* ➔ ~~*-y*~~ add *-ies*	*city* ➔ *cit**ies*** *baby* ➔ *bab**ies***
ends in *-o*, *-ch*, *-ss*, *-s*, *-sh*, and *-x* ➔ *add -es* Exception: For some *-o* words, add *-s*.	*watch* ➔ *watch**es*** *glass* ➔ *glass**es*** *photo* ➔ *photo**s***
irregular	*knife* ➔ *kni**ves***

books NOT ~~*a books*~~

a book

a ticket

an apple

book**s**

two ticket**s**

apple**s**

3A Simple present: *I / you / we / they*

03.09

	+		–	
I	*I **like***	*fish.*	*I **don't like***	*fish.*
you	*You **eat***	*meat.*	*You **don't eat***	*meat.*
we	*We **eat***	*a lot of vegetables.*	*We **don't eat***	*a lot of vegetables.*
they	*They **like***	*eggs.*	*They **don't like***	*eggs.*

*I **don't like** fish.* NOT ~~*I not like fish.*~~

> **Tip**
> *I **do not** like rice.* ➔ *I **don't like** rice.*

03.10

Yes/No questions	Short answers	
***Do** I **like** fish?*	*Yes, you **do**.*	*No, you **don't**.*
***Do** you **eat** meat?*	*Yes, I **do**.*	*No, I **don't**.*
***Do** we **eat** a lot of vegetables?*	*Yes, we **do**.*	*No, we **don't**.*
***Do** they **like** eggs?*	*Yes, they **do**.*	*No, they **don't**.*

***Do you** eat meat?* NOT ~~*You eat meat?*~~
*Yes, **I do**.* NOT ~~*Yes, I like.*~~
*No, **we don't**.* NOT ~~*No, we don't like.*~~

2A *be*: *it's / it's not*; Possessive adjectives

Part 1: *it's / it's not*

a Complete the sentences with *it's* or *they're*.

1 ___________ a beautiful town near Barcelona.
2 São Paulo and Rio de Janeiro are big cities. ___________ in Brazil.
3 My apartment is small. ___________ in a new part of town.
4 Our homes are old. ___________ in a nice part of town.
5 The apartments are in an old part of town. ___________ big and beautiful.
6 They're from a small town in China. ___________ near Beijing.

b Complete the sentences with *it's not* or *they're not*.

1 The houses are in Montana. ___________ in Idaho.
2 "Is this your apartment?" "No, ___________."
3 Mumbai is a big city. ___________ small.
4 They are from Costa Rica. ___________ a big country.
5 They are from Ottawa. ___________ from Vancouver.
6 Their apartments are very old. ___________ in a new part of town.

c Now go back to p. 16.

Part 2: Possessive adjectives

a Complete the sentences.

1 "Hi, I'm Jack. What's ___________ name?" "I'm Selim."
2 She's from Brazil and ___________ name's Maria.
3 They're from the U.S., and ___________ names are Sam and Erica.
4 We live in Cartagena. ___________ apartment is in an old part of town.
5 "Is this ___________ book?" "Yes, it is. Thank you."
6 They're from London, but ___________ parents are from Mumbai.

b Now go back to p. 17.

2B Plural nouns

a Write the plurals.

1 an egg ___________
2 a knife ___________
3 a girl ___________
4 a country ___________
5 a town ___________
6 a phone ___________
7 a house ___________
8 a city ___________

b Underline the correct words.

1 Bogotá is *big city* / *a big city*.
2 Villajoyosa is *a town* / *towns* in Spain.
3 It's *small* / *a small* house.
4 They're new *apartment* / *apartments*.
5 Two *bottle* / *bottles* of water, please.
6 He's a big *baby* / *babies*.
7 New York and Washington are *cities* / *citys* in the U.S.
8 Two *tickets* / *ticketes* to London, please.

c Now go back to p. 19.

3A Simple present: *I / you / we / they*

a Complete the sentences with the words in the box.

do (x2)	don't (x3)	eat

1 I like rice, but I ___________ like bread.
2 ___________ you like fruit?
3 **A** Do they eat meat? **B** Yes, they ___________.
4 We ___________ fruit every day.
5 I eat rice, but I ___________ like it.
6 **A** Do you like fish? **B** No, I ___________.

b Look at the information about the Brown family. Write five sentences about them.

meat	✓
fish	✗
vegetables	✓
rice	✓
bread	✗

They eat … They don't eat …

c Write sentences about things you eat and drink.

I eat rice. I eat vegetables every day. I don't like coffee …

d Now go back to p. 25.

3B Adverbs of frequency

03.20

We **always** have breakfast at 7:00.

I **usually** have a sandwich for lunch.

We **sometimes** eat fish for dinner.

I **never** eat cake.
NOT ~~*I never don't eat cake.*~~

Tip

Adverbs of frequency go **before** the verb.
NOT ~~***Always we have** breakfast at 7:00.*~~ OR ~~***We have always** breakfast at 7:00.*~~
The adverb of frequency ***sometimes*** can go **at the beginning of the sentence**, too.
***We sometimes eat** fish for dinner.* OR ***Sometimes we eat** fish for dinner.*

4A Simple present: *Wh-* questions

04.05

Wh-* questions with *be	
*What**'s** your name?*	*My name**'s** Lucia.*
*When **are** you home?*	*We**'re** home this evening.*
*Where **are** they from?*	*They**'re** from Brazil.*

NOT ~~*What **your name is**?*~~ OR ~~*Where **you are** from?*~~

Tip

Wh- word + *is*/*are* + person (*you*, *they*, etc.)?

04.06

***Wh-* questions with other verbs**	
*Where **do** you **live**?*	*I **live** in La Paz.*
*What **do** you **study**?*	*We **study** Chinese.*
*When **do** they **go** to school?*	*They **go** to school at 8:00.*

NOT ~~*Where **you live**?*~~ OR ~~*Where **live you**?*~~

Tip

Wh- word + *do* + person (*you*, *they*, etc.) + verb?

4B Simple present: *he / she / it* affirmative

04.14

	+	
he	*My brother **works*** *He **lives***	*in a hotel.* *in a small house.*
she	*Ingrid **lives*** *She **works***	*in Boston.* *in an office.*
it	*My room **has*** *It **has***	*a big window.* *a big table.*

Tip

*I/You/We/They **work** in a hotel.*
*He/She **works** in a hotel.*

SPELLING: verb + *-s*

most verbs → add ***-s***	*work* → *work**s*** *live* → *live**s***
consonant + ***-y*** → ~~***-y***~~ add ***-ies***	*study* → *stud**ies***
ends in ***-o***, ***-ch***, ***-ss***, ***-s***, ***-sh*** and ***-x*** → add ***-es***	*go* → *go**es*** *do* → *do**es*** *teach* → *teach**es***
irregular	*have* → ***has***

*He **studies*** NOT ~~*He **studys***~~
*She **has*** NOT ~~*She **haves***~~

3B Adverbs of frequency

a Put the words in the correct order to make sentences.

1 sometimes / at 10:00 / have dinner / we
2 I / in the evening / have coffee / never
3 have a sandwich / I / for lunch / usually
4 we / at home / always / have dinner
5 at lunchtime / always / eat fruit / I
6 usually / in a café / I / have lunch

b Look at Monica's schedule. Complete her sentences with adverbs of frequency.

1 "I ____________ have coffee in a small café."
2 "I ____________ eat breakfast."
3 "My friends and I ____________ have lunch at work."
4 "We ____________ have dinner at home."

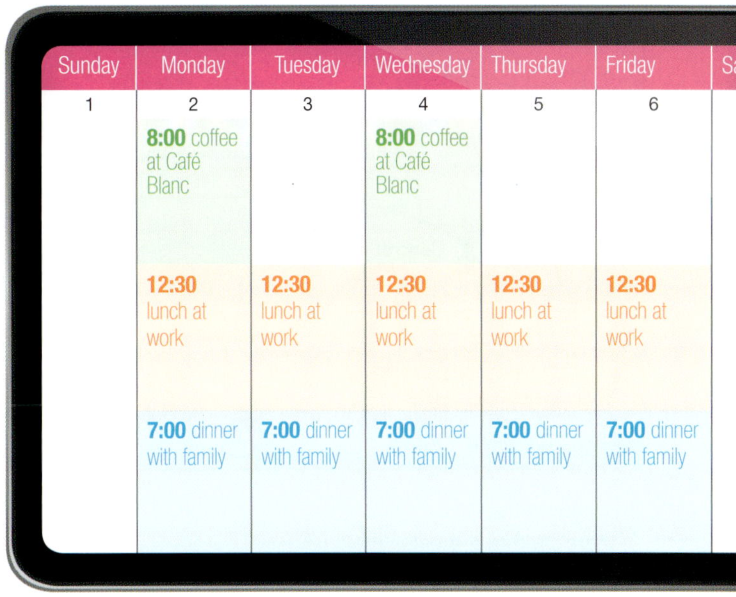

c Now go back to p. 27.

4A Simple present: *Wh-* questions

a Complete the questions with *'s, are,* or *do.*

1 Where ____________ they work?
2 What ____________ you eat for breakfast?
3 Where ____________ your home?
4 When ____________ you in class?
5 Where ____________ you study English?
6 Where ____________ you from?
7 What time ____________ you go to class every day?
8 When ____________ he at home?

b Write questions for the sentences. Use the question word in parentheses.

1 I work in Tokyo. (where)
Where do you work?
2 We go to work at 7:00 in the morning. (when)
3 I eat a sandwich for lunch. (what)
4 We study at a big language school in Quito. (where)
5 I study business at school. (what)
6 I go to my class at 6:00 in the evening. (when)

c Now go back to p. 33.

4B Simple present: *he / she / it* affirmative

a Underline the correct words.

1 She always *drink / drinks* tea for breakfast.
2 My son *studies / studys* Spanish in college.
3 He *works / workes* in a supermarket.
4 The car *have / has* new lights.
5 She has breakfast and then she *gos / goes* to school.
6 The dog *play / plays* in the backyard.

b Look at the picture. Complete the sentences about Carmen with the verbs in the box.

have drink eat live study

1 She ____________ in Madrid.
2 She ____________ English.
3 She ____________ bananas.
4 She ____________ coffee.
5 She ____________ a computer.

c Now go back to p. 35.

5A *there is / there are*: affirmative

On Regent Street, …
… **there's** a movie theater.
… **there are** two cafés.
… **there are** a lot of people.

There's = There is
There's** a café.* NOT ~~There** a café.*~~
***There are** three cafés.*
NOT ~~***There's three** cafés.*~~

05.02

	+	
Singular	***There's***	*a café.* *one café.*
Plural	***There are***	*cafés.* *three cafés.*

5B *there is / there are*: negative and questions

05.16

	–		–	
Singular	***There isn't***	*a shower.* *a blanket.*	***There's no***	*shower.* *blanket.*
Plural	***There aren't***	*any pillows.* *any rooms.*	***There are no***	*pillows.* *rooms.*

NOT ~~***There's isn't** shower.*~~ OR ~~***There's no** a shower.*~~
NOT ~~***There are no** any pillows.*~~

Tip
*There **is not** a hotel.* → *There **isn't** a hotel.* → *There**'s no** hotel.*
*There **are not** any cafés.* → *There **aren't** any cafés.* → *There **are no** cafés.*
Use *any* after *there are not* and *there aren't*.

05.17

	***Yes/No* questions**		**Short answers**	
Singular	***Is there***	*a café?*	*Yes, **there is**.*	*No, **there isn't**.*
Plural	***Are there***	*any small rooms?*	*Yes, **there are**.*	*No, **there aren't**.*

NOT ~~***There is** a café?*~~ OR ~~***There are** small rooms?*~~
NOT ~~*Yes, there's.*~~ OR ~~*No, there **not**.*~~

Tip
Use *any* after *Are there … ?*

5A *there is / there are*: affirmative

a Write three more sentences about Regent Street on page 122. Use *there's* or *there are* and the words in the box.

apartment car supermarket

1 ______________________________
2 ______________________________
3 ______________________________

b Look at the picture. Change the sentences to make them true.

1 There's a taxi.
2 There are two restaurants.
3 There's one store.
4 There are three women.
5 There are three girls.
6 There's a boy.
7 There are two schools.

c Now go back to p. 40.

5B *there is / there are*: negative and questions

a Complete the sentences with a negative (–) or question (?) form of *there is* or *there are*.

1 ____________ any cafés on my street.
2 ____________ a movie theater in this part of town.
3 ____________ a hotel near the subway station?
4 ____________ any stores near the hotel?
5 ____________ any restaurants on High Street.
6 ____________ a café near here?
7 ____________ a restaurant near the movie theater.
8 ____________ any supermarkets near the hostel?

b Add *any* to the sentences if possible.

1 There aren't good restaurants in this town.
2 Are there stores near the hotel?
3 Is there a TV in the room?
4 Sorry, there aren't available rooms.
5 There's a café on the first floor.
6 There are two movie theaters near here.

c Complete the conversation with the correct form of *there is / there are*.

A Excuse me, ____________ ____________ any hotels near here?
B No, ____________ ____________. But ____________ one near the train station.
A And ____________ ____________ a restaurant near the hotel?
B Yes, ____________ ____________. It's a very good one.

d Rewrite the sentences using *there's no* or *there are no*.

1 There isn't a TV in the room. There's no TV in the room.
2 There aren't hotels on this street. ____________
3 There aren't any pillows in the room. ____________
4 There isn't a swimming pool. ____________
5 There isn't a school in the town. ____________
6 There aren't gas stations on this road. ____________

e Now go back to p. 43.

6A Simple present: *he / she / it* negative

06.05

	–	
he	*He **doesn't work***	*on Monday.*
she	*She **doesn't study***	*Spanish.*
it	*The town **doesn't have***	*a bank.*

*He **doesn't work** on Monday.* NOT ~~*He doesn't works on Monday.*~~
OR ~~*He **don't works** on Monday.*~~
OR ~~*He **not works** on Monday.*~~

Tip

*I **do not work** at night.* → *I **don't work** at night.*
*He **does not work** at night.* → *He **doesn't work** at night.*

6B Simple present: *he / she / it* questions

06.13

	Yes/No questions		Short answers	
he	***Does** he*	***work** at a bank?*	*Yes, he **does**.*	*No, he **doesn't**.*
she	***Does** she*	***get up** early?*	*Yes, she **does**.*	*No, she **doesn't**.*
it	***Does** the party*	***start** at 9:00?*	*Yes, it **does**.*	*No, it **doesn't**.*

***Does he work** in a bank?* NOT ~~*Does he **works** … ?*~~
*Yes, **she does**.* NOT ~~*Yes, she **works**.*~~
*No, **she doesn't**.* NOT ~~*No, she **doesn't work**.*~~

06.14

	Wh- questions		
he	*Where*	***does** he*	***work**?*
she	*When*	***does** she*	***get up**?*
it	*What time*	***does** it*	***start**?*

*Where **does she** work?* NOT ~~*Where **she does** work?*~~
OR ~~*Where **she works**?*~~

Does she get up early?

6A Simple present: *he* / *she* / *it* negative

a Complete the sentences with *don't* or *doesn't*.

1 They ___don't___ speak French.
2 He ____________ like chocolate cake.
3 She ____________ eat eggs for breakfast.
4 We ____________ go to work early.
5 Eva and Ben ____________ like their jobs.
6 Penelope and her sister ____________ live in Spain.
7 Her brother ____________ work in a bank.
8 My sister, Lucia, and I ____________ eat fish.

b Make the sentences negative.

1 Pia works in a store. *Pia doesn't work in a store.*
2 My brother works in a car factory.
3 My parents like coffee.
4 We live near the subway station.
5 He studies Italian.
6 They go to work early.
7 Akira lives in Tokyo.
8 Their son works in a bank.

c Now go back to p. 49.

6B Simple present: *he* / *she* / *it* questions

a Complete the questions.

1 **A** He works in a restaurant.
  B ____________ he like it?
2 **A** I'm a taxi driver.
  B ____________ you meet interesting people?
3 **A** My brother's in London.
  B ____________ he live there?
4 **A** My children go to school at 7:30.
  B What time ____________ they get up?
5 **A** She often works in the evenings.
  B When ____________ she get home?

b Underline the correct words.

1 **A** Does your daughter like school?
  B Yes, she *likes* / *does*. She thinks it's great.
2 **A** Do you like ice cream?
  B *Yes* / *No*, I don't. I never eat it.
3 **A** Does he watch baseball?
  B No, he *don't* / *doesn't*. He only likes tennis.
4 **A** Do you start work early?
  B Yes, we *are* / *do*. We start at 5:00 in the morning!
5 **A** Does your wife work in a restaurant?
  B No, she *doesn't work* / *doesn't*. She's a hotel receptionist.

c Now go back to p. 51.

7A *this, that, these, those*

07.06

this, these = here, near me

"My brother wants **this** car."

"I love **these** flowers."

that, those = there, not near me

"My sister wants **that** car."

"I love **those** flowers."

Singular	***this*** *car*	***that*** *car*
Plural	***these*** *flowers*	***those*** *flowers*

this/that/these/those* + *be
That's *my car.*
These are *your flowers.*
Those are *my books.*
Is this *your bag?*

***this/that/these/those* + noun**
I like ***that car****.*
These flowers *are beautiful.*
Those books *are big.*
This bag *is red.*

7B Possessive *'s*

07.17

Kristina's Zane**'s** sister. ➔ Kristina is Zane**'s** sister.
Millie's Kristina**'s** friend. ➔ Millie is Kristina**'s** friend.
KRISTINA My brother**'s** jeans are light blue. NOT ~~***The jeans of my brother*** *are light blue.*~~
The girls**'** dresses are beautiful.

Zane and Kristina**'s** parents are Lara and Jim.

Tip

We use **'** after the *-s* for plural nouns ending in *-s*.
➔ *The* ***girls'*** *dresses are beautiful.* (2+ girls)

We use ***'s*** after a singular noun:
➔ *The* ***girl's*** *dresses are beautiful.* (1 girl)

7A *this, that, these, those*

a Underline the correct words.

1 Excuse me, is *this* / *these* your coat?
2 Who's *this* / *that* man in the next room?
3 How much are *those* / *that* watches?
4 This *is* / *are* my wife, Tammy.
5 Are *this* / *these* your glasses?

b Complete the sentences with *this*, *that*, *these*, or *those*.

1 "Look at ____________ beautiful house."

2 "____________ are our tickets."

3 "Who are ____________ people?"

4 "Is ____________ your phone?"

c Now go back to p. 57.

7B Possessive *'s*

a Complete the sentences with the words in parentheses.

1 It's Mara's skirt. (Mara / skirt)
2 It's ____________. (Esteban / shirt)
3 It's ____________. (Beth / dress)
4 They're ____________. (Luke / jeans)
5 They're ____________. (Sara / shoes)
6 It's ____________. (Matthew / jacket)

b Write new sentences. Use the names in parentheses.

1 **His** new jeans are dark blue. (Sam)
Sam's new jeans are dark blue.
2 **His** house is near the train station. (Jacob)
3 **Her** shoes are brown. (Vanessa)
4 I like **her** new coat. (my friend)
5 **Their** new car is blue. (Rob and Emma)
6 **Her** new dress is pretty. (Penelope)
7 He's **his** best friend. (Ryan)
8 **Their** room is on the first floor. (the boys)

c Now go back to p. 59.

8A Simple past: *be*

Part 1: Affirmative

08.02

	+	
I/you/he/she/it	*I* ***was*** *You* ***were*** *He/She* ***was*** *It* ***was***	*in Seattle yesterday.* *in Los Angeles yesterday.* *in Houston yesterday.* *fun.*
we/you/they	*We* ***were*** *You* ***were*** *They* ***were***	*in Cartagena last weekend.* *in São Paulo last weekend.* *in Paris last weekend.*

She ***was*** *in Houston yesterday.* NOT ~~*She* ***is*** *in Houston yesterday.*~~
OR ~~*She* ***were*** *in Houston yesterday.*~~

Tip
We often use past forms of *be* with past time expressions like *yesterday, last night, two days ago, on Saturday, this morning.* (See Vocabulary Focus 8A on p. 149.)

Part 2: Negative and questions

08.08

	–	
I/you/he/she/it	*I* ***wasn't*** *You* ***weren't*** *He/She* ***wasn't*** *It* ***wasn't***	*in Seattle yesterday.* *in Los Angeles yesterday.* *in Houston yesterday.* *fun.*
we/you/they	*We* ***weren't*** *You* ***weren't*** *They* ***weren't***	*in Cartagena last weekend.* *in São Paulo last weekend.* *in Paris last weekend.*

I ***wasn't*** *at home yesterday.* NOT ~~*I'm* ***not*** *at home yesterday.*~~
OR ~~I ***not was*** home yesterday.~~

Tip
I ***was not*** *in Seattle yesterday.* → *I* ***wasn't*** *in Seattle yesterday.*
You ***were not*** *in Los Angeles yesterday.* → *You* ***weren't*** *in Los Angeles yesterday.*

08.09

Yes/No questions		Short answers	
Were *you*	*in Los Angeles yesterday?*	*Yes, I* ***was***.	*No, I* ***wasn't***.
Was *she*	*in Houston yesterday?*	*Yes, she* ***was***.	*No, she* ***wasn't***.
Were *they*	*in Paris yesterday?*	*Yes, they* ***were***.	*No, they* ***weren't***.

08.10

Wh- questions		
Where	***was*** *she*	*yesterday?*
When	***was***	*the meeting?*
Where	***were*** *you*	*yesterday?*
When	***were*** *they*	*in San Francisco?*

Where ***were you*** *yesterday?* NOT ~~*Where* ***you were*** *yesterday?*~~

8B Simple past: affirmative

08.15

Regular verbs	+	
talk	*I* ***talked***	*to her yesterday.*
play	*They* ***played***	*tennis on Saturday.*
like	*He was nice – I* ***liked***	*him.*
arrive	*They* ***arrived***	*last night.*

I ***talked*** *to her.* NOT ~~*I* ***was talk*** *to her.*~~

SPELLING: *-ed* endings

most verbs → add ***-ed***	*talk* → *talk****ed*** *play* → *play****ed***
verb ends in ***-e*** → add ***-d***	*like* → *like****d***

08.16

Irregular verbs	+	
go	*I* ***went***	*to a party on Friday.*
have	*We* ***had***	*sandwiches for lunch.*
see	*I* ***saw***	*Peter yesterday.*

I ***went*** *to a party.* NOT ~~*I* ***goed*** *to a party.*~~
We ***had*** *sandwiches.* NOT ~~*We* ***did*** *have sandwiches.*~~

See Irregular verbs on p. 103.

Tip
The simple past form is the same for all persons, e.g., *I played tennis., He played tennis., We played tennis.*, etc.

8A Simple past: *be*

Part 1: Affirmative

a Complete the sentences with *was* or *were*.

1 I ______ at home yesterday.
2 He ______ in the office in the morning, but not in the afternoon.
3 We ______ at the movies last night.
4 They ______ in Buenos Aires last month.
5 Two nights ago you ______ at your sister's house.
6 The movie ______ really great.
7 You ______ at school last week.
8 Ben and Jorge ______ at the basketball game on Saturday.
9 The concert ______ very good.
10 This morning I ______ at a café.

b Now go back to p. 65.

Part 2: Negative and questions

Last night

a Complete the text with *was*, *were*, *wasn't*, or *weren't*.

"It [1]______ Saturday yesterday, but I [2]______ at work all morning. I [3]______ (not) at my desk – I [4]______ in a meeting. It [5]______ very boring. In the afternoon, I [6]______ at home with a book – it [7]______ great. In the evening, my friend Michelle and I [8]______ at the movies, but the movie [9]______ (not) very good. We [10]______ tired, so I [11]______ (not) out late."

The next day

b Put the words in the correct order to make questions.

1 last night / were you / at the movies?
Were you at the movies last night?
2 basketball game / was / on Saturday / he at the ?
3 were / the supermarket / they at / yesterday ?
4 you three / where were / years ago ?
5 interesting / movie / was the ?
6 China / you in / when were ?
7 was the / concert / where ?
8 a boring / was it / meeting ?

c Now go back to p. 65.

8B Simple past: affirmative

a Match verbs 1–6 with the past forms in the box.

arrived had watched saw stayed went

1 go ______
2 have ______
3 stay ______
4 see ______
5 watch ______
6 arrive ______

b Underline the correct words.

1 She *goed* / *went* to Spain last week.
2 I *was sees* / *saw* my sister last weekend.
3 It wasn't a very interesting evening. Everyone *talkd* / *talked* about work.
4 I *staied* / *stayed* in a cheap hotel near the train station.
5 We *watch* / *watched* Germany vs. Uruguay last night.
6 She *read* / *readed* a magazine in the backyard.

c Complete the text with the past form of the verbs in the box.

have (x2) go (x2) stay read talk watch ~~get~~

Last Saturday, Mr. Jones [1]___*got*___ up late, and he [2]______ a big breakfast. Then he [3]______ shopping. He [4]______ a pizza for lunch, and in the afternoon, he [5]______ to his mother on the phone for an hour. In the evening, he [6]______ at home, and he [7]______ baseball on TV. He [8]______ to bed at 10:30 and [9]______ a book until 11:00.

d Complete the sentences about you or your friends. Use the simple past.

1 Last weekend, ______.
2 Yesterday, ______.
3 This morning, ______.
4 Last Monday, ______.

e Now go back to p. 67.

9A Simple past: negative

She **didn't take** a taxi to the airport.

09.07

	–	
stay	*We* ***didn't stay***	*at a hostel.*
finish	*They* ***didn't finish***	*work early.*
see	*I* ***didn't see***	*them at the party.*
take	*She* ***didn't take***	*a taxi to the airport.*

I ***didn't see*** *them.* NOT ~~*I don't saw them.*~~
We ***didn't stay****.* NOT ~~*We didn't stayed.*~~

Tip

In the negative:

- add *didn't* before the verb
- the verb doesn't change

9B Simple past: questions

09.19

Yes/No questions		Short answers	
Did *you*	***see*** *the movie?*	*Yes, I/we* ***did****.*	*No, I/we* ***didn't****.*
Did *she*	***work*** *in a café?*	*Yes, she* ***did****.*	*No, she* ***didn't****.*
Did *they*	***go*** *to the party?*	*Yes, they* ***did****.*	*No, they* ***didn't****.*

Did *you* ***work*** *… ?* NOT ~~***Did*** *you* ***worked*** *… ?*~~
Did *she* ***go*** *… ?* NOT ~~***Did*** *she* ***went*** *… ?*~~
Yes, she ***did****.* NOT ~~*Yes, she* ***worked****.*~~
No, she ***didn't****.* NOT ~~*No, she* ***didn't work****.*~~

09.20

Wh- questions		
Where	***did*** *you*	***work****?*
Where	***did*** *she*	***go****?*
When	***did*** *they*	***arrive****?*

Where ***did*** *you* ***work****?* NOT ~~*Where you* ***worked****?*~~
OR ~~*Where did you* ***worked****?*~~
Where ***did*** *she* ***go****?* NOT ~~*Where did she* ***went****?*~~

10A Present continuous: affirmative

We use the present continuous to talk about now.

10.07

	+
I	***I'm writing*** *an email.*
you	***You're working*** *a lot.*
he/she	*He****'s****/She****'s studying****.*
it	*It****'s raining****.*
we	*We****'re watching*** *TV.*
they	*They****'re eating*** *a big dinner.*

I'm working *hard.* NOT ~~*I working hard.*~~ OR ~~*I'm work hard.*~~
I'm having *breakfast.* NOT ~~*I'm haveing breakfast.*~~
I'm sitting *in the car.* NOT ~~*I'm siting in the car.*~~

"It's raining and I'm writing this email …"

Tip

I'm writing *an email.* → *I* ***am writing*** *an email.*
*We****'re watching*** *TV.* → *We* ***are watching*** *TV.*
*He****'s studying****.* → *He* ***is studying****.*

9A Simple past: negative

a Complete the sentences with the simple past negative form of the verbs in parentheses.

1 I _didn't play_ baseball. (play)
2 I ___________ early. (get up)
3 I ___________ cereal for breakfast. (have)
4 I ___________ my phone. (use)
5 I ___________ my emails. (read)
6 I ___________ a friend. (visit)
7 I ___________ shopping. (go)
8 I ___________ any photos. (take)
9 I ___________ to the radio. (listen)

b Look at the pictures. Complete the sentences with the verbs in the box. Make one affirmative and one negative sentence.

arrive play go (x2) have ~~get up~~

1 Last week, John _didn't get up_ at 6:00. He _got up_ at 7:00.

2 He ___________ to work by bus. He ___________ to work by train.

3 He ___________ at work at 9:00. He ___________ at work at 10:00.

4 He ___________ pizza for lunch. He ___________ spaghetti.

5 After work, he ___________ baseball. He ___________ tennis.

6 In the evening, he ___________ to the movies. He ___________ to a restaurant.

c Now go back to p. 73.

9B Simple past: questions

a Put the words in the correct order to make questions.

1 you go / where did / on vacation?
2 see / what did / you ?
3 you have / did / a good time ?
4 you / meet / who did ?
5 you / what did / eat ?
6 like it / you / did ?

b Complete the questions with *did* or *do/does*.

1 Where ___________ you go last night?
2 ___________ you see Jim yesterday?
3 What time ___________ he go to work every day?
4 ___________ they go to the movies every Saturday?
5 What ___________ you do after class last week?
6 What time ___________ their classes usually start?
7 What time ___________ she start work yesterday?
8 Who ___________ you see at the party last night?

c Complete the answers to the questions.

1 **A** Did you go home early?
B Yes, _I_ _did_. I left at 4:00.
2 **A** Did they enjoy their vacation?
B No, ______ ______. It was boring.
3 **A** Did he watch the soccer game?
B No, ______ ______. He was at the movies.
4 **A** Did you go to the supermarket?
B Yes, ______ ______. We got some bread and cheese.
5 **A** Did your sister work in a restaurant?
B No, ______ ______. She worked in a café.

d Now go back to p. 75.

10A Present continuous: affirmative

a Write the *-ing* forms of the verbs.

1 eat ___________
2 cook ___________
3 talk ___________
4 listen ___________
5 get ___________
6 have ___________
7 wear ___________
8 go ___________

b Complete the sentences with the present continuous form of the verbs in parentheses.

1 I (wear) jeans and a T shirt.
2 We (listen) to Drake's new song.
3 Lee (study) in her bedroom.
4 They (have) dinner at the moment.
5 Rob and Ben (play) soccer in the park.
6 He (watch) a movie in the living room.
7 Our children (cook) dinner for us.
8 I (write) this email at work.

c Now go back to p. 81.

10B Present continuous: negative and questions

10.15

	–
I	*I'm **not waiting** for the bus.*
you	*You**'re not listening**!*
he/she	*She**'s not reading** a book.*
it	*It**'s not raining**.*
we	*We**'re not staying** in a hostel.*
they	*They**'re not working**.*

*She**'s not reading**.* NOT ~~*She not reading.*~~
OR ~~*She's not read.*~~

10.16

***Yes/No* questions**		**Short answers**	
***Are** you*	***waiting** for the bus?*	*Yes, I **am**.*	*No, I**'m not**.*
***Is** she*	***reading** a book?*	*Yes, she **is**.*	*No, she**'s not**.*
***Is** it*	***raining**?*	*Yes, it **is**.*	*No, it**'s not**.*
***Are** they*	***working**?*	*Yes, they **are**.*	*No, they**'re not**.*

***Are you** waiting?* NOT ~~*You waiting? You are waiting?*~~

10.17

	***Wh-* questions**		
you	*What*	***are** you*	***doing**?*
he/she	*Where*	***is** he*	***going**?*
it	*Why*	***is** it*	***raining**?*
they	*What*	***are** they*	***watching**?*

*What **are you** doing?* NOT ~~*What you are doing?*~~

11A Object pronouns

Subject pronouns	**Object pronouns**	11.08
I	**me**	***I** talked to Mark last night. He called **me**.*
you	**you**	***You** were in town yesterday. I saw **you**.*
he	**him**	***He**'s a great singer. I like **him**.*
she	**her**	***She** lives nearby. I often visit **her**.*
it	**it**	*I live near Greenport. **It**'s a nice town. I like **it**.*
we	**us**	***We** were at the party. Did you see **us**?*
they	**them**	*These shoes are nice, but **they**'re expensive. I can't buy **them**.*

*He called **me**.* NOT ~~*He called I.*~~

Tip

We use *it* and *them* to talk about things and places.

***It** isn't a very interesting book. I don't want to finish **it**.*

NOT ~~***She** isn't an interesting book. I don't want to finish **her**.*~~

***It**'s a nice town. I like **it**.*

NOT ~~***He**'s a nice town. I like **him**.*~~

10B Present continuous: negative and questions

a Complete the sentences using the negative form of the present continuous.

1 She's not studying (study). She's watching TV.
2 They ______ (have) lunch. They're having breakfast.
3 I ______ (work). I'm at home.
4 He ______ (play) baseball. He's watching the game.
5 We ______ (stay) in a hotel. We're camping.
6 Are you OK? You ______ (eat).

b Put the words in the correct order to make questions.

1 wearing / a coat / you / why / are ?
2 working / she / is ?
3 you / doing / are / what ?
4 are / where / going / you ?
5 she / is / texting / who ?
6 a computer game / playing / he / is ?

c Write two questions to ask your partner about now. Use the present continuous. Ask and answer your questions.

d Now go back to p. 83.

11A Object pronouns

a Underline the correct words.

1 We're waiting at the train station. Please come and meet *we* / *us*.
2 She was in town. We saw *her* / *him* there.
3 My parents live in London. I love to visit *them* / *they* on weekends.
4 I bought a pizza. Do you want to have *it* / *her* for dinner?
5 Where are my keys? Do you have *they* / *them* in your bag?
6 Here's a photo of my new boyfriend. I met *it* / *him* two months ago at a party.

b Complete the text with the words in the box.

he	she	it	we	me	him	her	us

c Write sentences about your favorite things and people. Use pronouns in your sentences.

d Now go back to p. 89.

JULIE THOMPSON, ACTOR
MY FAVORITE THINGS AND PEOPLE ...

1 My car

It's a very old Volkswagen, but I use [1]______ every day.

2 My brother

[2]______ works in Japan, so we don't see [3]______ very often, but he always stays with [4]______ on New Year's Eve.

3 The singer Lana del Rey

I think [5]______'s a wonderful singer. I can listen to [6]______ for hours.

4 My husband, Paul

We got married 30 years ago and [7]______'re very happy. He always listens to [8]______ when I have problems.

11B *can* for ability

> **Tip**
> I **cannot** swim. ➔ I **can't** swim.
> For all persons (*I/you/he/she/it/we/they*), *can/can't* and the verb don't change.

Part 1: Affirmative and negative

We use *can* to talk about things we know how to do.

11.09

+	I/You/He/She/It/We/They	**can**	**swim**.
–		**can't**	**fly**.

I **can swim** *well.* NOT ~~*I can to swim well.*~~
She **can swim** *well.* NOT ~~*She cans swim well.*~~
He **can't swim** *well.* NOT ~~*He not can swim well.*~~

Part 2: Questions

11.14

Yes/No questions	+	–
Can *you* ***swim?***	*Yes, I* ***can.***	*No, I* ***can't.***
Can *she* ***swim?***	*Yes, she* ***can.***	*No, she* ***can't.***
Can *they* ***swim?***	*Yes, they* ***can.***	*No, they* ***can't.***

Can you *swim?* NOT ~~*You can swim?*~~
Yes, ***I can.*** NOT ~~*Yes, I swim.*~~
No, ***I can't.*** NOT ~~*No, I not swim.*~~

12A *be going to*: affirmative and negative

Part 1: Affirmative

We use *be* + *going to* to talk about things we plan to do in the future.

12.02

	+		
I	*I'm*	**going to**	***get*** *some coffee.*
you/we/they	*You're*		***go*** *shopping.*
he/she/it	*She's*		***have*** *chicken tonight.*

I'm going to take *a bath.* NOT ~~*I going to take a bath.*~~
OR ~~*I'm going take a bath.*~~
OR ~~*I'm go to take a bath.*~~

Part 2: Negative

12.08

	–		
I	***I'm not***	**going to**	***go*** *on vacation.*
you/we/they	***You're not***		***read*** *a book.*
he/she/it	***She's not***		***visit*** *her sister.*

*We****'re not going to take*** *a bath.*
NOT ~~*We're going not to take a bath.*~~

12B *be going to*: questions

12.16

Yes/No questions			Short answers	
Am *I*	**going to**	***see*** *you soon?*	*Yes, you* ***are.***	*No, you****'re not.***
Are *you*		***go*** *out?*	*Yes, I* ***am.***	*No, I****'m not.***
Is *he*		***leave*** *home?*	*Yes, he* ***is.***	*No, he****'s not.***

Are you going to *... ?* NOT ~~*You are going to ... ?*~~
Yes, ***I am.*** NOT ~~*Yes, I'm going.*~~

12.17

	Wh- questions			
I	*When*	***am*** *I*	**going to**	***see*** *you?*
you/we/they	*What*	***are*** *you*		***do?***
he/she/it	*Where*	***is*** *he*		***live?***

What ***are you going to*** *do?* NOT ~~*What you going to do?*~~
OR ~~*What you are going to do?*~~

11B *can* for ability

Part 1: Affirmative and negative

a Complete the sentences with *can* or *can't*.

1 I studied Spanish at college for three years. I ____________ speak with Spanish people.
2 Her meals are terrible. She ____________ cook!
3 My brother and I don't like the ocean or swimming pools. We ____________ swim.
4 I went to guitar lessons. Now I ____________ play some easy songs.
5 I don't have a bicycle, but I ____________ ride one.
6 I don't like that band. They ____________ sing.

b Now go to p. 91.

Part 2: Questions

a Put the words in the correct order to make questions.

1 you ride / can / a horse ?
2 well / cook / can he ?
3 sing and / can / play the guitar / they ?
4 can / draw pictures / she ?
5 speak / both Japanese / can you / and Mandarin ?
6 he drive / a car and / can / a bus ?

b Now go back to p. 91.

12A *be going to*: affirmative and negative

Part 1: Affirmative

a Complete the sentences with *going to* and the verb in parentheses.

1 I'm hungry. I'm ____________ (eat) a sandwich.
2 The house is dirty. He's ____________ (clean) it today.
3 We're bored. We're ____________ (watch) a movie.
4 It's very cold today. I'm ____________ (wear) a coat.
5 She's tired. She's ____________ (go) to bed.

b Now go back to p. 96.

Part 2: Negative

a Put the words in the correct order to make sentences.

1 his homework on / he's going / the weekend / to do
2 visit my parents / not / next week / we're / going to
3 going to / Friday night / I'm / party on / have a
4 they're not / to play soccer / going / on Saturday
5 not / cook dinner / she's / going to / this evening
6 to meet / tomorrow evening / we're going / some friends

b Complete the conversation with the correct form of *be going to* and the verb in parentheses.

A What are your plans for this evening?
B I [1]____________ (stay) home.
A That's not very interesting.
B Maybe not. But I [2]____________ (cook) a nice dinner.
A OK, and then maybe watch a movie?
B No, I [3]____________ (not / watch) a movie. I [4]____________ (read) a book. And you?
A Well, I [5]____________ (not / cook) dinner. I [6]____________ (get) a pizza and then I [7]____________ (go) to a party. Do you want to come?
B No, thanks. I [8]____________ (have) a quiet evening.

c Now go back to p. 97.

12B *be going to*: questions

a Make questions with *be going to*.

1 you / see / a movie / tonight?
Are you going to see a movie tonight?
2 what / you / do / this evening?
3 they / go / Italy / next summer?
4 when / you / have / lunch?
5 how / she / get to / the airport?
6 when / we / clean / the apartment?

b Complete the questions with *be going to* and the words in parentheses.

1 **A** ____________ home tonight? (you / stay)
B No, we're not. We're going to go out.
2 **A** What ____________? (she / buy)
B A new coat.
3 **A** ____________ shopping? (you / go)
B Yes, I am. Do you want to come with me?
4 **A** Who ____________? (they / invite)
B Oh, just a few friends. They don't want to have a big party.
5 **A** ____________ TV? (he / watch)
B No, he's not. He's going to work.

c Now go back to p. 99.

VOCABULARY FOCUS

1A Countries

a 01.11 Listen and write the countries on the map.

the U.S. Brazil the U.K. / Britain
Ecuador Spain Mexico Colombia
China Japan

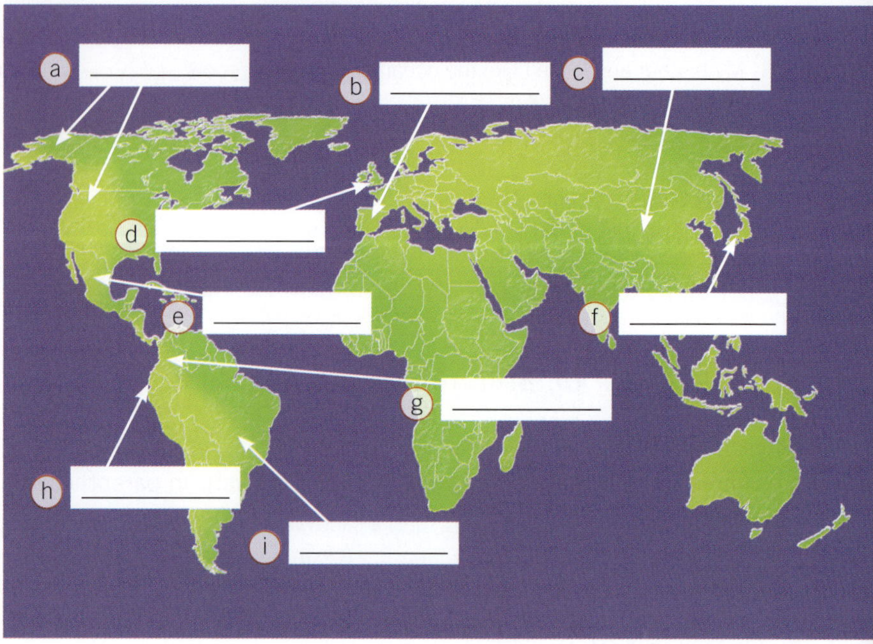

Tip
the U.S. = the United States of America
the U.K. = the United Kingdom

b 01.11 Listen again and practice saying the countries.

c Add the name of your country in English to the list in a. Practice saying it.

d Now go back to p. 9.

1B Nationalities

a Complete the charts with countries from page 9.

Country	Nationality
	-ian
Australia	Australian
1 ________	Brazilian
Canada	Canadian
2 ________	Colombian
Ecuador	Ecuadorian
Italy	Italian

Country	Nationality
	-an
3 ________	Mexican
4 ________	American
	-ish
5 ________	Spanish
6 ________ / Britain	British
	-ese
7 ________	Chinese
8 ________	Japanese

b 01.14 Listen and repeat the countries and nationalities.

c Write your nationality.

I'm ________.

d Work in pairs.

Student A: Say a country.
Student B: Say the nationality.

Canada
Canadian

Then switch roles.

e Now go back to p. 10.

2A Common adjectives

a 02.09 Listen and repeat the adjectives.

1 small

big

2 old

new

3 good

bad

4 happy

sad

5 interesting

boring

6 easy

difficult

7 right

wrong

8 beautiful

9 funny

b Work in pairs.

Student A: Say an adjective.
Student B: Say the opposite.

happy

sad

c Complete the sentences with an adjective. There is no correct answer.

1 New York is a ___________ city.
2 Harry Potter books are ___________.
3 My house is very ___________.
4 The English language is ___________ for me.
5 My best friend is ___________.

Tell a partner your sentences. Are the adjectives the same?

d Now go back to p. 17.

2B Common objects 1

a book (books)

a bottle of water (bottles of water)

a computer (computers)

a key (keys)

a newspaper (newspapers)

a knife (knives)

a phone (phones)

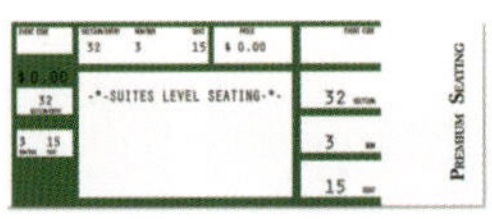
a ticket (tickets)

a watch (watches)

an umbrella (umbrellas)

a 02.12 Listen and repeat the objects.

b Write three objects on three pieces of paper. Don't show your partner!

a phone | an umbrella | a book

c Guess your partner's words.

Is it a watch?
No.
Is it a book?
Yes.

d Now go back to p. 18.

5B Hotels

a 05.11 Listen and repeat the words.

bathtub

room

bed

pillow

shower

Wi-Fi

blanket

parking

TV

towel

There's parking at the hotel. NOT ~~*There's a parking at the hotel.*~~ OR ~~*There are parking at the hotel.*~~

There's Wi-Fi in the room. NOT ~~*There's a Wi-Fi in the room.*~~ OR ~~*There are Wi-Fi in the room.*~~

b Which word is different in each group? Compare your answers with your partner.

1 shower pillow bathtub
2 TV Wi-Fi room
3 shower blanket pillow
4 parking towel blanket
5 bed room bathtub

c Now go back to p. 42.

3A Food 1

a 03.04 Listen and repeat the words.

fruit

vegetables

meat

fish

eggs

bread

rice

b Talk to a partner. What food is in the pictures?

1

2

3

4

5

6

c Match pictures 1–6 with the words in the box.

coffee soda juice milk tea water

1

2

3

4

5

6

d 03.05 Listen and check your answers in c. Practice saying the words.

e Talk to your partner. Which drinks are in the pictures?

I think it's tea.

Maybe it's juice.

f Now go back to p. 24.

3B Food 2

a 03.11 Listen and repeat the words.

breakfast

lunch

dinner

I have breakfast at 7:30. NOT ~~*I have a breakfast at 7:30.*~~
She has lunch at 12:30. NOT ~~*She has a lunch at 12:30.*~~
We have dinner at 7:00. NOT ~~*We have a dinner at 7:00.*~~

b 03.12 Match the words in the box with pictures 1–12. Listen and check your answers. Then listen and repeat.

orange sandwich butter cookie banana pizza potato tomato apple ice cream cheese cake

1 
2 
3 
4 
5 
6 
7 
8 
9 
10 
11 
12 

c Which food in b do you eat for ... ?

- breakfast
- lunch
- dinner

d Now go back to p. 27.

2B Numbers 1

a 02.19 Listen and repeat the numbers.

1	2	3	4	5	6	7	8	9	10
one	two	three	four	five	six	seven	eight	nine	ten
11	12	13	14	15	16	17	18	19	
eleven	twelve	thirteen	fourteen	fifteen	sixteen	seventeen	eighteen	nineteen	

thirteen NOT ~~threeteen~~, *fifteen* NOT ~~fiveteen~~

20	30	40	50	60	70	80	90
twenty	thirty	forty	fifty	sixty	seventy	eighty	ninety

thirty NOT ~~threety~~, *forty* NOT ~~fourty~~, *fifty* NOT ~~fivety~~

b 02.20 Listen to a–g. Underline the number you hear.

a 13 / 30
b 14 / 40
c 15 / 50
d 16 / 60
e 17 / 70
f 18 / 80
g 19 / 90

c Now go back to p. 19.

3B Time

a 03.15 Match the clocks with the times in the box. Listen and check.

two o'clock twenty after two (a) quarter after two
two thirty (a) quarter to two twenty to two

b 03.15 Listen again and repeat the times.

c Complete the sentences.

1 My English class is at ________________.
2 My favorite TV show is at ________________.
3 My school / job starts at ________________.

Tell a partner your sentences.

d Now go back to p. 27.

4B Numbers 2

a 04.13 Listen and repeat the numbers.

21	34	42	57	63	79	85	99	100
twenty-one	thirty-four	forty-two	fifty-seven	sixty-three	seventy-nine	eighty-five	ninety-nine	a/one hundred

thirty-four NOT ~~*thirty and four*~~ OR ~~*four and thirty*~~

b Work with a partner.
Student A: Say a number in the box.
Student B: Say the next two numbers.

52 41 29 68 98 36 82 75 59

fifty-two

fifty-three, fifty-four

c Now go back to p. 35.

4A Common verbs

a 04.02 Listen to the sentences. Repeat the verbs.

1 We **live** in a big house.

2 I **work** in a factory.

3 I **speak** Spanish.

4 We **study** at school.

5 I **go** to the movies every weekend.

6 I **teach** young children.

7 We **play** tennis on Saturdays.

8 I **meet** my friends for coffee every day.

b Complete the phrases with verbs in a.

1 ___*work*___ in an office / in a bank
2 ________ soccer / the guitar
3 ________ in an apartment / in New York
4 ________, 5 ________ and 6 ________ Italian
7 ________ in college
8 ________ people / a friend
9 ________ to the gym / home

c Write two sentences about you with phrases in a and b.

I study English. I play soccer.

Tell a partner your sentences.

d Now go back to p. 32.

4B Family and people

a ▶ 04.09 Listen and repeat the words.

b Look at the words in a. Complete 1–10.

c ▶ 04.10 Listen and repeat the words.

d Complete the sentences with words from a and c.

1 They have three c_________n, a b_________y and two g_________s.
2 I'm Olivia and this is David. He's my h_________d.
3 That w_________n is my s_________r.
4 They have a new b_________y. It's a g_________l. Her name's Lucia.
5 My yoga class has ten p_________e: nine w_________n and only one m_________n!

e Now go back to p. 34.

5A Places in a town

a 05.04 Listen and repeat the places.

subway station

supermarket

school

hotel

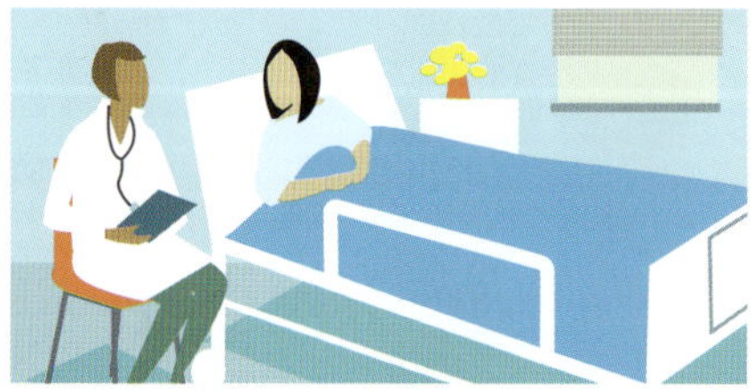
hospital

movie theater

restaurant

bank

store

café

swimming pool

park

museum

beach

bus stop

b Talk to your partner. Where are these signs?

I think 1 is at a swimming pool, or maybe a beach.

1

2

3

4

5

6

7

8

c Now go back to p. 41.

6A Jobs

a 06.03 Listen and repeat the jobs.

soccer player

student

receptionist

server

taxi driver

factory worker

bank teller

sales assistant

businessman / businesswoman

chef

office worker

IT worker

teacher

doctor

b Cover the words and pictures in a. Correct the spelling in each job. Then check your answers.

1 studint
2 servar
3 factery worker
4 sales asistant
5 taxi drivar
6 socer player
7 receptonist
8 bank tellr
9 ofice worker

c Do you know people who do the jobs in a? Tell your partner.

My father is a taxi driver.

My friend Kumiko is a chef.

d Now go back to p. 49.

6B Daily routine

a 06.08 Listen to Danny's daily routine and complete the times.

1 Danny **wakes up** at ___________.

2 He **gets up** at ___________.

3 He **has breakfast** at ___________.

4 He **goes to work** at ___________.

5 He **starts work** at ___________.

6 He **has lunch** at ___________.

7 He **finishes work** at ___________.

8 He **gets home** at ___________.

9 He **has dinner** at ___________.

10 He **goes to bed** at ___________.

b 06.09 Listen and repeat the verb phrases.

wake get	up	have	breakfast lunch dinner coffee	go	to school to work to bed	start finish	work	get arrive	home	take	a shower

have breakfast/lunch/dinner NOT *~~have the breakfast, have a lunch~~*
go to work NOT *~~go to the work~~*
go to bed NOT *~~go in the bed~~*

c Read about Pablo's daily routine. Then complete the sentences about him with words in a and b.

> I sleep from 11:00 to 7:00 every night.
> In the morning, I get up and have breakfast. I finish at 7:30.
> It's 30 minutes by bus to go to work.
> I work from 8:30 until 12:30, then I have lunch for half an hour.
> Then I work for three hours until I go home.

1 He _______________ at 7:00.
2 He _______________ at 7:30.
3 He _______________ at 8:00.
4 He _______________ at 8:30.
5 He _______________ at 12:30.
6 He _______________ at 4:00.
7 He _______________ at 11:00 at night.

d Now go back to p. 50.

7A Common objects 2

a 07.01 Listen and repeat the objects.

a bag (bags)

a chair (chairs)

a clock (clocks)

a cup (cups)

a glass (glasses)

a guitar (guitars)

a lamp (lamps)

a picture (pictures)

a plant (plants)

a plate (plates)

a soccer ball (soccer balls)

a speaker (speakers)

a suitcase (suitcases)

b Work in groups of three. Cover the pictures and make sentences. Add one more object each time.

At home, I have a guitar.

At home, I have a guitar and ten plates.

At home, I have a guitar, ten plates, and three big plants.

c Now go back to p. 56.

10B Place phrases with prepositions

a 10.08 Listen and repeat the phrases.

in the car

in a taxi

in a hotel

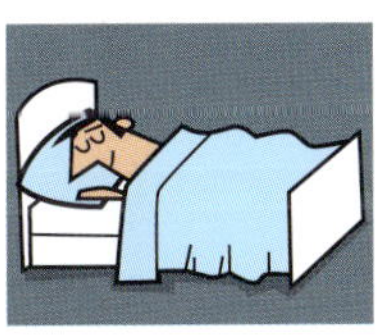
in bed

in/at a restaurant

in/at a café

at the subway station

at the airport

at the bus stop

at the movies

at a party

at home

at work

at school

on a bus

on a train

on a plane

on vacation

b Correct the phrases with prepositions.

1 It's 10:00, but he's still at the bed.
2 I'm waiting for the plane on the airport.
3 I can't talk now. I'm on the car. I'm driving home.
4 Are you in home or are you at the work?
5 I'm having coffee on a café.
6 John's not here. He's still in the vacation.

c Think about people you know. Where are they now?

I think my sister is on a plane.

My husband is at work.

d Now go back to p. 82.

7B Clothes and colors

a 07.13 Listen and repeat the clothes.

1

2

3

4

5
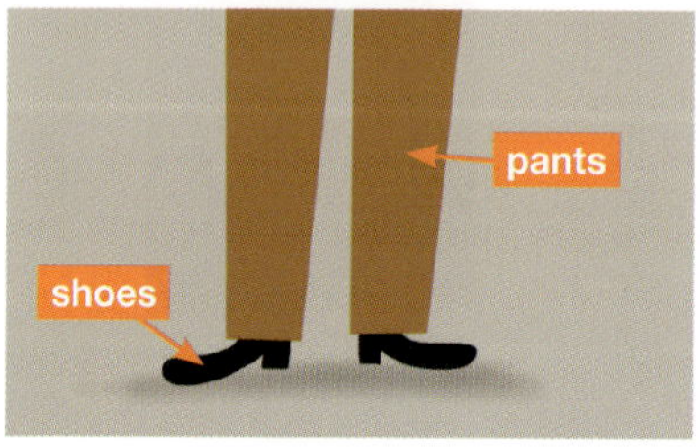

6

b 07.14 Listen and repeat the colors.

light blue	dark blue	light brown	dark brown	light green	dark green	light gray	dark gray	red	black	white	yellow

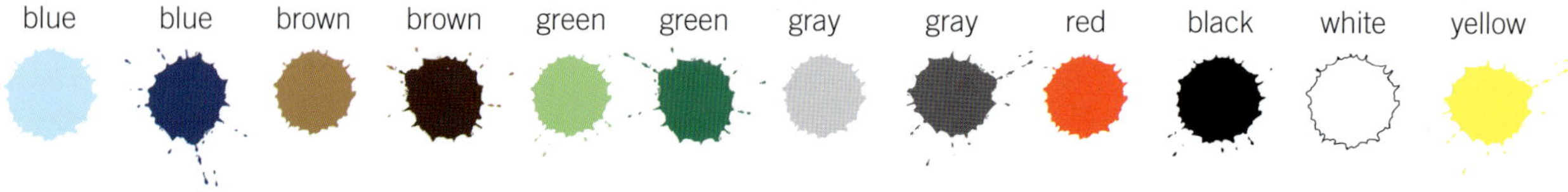

c What do the people usually wear? Write sentences.

1 *Enrico usually wears a dark gray jacket and a light blue shirt.*

2 ______________________

3 ______________________

4 ______________________

5 ______________________

6 ______________________

d Now go back to p. 59.

8A Past time expressions

a 08.03 Listen and repeat the days of the week.

b Complete the sentences.

1 Today is ____________.
2 Yesterday was ____________.
3 My favorite day is ____________, because ________________________________.

Tell a partner your answer in 3.

My favorite day is …

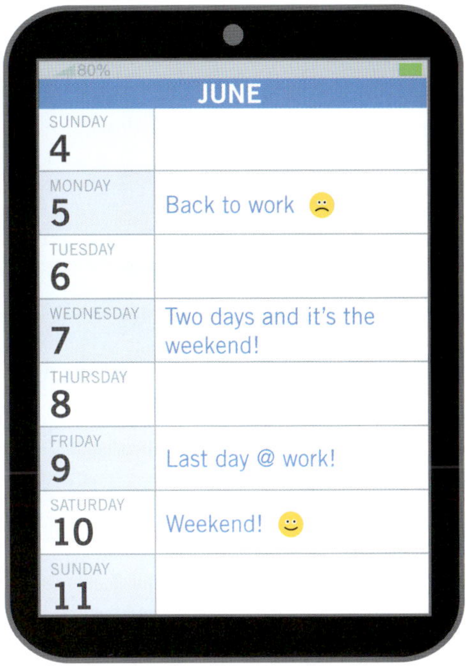

c 08.04 Listen and repeat the past time expressions.

yesterday

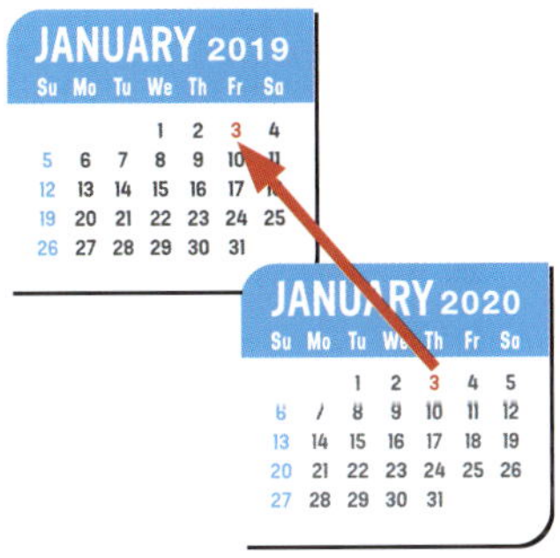

a year ago

last weekend

two days ago *or* on Monday

last night

this morning

d 08.05 Complete the chart with words in the box. Listen and check.

ago last on this

1 ______	night Sunday month weekend
a week two months ten years	2 ______
3 ______	morning afternoon
4 ______	Monday Friday

two months ago NOT ~~*before two months ago*~~
on Monday NOT ~~*at Monday*~~

e Complete the sentences with words from c and d.

1 I was in Barcelona ____________ weekend.
2 They were at the World Cup ____________ year ago.
3 Were you at home ____________ morning?
4 I was at a meeting two days ____________.
5 We were at work ____________ Friday.
6 He was at his friend's house ____________ night.

f Now go back to p. 65.

8B Free time activities

a 08.20 Listen to five people talk about free time activities. Put their activities in the correct order.

1 go (**simple past**: *went*)

☐ I went to the movies.

☐ I went to a party.

☐ I went shopping.

☐ I went to a café.

2 have (**simple past:** *had*); take (**simple past:** *took*)

☐ I had a pizza.

☐ I had a glass of water.

☐ I had coffee.

☐ I took a shower.

3 listen (**simple past:** *listened*); watch (**simple past:** *watched*)

☐ I listened to a podcast.

☐ I watched a soccer game.

☐ I listened to music.

☐ I watched a movie on TV.

4 read (**simple past:** *read* (/red/)

☐ I read a book.

☐ I read a magazine.

☐ I read the newspaper.

5 play (**simple past:** *played*)

☐ I played the guitar.

☐ I played a video game.

☐ I played soccer.

b 08.21 Listen and repeat the present and past verbs in a.

c Complete the sentences with the correct simple past verb.

1 We ____________ basketball on TV last night.
2 He had breakfast and ____________ the newspaper.
3 I ____________ to a party last night until 2:00.
4 I ____________ to music on the bus this morning.
5 We went to a café and ____________ a pizza.

d Write two true sentences about a free time activity in a.

On Friday, I went to a party.

e Read the first part of your sentences in d. Stop at the verb! Your partner guesses the second part of the sentence.

On Friday, I went …

… to the movies … ?

No, try again!

f Now go back to p. 67.

9A Transportation

a 09.02 Listen and repeat the words.

b Cover the transportation pictures in a. What do these signs show?

1 

2 

3 

4 

5 

6 

7 

8 

c Which kind of transportation do you prefer? Why?

d Notice how we use *go by* and *take* with different kinds of transportation.

go by	bus train plane tram

take	a bus a train a taxi a tram

go by bus NOT ~~*go with bus, go by the bus*~~
We can also use *take the bus, take the train,* or *take the tram*. NOT ~~*take the taxi*~~

e 09.03 Check (✓) the activity you see. Then listen and check.

1 

- ☐ I go to work by train.
- ☐ I drive to work.

2 

- ☐ He takes a taxi to school.
- ☐ He takes a bus to school.

3 

- ☐ She drives to work.
- ☐ She takes a tram to work.

4 

- ☐ She takes the subway to see her parents.
- ☐ She goes by plane to see her parents.

5 

- ☐ They always walk to school.
- ☐ They take the subway to school.

f Think of three places you went to in the last year. Write how you got there.

I drove to a friend's house yesterday.
I flew to Turkey last summer.

Tell a partner your sentences.

g Now go back to p. 72.

9B The seasons and the weather

a 09.12 Listen and repeat the seasons.

spring

summer

autumn/fall

winter

b Look at pictures 1–5 below. Which season do you think it is in each picture?

c 09.13 Complete the sentences with the words in the box. Listen and check.

windy sunny snowy rainy cloudy

1 It often **rains** in Vancouver. (verb)
There's a lot of **rain** in Vancouver. (noun)
It's often __________ in Vancouver. (adjective)

2 It often **snows** in Antarctica. (verb)
There's always **snow** in Antarctica. (noun)
It's always __________ in Antarctica. (adjective)

3 There's a lot of **wind** in my town. (noun)
It's often __________ in my town. (adjective)

4 It's very **sunny** and **hot** today. (adjectives)
It was __________ and **warm** yesterday. (adjectives)

5 There are a lot of **clouds** today. (noun)
It's __________ and **cold** today. (adjectives)

d Underline the correct words.

1 Do you like hot and *sun* / *sunny* weather?
2 Is the weather *cloudy* / *cloud* today?
3 Is winter cold and *snow* / *snowy* in your country?
4 Is summer hot and *sunny* / *sun* in your country?
5 Does it *rainy* / *rain* in the fall in your country?

e Ask and answer the questions in d with a partner.

f Now go back to p. 75.

10A The home

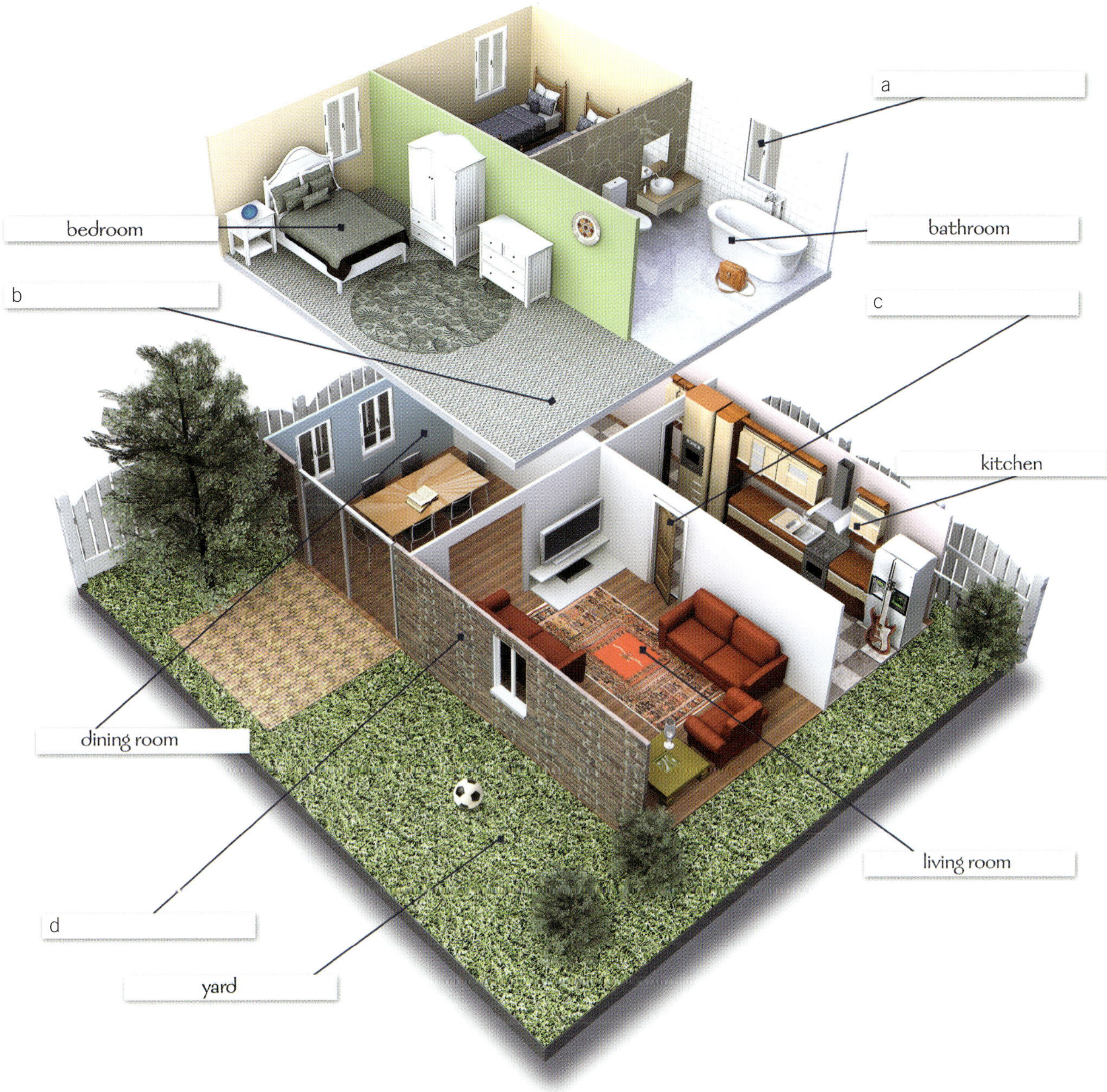

a Look at the picture. Where are objects 1–6? Ask and answer questions with a partner.

1 the glass
2 the bag
3 the book
4 the soccer ball
5 the guitar
6 the plate

Where's the glass?

It's in the living room.

b 10.02 Match the words in the box with a–d in the picture. Listen and check.

wall window floor door

c Complete the sentences with the correct words.

1 My family has dinner in the d__________ r__________ every evening.
2 We have a small y__________ behind our house. We often sit there on summer evenings.
3 My bedroom has a large w__________, and I can see the mountains.
4 I don't need a chair – I can sit on the f__________.
5 There are a lot of pictures on the w__________ in the dining room.
6 After dinner I like to read in the l__________ r__________.
7 My brother is always in the b__________ – he likes long showers.
8 There are two d__________s in the dining room – one goes to the kitchen, the other to the living room.

d Now go back to p. 80.

11A Life events

a Put the life events in the order you think is correct.

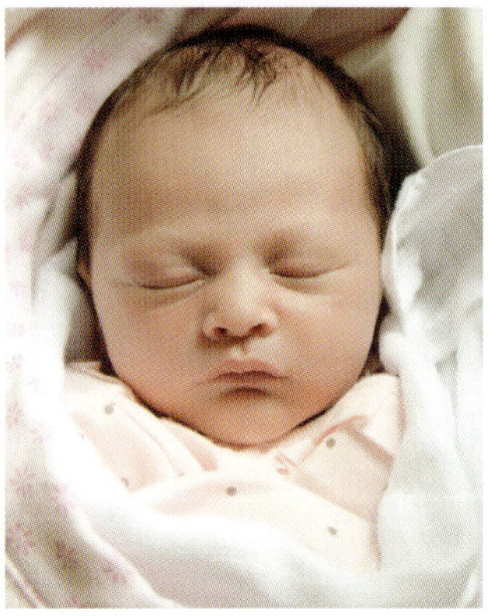

☐ be born
(**simple past:** *was born*)

☐ finish college
(**simple past:** *finished*)

☐ grow up
(**simple past:** *grew up*)

☐ get married
(**simple past:** *got*)

☐ go to school
(**simple past:** *went*)

☐ have a baby
(**simple past:** *had*)

☐ finish school
(**simple past:** *finished*)

☐ stop working
(**simple past:** *stopped*)

☐ go to college
(**simple past:** *went*)

☐ die
(**simple past:** *died*)

b 11.04 Listen and repeat the verb phrases in a.

c Complete the sentences with the verbs in parentheses.

1 I ____________ (go to) college when I was 18, and I ____________ (finish) college when I was 24.
2 Nelson Mandela ____________ (be born) in 1918, and he ____________ (die) in 2013.
3 My father ____________ (stop) working when he was 68.
4 She ____________ (get married) when she was 25, and she ____________ (have) a baby two years later.
5 I ____________ (finish) school when I was 16, and I ____________ (get) a job in a car factory.
6 Michelle Obama ____________ (be born) in 1964, and she ____________ (grow up) in Chicago.

d 11.05 Look at the answers and complete the questions. Listen and check.

1 **Q** ________________ go to school? **A** In New York.
2 **Q** ________________ finish? **A** In 2016.
3 **Q** ________________ do after that?
A I went to Canada.
4 **Q** ________________ go there?
A My brother lives there.
5 **Q** ________________ like it? **A** Yes, I had a great time.

e Ask and answer the questions in d with a partner. Say answers that are true for you.

f Now go back to p. 89.

11B Abilities

a 11.10 Listen and repeat the verbs.

swim
(**simple past:** *swam*)

cook
(**simple past:** *cooked*)

paint
(**simple past:** *painted*)

sing
(**simple past:** *sang*)

dance
(**simple past:** *danced*)

drive a car
(**simple past:** *drove*)

play volleyball

play cards

(**simple past:** *played*)

ride a horse

ride a bike

(**simple past:** *rode*)

run
(**simple past:** *ran*)

b 11.11 Complete the phrases with verbs in a. Listen and check.

1 ____________ a picture

2 ____________ a motorcycle

3 ____________ a song

4 ____________ dinner

5 ____________ basketball

6 ____________ to work

c Write four sentences about what you did:

- yesterday
- last night
- last weekend
- last Monday

Yesterday I drove my car to work.
I danced at a party last weekend.

Tell a partner your sentences.

Last night …

d Now go back to p. 91.

12A Months and future time expressions

a 12.03 Listen and repeat the months.

1 December, January, February
2 March, April, May
3 June, July, August
4 September, October, November

b Which seasons are 1–4 in a in your country?

c 12.04 Listen and repeat the time expressions.

tomorrow

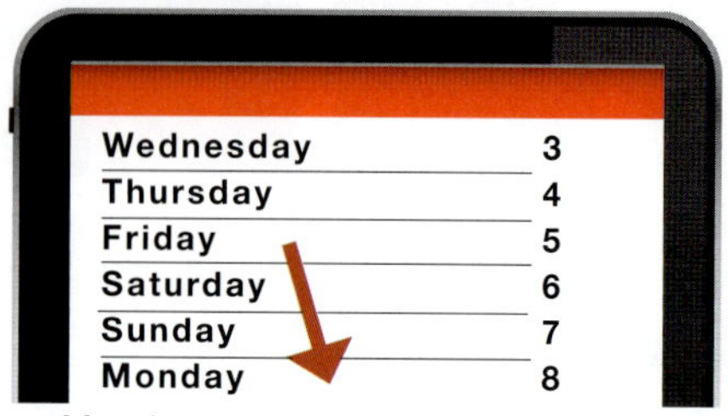

on Monday

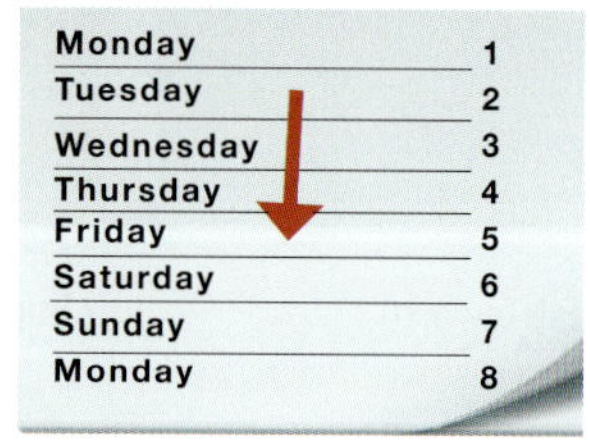

this Friday

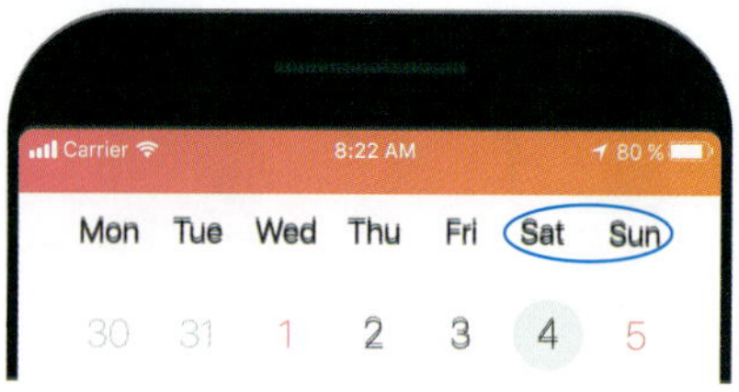

on the weekend

next Tuesday

in two weeks

d Complete groups 1–4 with words and phrases in the box. Some of them can go in more than one group.

Thursday	three months	June	winter	year	the winter

1 **on** Monday, Tuesday, Wednesday …
2 **this** afternoon, Monday, week, March, month, summer …
3 **in** March, the summer, two weeks …
4 **next** Monday, week, March, month, summer …

e Complete the sentences with a time expression.

1 I'm going to have (*meal*) ____________.
2 I'm going to go on vacation ____________.
3 I'm going to visit a friend ____________.
4 I'm going to buy a new (*object*) ____________.

Tell a partner your sentences.

I'm going to visit a friend tomorrow.

Ordinal numbers

a 12.05 Listen and repeat the ordinal numbers.

1 first, 2 second, 3 third, 4 fourth, 5 fifth, 6 sixth, 7 seventh, 8 eighth, 9 ninth, 10 tenth, 11 eleventh, 12 twelfth, 13 thirteenth, 14 fourteenth, 20 twentieth, 21 twenty-first, 22 twenty-second, 30 thirtieth, 31 thirty-first

b Work with a partner.
Student A: Say a number.
Student B: Say the ordinal number.

fifteen

fifteenth

c Now go back to p. 97.

12B Common verbs and collocations

a 12.11 Listen and repeat the phrases.

clean (**simple past:** *cleaned*)

clean a room / your apartment

exercise (**simple past:** *exercised*)

exercise at the gym

go (**simple past:** *went*)

go to the beach

go to a museum

make (**simple past:** *made*)

make a cake

play (**simple past:** *played*)

play sports

visit (**simple past:** *visited*)

visit a friend

visit Paris

invite (**simple past:** *invited*)

invite someone to a party

invite someone for a meal

use (**simple past:** *used*)

use a computer

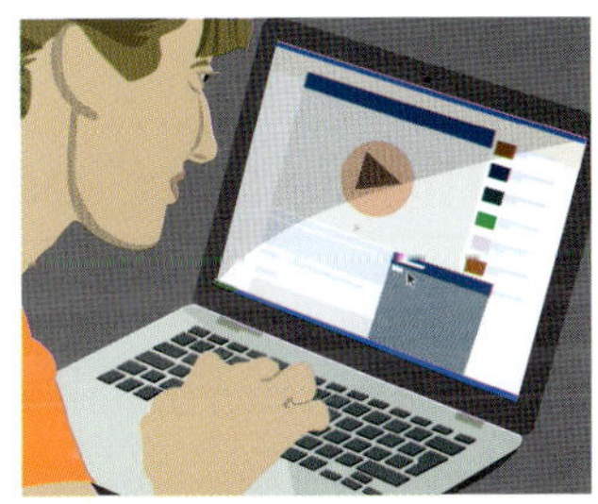

use the Internet

do (**simple past:** *did*)

do yoga

do your homework

do laundry

b Underline the correct words.

1 He eats a lot and he never *plays* / *makes* sports.
2 It's my birthday next week. I'm going to *visit* / *invite* some friends to my apartment for dinner.
3 She's going to *paint* / *draw* the walls of her room dark green. Don't ask me why!
4 We were in Mexico and we *visited* / *went* Palenque.
5 I'm going to *do* / *make* some coffee.
6 A woman comes on Wednesday. She cleans and *does* / *makes* laundry for us.
7 Excuse me, can I *clean* / *use* your phone? I need to call my sister.

c Write three sentences with the phrases in a.

I'm going to clean my bedroom tomorrow.

Tell a partner your sentences.

d Now go back to p. 99.

1C Capital letters and periods

a Look at the sentence. Read the information about capital letters and periods.

My name's Sophia Taylor.

Capital letters

We use capital letters (*A, B, C, D …*):

- for names (*Sophia Taylor, Ben Wilson, Maria González*)
- names of places (*Toronto, Canada, High Street*)
- for nationalities (*Italian, British, Chinese*)
- at the beginning of a sentence (*My name's …*)

Periods

. = period

We usually use periods at the end of sentences.

My name's Sophia Taylor.

b Write the capital letters.

1 a A
2 b
3 d
4 e
5 g
6 h
7 q
8 r
9 t

c Add capital letters and periods to each sentence.

> they're married. (T)
1 we're from brazil
2 he's a student
3 this is ruben
4 i'm in a class with amy lee
5 my name is sandro
6 their apartment is in mexico city it's small

d Now go back to p. 13.

2C The alphabet and spelling

Part 1: The alphabet

a 02.26 Listen to how we say the letters of the alphabet.

/eɪ/ (*day*)	/i/ (*we*)	/e/ (*ten*)	/aɪ/ (*hi*)	/oʊ/ (*no*)	/u/ (*you*)	/ɑ/ (*car*)
Aa	Bb	Ff	Ii	Oo	Qq	Rr
Hh	Cc	Ll	Yy		Uu	
Jj	Dd	Mm			Ww	
Kk	Ee	Nn			("double u")	
	Gg	Ss				
	Pp	Xx				
	Tt					
	Vv					
	Zz					

b Add the letters to the group with similar sounds. Say the letters.

R H Q O Z Y C F

1 (**you**) U, Q, W
2 (**day**) J, __, A, K
3 (**hi**) I, __
4 (**we**) T, __, B, D, E, G, P, V, __
5 (**ten**) N, L, __, M, S, X
6 (**car**) __
7 (**no**) __

c Now go back to p. 20.

Part 2: Spelling

Some words in English have double letters in their written form.

*umbre**ll**a*

Other words in English have letters in their written form that might seem different from what you hear.

***c**ity*

d 02.30 Correct the spelling. Listen and check. Then practice spelling the words.

1 adress
2 bok
3 umbrela
4 hapy
5 smal
6 dificult
7 intresting
8 rite
9 rong
10 nife

e Now go back to p. 21.

3C Contractions

a Look at the sentences and read about contractions.

I'm at a café with Hannah. **She's** my friend from work.

I'm (contraction) = *I am* *She's* (contraction) = *She is*
We use contractions in speaking and writing, usually in informal situations.

***be*: affirmative and negative**

+		–	
Full form	**Contraction**	**Full form**	**Contraction**
I am	*I'm*	*I am not*	*I'm not*
you are	*you're*	*you are not*	*you're not / you aren't*
we are	*we're*	*we are not*	*we're not / we aren't*
he is	*he's*	*he is not*	*he's not / he isn't*
she is	*she's*	*she is not*	*she's not / she isn't*
it is	*it's*	*it is not*	*it's not / it isn't*
they are	*they're*	*they are not*	*they're not / they aren't*

***It is** a pizza.* → ***It's** a pizza.*

Simple present: negative

Full form	Contraction
I/you/we do not	*I/you/we don't*

*I **do not** eat fish.* → *I **don't** eat fish.*

b Match the contractions in the box with 1–8.

we're not it's not don't I'm you're she's they're we're

1 you are ____________
2 she is ____________
3 I am ____________
4 do not ____________
5 they are ____________
6 we are not ____________
7 we are ____________
8 it is not ____________

c Add the words in parentheses to each sentence. Use contractions.

1 ____________ from Sweden. (He is)
2 ____________ tomatoes. (They are)
3 ____________ five o'clock. (It is not)
4 I ____________ have a big meal in the evening. (do not)
5 ____________ a teacher. (You are not)
6 ____________ OK. (I am)
7 We ____________ eat meat. (do not)
8 ____________ Spanish. (I am not)

d Now go back to p. 29. Try to use contractions in your text message.

4C Word order

a Look at the examples and the word order.

Word order

- **subject + verb**
I work.
You don't work.
- **subject + verb + object**
Emma and Charlotte don't have a brother.
They speak Spanish.
- **subject + verb + preposition + noun**
My daughters are in college.
They don't live in an apartment.
- **subject + verb + object + preposition + noun**
I don't have a phone in my bag.
I like milk in my coffee.

We can use *here* or *there* after a verb.
*I live **there**.*
*You don't work **here**.*

b Check (✓) the correct sentences.

1 a ☐ Tennis we play.
b ☐ We play tennis.
2 a ☐ I don't teach children.
b ☐ Don't teach children I.
3 a ☐ They there don't study.
b ☐ They don't study there.
4 a ☐ My sister in Japan lives.
b ☐ My sister lives in Japan.
5 a ☐ These are my friends.
b ☐ These my friends are.
6 a ☐ I have an apartment in New York.
b ☐ I in New York have an apartment.

c Put the words in the correct order to make sentences. Remember to use capital letters and periods.

1 don't speak / they / German
2 there / have coffee / you
3 we / in a factory / don't work
4 teaches / at the university / my dad / Italian
5 the computer / I / at the office / don't like
6 have / in Canada / a nice house / they

d Now go back to p. 37.

5C *and* and *but*

a Look at the sentences and read about *and* and *but*.

There's a beautiful park near the hotel, **and** there are stores on the next street.
Our hotel is in a nice part of town, **but** it's really small.

☺	***and***	☺
There's a beautiful park near the hotel,	*and*	*there are stores on the next street.*

☹	***and***	☹
The hotel's not very big,	*and*	*it's not near Sebastien's apartment.*

☹	***but***	☺
The hotel is really small,	*but*	*it's in in a nice part of town.*

☺	***but***	☹
His apartment is nice,	*but*	*it's not near our hotel.*

b Underline the correct words.

1 I love New York City, but it's very *expensive / nice*.
2 The hotel has free Wi-Fi, and *there's / it doesn't have* a TV in every room.
3 Libya is a very hot country, but *the old houses are always cool / it's sometimes 55°C*.
4 There are a lot of expensive hotels, but *there are a lot of / there aren't any* cheap hostels.
5 There are a lot of good books in the bookstore, and *they are very boring / the sales assistants are very friendly*.
6 The Maris Hotel is beautiful, and *it's near the ocean / the restaurant isn't very good*.

c Add *and* or *but* to each sentence.

1 I live in Spain, ______ I don't speak Spanish.
2 The food is good, ______ it's very expensive!
3 Their house is nice, ______ it's near the bus station.
4 This hotel room is small, ______ the shower is cold.
5 The city has a good university, ______ I'd like to study there.
6 There isn't a supermarket here, ______ there is a market on the next street.

d ⋙ Now go back to p. 45. Try to use *and* and *but* in your writing.

6C *because* and *also*

a Look at the sentences and read about *because* and *also*.

I walk to work every day **because** my apartment is near the office.
We go out to a café for coffee every day. We **also** have lunch there.

We use *because* and *also* to join ideas.

- *Because* joins two ideas in one sentence. We use *because* to give a reason. It answers the question *Why?*

  Why do you like your job?

  It's interesting.

  *I like my job **because** it's interesting.*
  *He sleeps in the morning **because** he works at night.*
- *Also* joins two ideas in two sentences. It means *and*.
  He plays baseball and tennis. He plays soccer.
  *He plays baseball and tennis. He **also** plays soccer.*
  (= He plays baseball, tennis, and soccer.)
- We use *also* before the verb:
  *He sleeps in the morning. He **also** sleeps in the afternoon.*
- We use *also* after *be*:
  *I'm a doctor. I'm **also** a teacher.*

b Underline the correct answers.

1 She plays basketball *also she teaches basketball. / . She also teaches basketball.*
2 I feel good in the morning *because I sleep for seven hours at night. / . Because I sleep for seven hours at night.*
3 I speak English. I also speak Italian because my parents *Italian / are Italian*.
4 Michael works at night. His wife *also works / works also* at night.
5 We always eat at home because *like / we like* cooking.
6 He's a student. He *also is / 's also* a waiter.

c Use *because* and *also* to join the ideas.

> I want to go shopping. I need some cups. (because)
I want to go shopping because I need some cups.
> She teaches English at the school. She teaches Turkish. (also)
She teaches English at the school. She also teaches Turkish.

1 I don't like my job. It's boring. (because)
2 She doesn't have breakfast. She isn't hungry in the morning. (because)
3 I need to make lunch. I need to go to the supermarket. (also)
4 The children are nice. They're very funny. (also)

d ⋙ Now go back to p. 53. Try to use *because* and *also* in your writing.

7C Commas, exclamation points, and question marks

a Look at the sentences and read about commas, exclamation points, and question marks.

Women's coats, blouses, jeans, bags – all in good condition.
Not expensive!
How much are they?

, = comma   ! = exclamation point   ? = question mark

Commas

- We use commas in lists of nouns (things or people).
  Beautiful things for your home – ***chairs, lamps, small tables***
- We often finish a list with *and* + noun. We use a comma before *and* in lists.
  I'd like a bag, a coat, ***and a blouse****.*

Exclamation points

- We use exclamation points to mean *Look at this* or *This is important.*
  Not expensive!

Question marks

- We use question marks at the end of questions.
  How much are they?

b Add commas to each list.

1 For sale: old books newspapers magazines.
2 I love old cups plates and glasses.
3 She's wearing black pants a white shirt a gray jacket and black shoes.
4 They sell radios clocks pictures lamps tables chairs …
5 For sale: coats jackets hats shoes shirts dresses …
6 We need bread milk cheese and apples.

c Add a question mark (?) or an exclamation point (!) to each sentence.

1 How old are these things
2 Thank you
3 Write soon
4 New bookstore
5 Can I pay by credit card
6 How much are they

d Now go back to p. 61. Try to use commas, exclamation points, and question marks in your email.

8C Writing short emails, notes, and texts

a Look at the text and read about writing short emails, notes, and texts.

LOGAN

Hi Daniel!
Thank you for the tour of Newport yesterday. It was great to see a new town and meet your friends. I had a lot of fun! Here is a picture of all of us at lunch. I hope we can do it again some time soon.
See you soon!

1 We start **emails and notes** like this:
- *Dear* (name),
- *Hi* (name),

We are usually less formal in **texts**:
- *Hi* (name)*!*
- *Hey* (name).

2 In the main part, we use phrases like these:
- *I want to say …*
- *Thanks for your email/note/text.*
- *Thank you for …*
- *Here is/are …*
- *I was …*
- *It was …*
- *I hope …*

We often use the simple past, e.g., *I* ***had*** *a lot of fun. I* ***stayed*** *at home. I* ***went*** *into town.*

3 We finish **emails and notes** like this:
- *Best,* (name)
- *Thanks,* (name)
- *See you soon,* (name)

We don't usually finish a **text** with our name.
- *See you soon.*
- *Talk to you later!*

b Put a–e in the correct order to make a note.

a The food was great, and it was good to talk! I went home and watched a movie in the afternoon.
b I hope we can go to the concert on Friday.
c Hi Laura,
d See you soon,
Matt
e I want to say thank you very much for lunch yesterday.

c Complete the email with the words and phrases in the box.

hope	sorry	It was	Here are	Dear	talked

Reply Forward

1 _______ Allie,
2 _______ some photos of the party on Saturday night. I'm 3 _______ I was late!
4 _______ good to meet your friends. I
5 _______ to Emma and Marco – they're really nice!
I 6 _______ we can meet for coffee next week.
Best,
Janelle

d Now go back to p. 69.

9C Making the order clear

a Look at part of Sara's online post and read about making the order clear with *first, next, then.*

***First**, we went for a walk to the old part of the city.*
***Next**, we had lunch at a small restaurant.*
***Then**, we went shopping at a market, and I saw some beautiful things.*

When we write about events in the past, it's good to make the order clear. We use phrases like:

- *First, …*
  ***First**, we flew to Istanbul.*
- *Next, … Then, … After that, …*
  ***After that**, we took a bus to Claudia's town.*
  ***Then**, we went shopping.*

We usually use *Next* for the middle event, not the last event.
*First, we went to the zoo. **Next**, we had lunch. Then, we went shopping.*

b Underline the correct words.

The weather was very bad! [1] *Then, / First,* it rained. [2] *First, / Next,* it was very windy. [3] *Then, / After,* it snowed!

[4] *First, / Next,* we camped in Anton's backyard. [5] *First, / After that,* we stayed in a hotel.

Last summer I went to Canada with Veronica and Elijah. [6] *First, / Then,* we went to Toronto. It was great. [7] *Next, / First,* we went to Thunder Bay for three days. [8] *After this, / After that,* we stayed with Elijah's family in Vancouver.

c Add the words and phrases in parentheses in the correct place to make the order clear.

> We visited Emma's family in the country. We went to the city. (*then, first,*)
First, we visited Emma's family in the country. Then, we went to the city.

1 I went to a café. I went to the park. (*first, after that,*)
2 It was sunny and warm. It was sunny and cold. (*then, first,*)
3 We went to a restaurant. We saw a movie. We went home. (*next, first, then,*)
4 I finished work. I went for a walk by the river. I met her at the bus station. (*first, after that, next,*)

d Now go back to p. 77. Try to make the order clear in your online post.

10C Word order in questions

a Look at part of Anthony's message to Owen and read about word order in questions.

First, where can I find a taxi at the train station? And how much is it from the station to the hotel?

Yes/No questions		
Do	they	have a yard?
Did	Eduardo	visit you?
Can	you	call me, please?
Is	she	working?

Wh- questions			
How many rooms	does	your house	have?
Where	can	I	find a taxi?
When	did	the train	leave?
What	is	Selma	doing?

Questions with *be* are different.

Yes/No questions with *be*	
Is	Grace's apartment big?
Were	you at work today?

Wh- questions with *be*		
Where	was	your phone?
How much	is	it from the station to the hotel?

b Underline the correct words.

1 Where *are you / you are* going?
2 Who *is that / that is*?
3 *Did you use / You did use* your phone on the plane?
4 *You can / Can you* help me?
5 How many taxis *there were / were there*?
6 What movie *is your sister watching / is watching your sister*?
7 *There is / Is there* a yard?
8 How *you do often / often do you* watch TV?

c Put the words in the correct order to make questions. Add capital letters and question marks.

there / at the station / a café / is
Is there a café at the station?

1 where / the bus stop / is
2 do / when / start / work / you
3 you / the tickets / buy / did
4 some bread / you / buy / can
5 doing / what / you / are
6 the movie / is / what time

d Now go back to p. 85.

11C Pronouns

a Look at part of Leah's email to Hailey and read about subject and object pronouns.

… I study with a girl named Megan. She's from Ann Arbor … She and her boyfriend Chris helped me a lot … I often see them at the library … I also know my brother, of course! … It's good to have him in the same city.

We use subject and object pronouns so that we don't repeat nouns and names.

*I study with **a girl named Megan**. **She**'s from Ann Arbor and **she**'s really nice.*

*I also know **my brother**, of course! **He**'s really busy …*

*I study with **a girl named Megan** … She and **her boyfriend Chris** helped me a lot … I often see **them** at the library.*

Read more about pronouns in Grammar Focus 11A on p. 132.

We often use *you* to mean "people in general / everyone."
***You** can study English online.*

b Underline the correct words.

Seemа Bhadoria is a young woman from India. People call [1]*she / her* "The Strong Woman." [2]*She / Her* can pull a truck with her teeth.
The Bajau Laut people can swim underwater for a long time. [3]*They / Them* are amazing humans. Did you read about [4]*they / them*?

William Higinbotham was a scientist. [5]*It / He* lived from 1910 to 1994. At a science lab, [6]*it / he* invented a machine called "Tennis for Two." [7]*It / You* could play tennis! [8]*It / He* was the first video game in the world, but he didn't make any money from [9]*it / them*.

c Switch the underlined words with the subject and object pronouns in the box.

he her him him it it me
us she she ~~they~~ they we

> I met a doctor and an IT worker. The doctor and the IT worker live in Madrid.
They live in Madrid.

1 Why is my sister eating that sandwich? My sister made that sandwich for me!
2 Do you like this picture of my wife and me? Valerie gave this picture to my wife and me.
3 My friends have a baby boy named Luke. My friends talk about the baby boy named Luke all the time!
4 Neil and Andy are students. Neil, Andy, and I met in college.
5 I'm Tony Smith, from school. Do you remember Tony Smith?
6 That's Ellie, and that's Jack. Jack likes Ellie, but Ellie doesn't like Jack!

d Now go back to p. 93. Try to use pronouns in your email.

12C Paragraphs

a Look at Carlos's email to his friends and read about paragraphs.

Reply
Hi guys,
It's my birthday on Saturday. Do you want to come to my party?
It's at my apartment at 2:00. We're going to watch my favorite soccer team play on TV at 3:00.
I hope to see you then!
Carlos

Paragraph 1 = invitation

Paragraph 2 = making plans for the time and place

Paragraphs divide writing into groups of ideas. We use them to make our writing clear. In Carlos's email, he uses two paragraphs – one for the invitation and the other for making plans.
To start a new paragraph, write the next sentence on a new line, like this:

Reply
I'm sorry, I can't go. I have to work.

Do you want to meet on Tuesday?

Reply
~~I'm sorry, I can't go. I have to work. Do you want to meet on Tuesday?~~

b Match paragraphs a–b with 1–2.

Reply
1 ______
We could meet tomorrow. I'm free in the afternoon. What do you think?

Reply
There's a new restaurant in town. It looks really good.
2 ______

a Reply
Thanks for the lunch invitation, but I can't come today. I'm busy.

b Reply
Do you want to go there on Saturday?

c Rewrite the emails with two paragraphs.

1 Do you have any plans for the weekend? I'd like to see a movie. We could meet at the movie theater at 6:30. Is that OK with you?
2 It's my birthday next Friday. I'm going to be 25! Do you want to come here for dinner on Saturday? I'm going to invite a few friends.

d Now go back to p. 101. Try to use paragraphs in your invitations.

Acknowledgments

The authors and publishers acknowledge the following sources of copyright material and are grateful for the permissions granted. While every effort has been made, it has not always been possible to identify the sources of all the material used, or to trace all copyright holders. If any omissions are brought to our notice, we will be happy to include the appropriate acknowledgments on reprinting and in the next update to the digital edition, as applicable.

Key:
U = Unit, CL = Classroom Language, C = Communication Plus, G = Grammar Focus, V = Vocabulary Focus

Photographs
All the photographs are sourced from Getty Images.
Front cover photography by Don Mason/Getty Images.
CL: Alexis84/iStock/Getty Images Plus; Witthaya Prasongsin/Moment; Eric Audras/PhotoAlto; Image Source; Farknot_Architect/iStock/Getty Images Plus; SDI Productions/E+; F. Lukasseck/Radius Images; **U1:** Oliver Burston/Ikon Images/Getty Images Plus; Alex Goodlett/Getty Images Sport; Sean M. Haffey/Getty Images Sport; Clive Brunskill/Getty Images Sport; Chris Brunskill/Fantasista/Getty Images Sport; Lucas Uebel/Getty Images Sport; Jordan Mansfield/Getty Images Sport; Visual China Group; Clasos/LatinContent Editorial; Franckreporter/E+; Phillip Waterman/Cultura; Jacoblund/iStock/Getty Images Plus; **U2:** Jeff Kowalsky/AFP; Janoka82/iStock/Getty Images Plus; Chiyacat/iStock/Getty Images Plus; Karol Kozlowski/robertharding/Getty Images Plus; Charlie Dean/Caiaimage; Fuse/Corbis; Thinkstock/Stockbyte; Tassii/iStock/Getty Images Plus; ER Productions Limited/DigitalVision; Tulcarion/E+; **U3:** Caiaimage; Mphillips007/iStock/Getty Images Plus; AlexPro9500/iStock/Getty Images Plus; Anilakkus/iStock/Getty Images Plus; Baibaz/iStock/Getty Images Plus; pidjoe/iStock/Getty Images Plus; Stockcam/E+; Dszc/iStock/Getty Images Plus; Lane Oatey; Gurpal Singh Datta; Eli_asenova/E+; Vitalina/iStock/Getty Images Plus; JohnGollop/E+; JoeGough/iStock/Getty Images Plus; VvoeVale/iStock/Getty Images Plus; Hispanolistic/E+; Skynesher/E+; Monkeybusinessimages/iStock/Getty Images Plus; XiXinXing; Ridofranz/iStock/Getty Images Plus; Nadofotos/iStock/Getty Images Plus; Vinnstock/iStock/Getty Images Plus; Creacart/iStock/Getty Images Plus; Erstudiostok/iStock/Getty Images Plus; Portra/E+; Bim/E+; **U4:** Michael Cogliantry/Taxi/Getty Images Plus; Compassionate Eye Foundation/Robert Kent/; PeopleImages/E+; Kali9/E+; Efenzi/iStock/Gett; Henryk Sadura/Moment; Sergio Monti/EyeEm; Bojan89iStock/Getty Images Plus; Sambrogio/E+; Albert L. Ortega/Getty Images Entertainment; Mike Coppola/WireImage; Christopher Polk/Getty Images Entertainment; Kevork Djansezian/Getty Images Entertainment; Quality Sport Images/Getty Images Sport; Dimitrios Kambouris/WireImage; Aldomurillo/E+; Westend61; Kathleen Finlay/Cultura; Ariel Skelley/DigitalVision; Morsa Images/E+; **U5:** Pierre Dunnigan/500px; Miroslav_1/iStock Editorial/Getty Images Plus; IPGGutenbergUKLtd/iStock/Getty Images Plus; Andreka/iStock/Getty Images Plus; Monkeybusinessimages/Getty Images Plus; YinYang/E+; JackF/iStock/Getty Images Plus; Hispanolistic/E+; MangoStar_Studio/iStock/Getty Images Plus; Jupiterimages/Goodshoot/Gett; Yogenyogeny/iStock/Getty Images Plus; northlightimages/iStock/Getty Images Plus; Jupiterimages/Stockbyte; Micah Wright/First Light/Getty Images Plus; Kitti Boonnitrod/Moment; Tpopova/iStock/Getty Images Plus; Anadolu Agency; Lorado/E+; Chalffy/iStock; **U6:** Westend61; Hugh Sitton/Corbis/Getty Images Plus; Klaus Vedfelt/DigitalVision; FG Trade/E+; Philipp Nemenz/Cultura; Andresr/E+; Commercial Eye/Stone/Gett; TAGSTOCK1/iStock/Getty Images Plus; DragonImages/iStock/Getty Images Plus; Peopleimages/E+; Skynesher/E+; Jetta Productions Inc/DigitalVision; Rowan Jordan/iStock/Getty Images Plus; Kurt Budiarto Photography/Moment Open; Niqin/E+; Adamkaz/E+; Mediaphotos/iStock/Getty Images Plus; Robert Daly/Caiaimage; **U7:** Cristina Arias/Cover; Danita Delimont; Dial-a-view/E+; Victor VIRGILE/Gamma-Rapho; Stefania D'Alessandro/WireImage; JP Yim/Getty Images Entertainment; Michael Loccisano/Getty Images Entertainment; Jamie McCarthy/WireImage; Aldomurillo/E+; Mint Images; Neustockimages/iStock/Getty Images Plus; Kettaphoto/iStock/Getty Images Plus; **U8:** FEBRUARY/Moment; Doble.d/Moment Open; Bay Area News/MediaNews Group; KeithBinns/E+; Tier Und Naturfotografie J und C Sohns/Photographer's Choice RF; UrosPoteko/iStock/Getty Images Plus; Mauriliers Schoenmaekers/500px; GK Hart/Vikki Hart/Photodisc; Andrew_Howe/E+; Geoff Scott-Simpson/Moment Open; Westend61; Mark Hunt; Pixelfit/E+; **U9:** Jeremy Maude/Photodisc; Nelsonarts/iStock/Getty Images Plus; Tatsiana Volskaya/Moment; StockstudioX/E+; GM Visuals/Royalty-free; Pigphoto/iStock/Getty Images Plus; Czekma13/iStock/Getty Images Plus; Allou/iStock/Getty Images Plus; J-wildman/Getty Images Plus; Jose Luis Pelaez Inc/DigitalVision; Simon Dux/iStock Editorial/Gett; Michael Lee/Moment; AntonioGuillem/iStock/Getty Images Plus; PRImageFactory/iStock/Getty Images Plus; Billnoll/E+; Danita Delimont; Floortje/E+; **U10:** Zero Creatives/Cultura; Cavan Images; KatarzynaBialasiewicz/iStock/Getty Images Plus; Gerenme/E+; Russwitherington1/iStock/Gett; Jacek Kadaj/Moment; John Keeble/Moment; JohnnyGreig/E+; Ppa5/iStock/Getty Images Plus; ExcellentPhoto/iStock/Getty Images Plus; FotoTravel/iStock/Getty Images Plus; Kohei Hara/DigitalVision; Flashpop/DigitalVision; PhotoAlto/Frederic Cirou; Luis Alvarez/DigitalVision; Jamie Squire/Getty Images Sport; David Madison/Photographer's Choice/Getty Images Plus; Baona/iStock/Getty Images Plus; **U11:** Sovfoto/Universal Images Group; Sven Creutzmann/Mambo Photo/Hulton Archive; Hill Street Studios/DigitalVision; Timothy Allen/Photolibrary/Getty Images Plus; OSTILL/iStock/Getty Images Plus; Kupicoo/E+; Vadimguzhva/iStock/Getty Images Plus; Artem Ermilov/iStock/Getty Images Plus; Hispanolistic/E+; Roy Mehta/The Image Bank/Getty Images Plus; Steve Cohen/Photolibrary; Greg Epperson/Photolibrary/Getty Images Plus; **U12:** Peter Cade/The Image Bank/Getty Images Plus; Westend61; DavidCallan/iStock; Simonkr/E+; Mint Images; AJ_Watt/E+; Cavan Images; Tim Kitchen/The Image Bank/Getty Images Plus; Synergee/E+; Wavebreakmedia/iStock/Getty Images Plus; Santypan/iStock/Getty Images Plus; Paul Bradbury/OJO Images; Vm/E+; Martin-dm/E+; **C:** Monkeybusinessimages/iStock; Vadimguzhva/iStock/Getty Images Plus; Ajr_images/iStock/Getty Images Plus; Adamkaz/iStock/Getty Images Plus; Juanmonino/E+; Drbimages/E+; Stevecoleimages/E+; Juanmonino/iStock/Getty Images Plus; Maskot; Leland Bobbe/Image Source; **G:** Eugenesergeev/iStock Editorial/Getty Images Plus; Chelsea Lauren/WireImage; **V:** Bravo1954/E+; Hyrma/iStock/Getty Images Plus; Sohel Parvez Haque/EyeEm; Devonyu/iStock/Getty Images Plus; Vofpalabra/iStock/Getty Images Plus; Eskymaks/iStock/Getty Images Plus; Guvendemir/iStock; MicroStockHub/iStock/Getty Images Plus; L_Mirror/iStock/Getty Images Plus; Carlosalvarez/E+; Steve@Colorado/E+; Christina Lease/Lonely Planet Images/Getty Images Plus; Judd Pilossof/Photolibrary/Getty Images Plus; Andrea Bricco/StockFood Creative/Getty Images Plus; Gbh007/iStock/Getty Images Plus; Twomeows/Moment Open; Ma-k/E+; Pjohnson1/E+; Seregam/iStock/Getty Images Plus; Subjug/iStock/Getty Images Plus; Juanmonino/E+; Animaflora/iStock/Getty Images Plus; Kirin_photo/E+; LindasPhotography/iStock/Getty Images Plus; Akepong Srichaichana/EyeEm; Chee Siong Teh/EyeEm; Ligorko/iStock/Getty Images Plus; Caziopeia/E+; Dimitris66/iStock/Getty Images Plus; Kutaytanir/E+; Hidesy/iStock/Getty Images Plus; Unpict/iStock/Getty Images Plus; RedHelga/iStock/Getty Images Plus; Bestfotostudio/iStock/Getty Images Plus; Gannet77/iStock/Getty Images Plus; Radionphoto/iStock/Getty Images Plus; Ariel Skelley/DigitalVision; Monty Rakusen/Cultura; Alvarez/E+; Monkeybusinessimages/iStock/Getty Images Plus; Image Source/DigitalVision; FatCamera/E+; PeopleImages/iStock/Getty Images Plus; Hoxton/Tom Merton; Wavebreakmedia/iStock/Getty Images Plus; Vav63/iStock/Getty Images Plus; Skrow/iStock/Getty Images Plus; Monticelllo/iStock/Getty Images Plus; Classen Rafael/EyeEm; Dan Thornberg/EyeEm; CostinT/E+; MortenBjerregaard/iStock/Getty Images Plus; Danielsbfoto/iStock/Getty Images Plus; Rosemary Calvert/The Image Bank/Getty Images Plus; Hudiemm/iStock/Getty Images Plus; Suradech14/iStock/Getty Images Plus; Golibtolibov/iStock/Getty Images Plus; Yevgen Romanenko/Moment; MDHayes/iStock/Getty Images Plus; John Seaton Callahan/Moment; Tramino/iStock; Oliver Strewe/Lonely Planet Images/Getty Images Plus; FotografiaBasica/iStock/Getty Images Plus; Marin Tomas/Moment; Rainer Grosskopf/Photolibrary/Getty Images Plus; John & Lisa Merrill/Photolibrary/Getty Images Plus; Jodie Wallis/Moment; Photographer Nick Measures/Moment; Fuse/Corbis; Real444/E+; IB/iStock/Getty Images Plus; Iliana Mestari/Moment; Vanessa Davies/Dorling Kindersley/Getty Images Plus; Skynesher/E+; Mark Williamson/Photodisc; Mlenny/Stock/Getty Images Plus; Prasit photo/Moment; Eli_asenova/E+; Quim Llenas/Getty Images Entertainment; PeTer_Lau; RUSS ROHDE/Cultura; Image Source; Shapecharge/E+; Lukasz Olek/Caiaimage; Jupiterimages/Stockbyte; UntitledImages/E+.

The following images are sourced from other Sourced/libraries. **U3:** Danita Delimont/Alamy; **U5:** © Gehry Partners, LLP, © Frank O. Gehry and © Iwan Baan 2014; **U7**: Alamy/LOOK Die Bildagentur der Fotografen GmbH; Bennyartist/Shutterstock; StudioSmart/Shutterstock; Raulin/Shutterstock; PodPad/Shutterstock; Ruslan Semichev/Shutterstock; **U11:** Emilio Segre Visual Archives/American Institute of Physics/Science Photo Library; Courtesy Brookhaven National Laboratory; CB2/ZOB/Wenn/Newscom; Sanjeev Gupta/EPA/Shutterstock.

Commissioned photography by Gareth Boden:U1; U2; U8

We are grateful to The Stephen Perse 6th Form College, Cambridge, for their help with the commissioned photography.

Illustrations
Illustrations by QBS Learning; Mark Bird; Mark Duffin; Sally Elford; John Goodwin (Eye Candy Illustration); Dusan Lakicevic (Beehive Illustration); Roger Penwill; Gavin Reece (New Division); Martin Sanders (Beehive Illustration); Sean 290 (KJA Artists); David Semple; Marie-Eve Tremblay (Colagene); Andrea Turvey (Eye Candy Illustration); Gary Venn (Lemonade Illustration).

Typeset by QBS Learning.

Audio by John Marshall Media.

Corpus
Development of this publication has made use of the Cambridge English Corpus(CEC). The CEC is a computer database of contemporary spoken and written English, which currently stands at over one billion words. It includes British English, American English and other varieties of English. It also includes the Cambridge Learner Corpus, developed in collaboration with the University of Cambridge ESOL Examinations. Cambridge University Press has built up the CEC to provide evidence about language use that helps us to produce better language teaching materials.

English Profile
This product is informed by English Vocabulary Profile, built as part of English Profile, a collaborative program designed to enhance the learning, teaching and assessment of English worldwide. Its main funding partners are Cambridge University Press and Cambridge Assessment English and its aim is to create a "profile" for English, linked to the Common European Framework of Reference for Languages (CEFR). English Profile outcomes, such as the English Vocabulary Profile, will provide detailed information about the language that learners can be expected to demonstrate at each CEFR level, offering a clear benchmark for learners' proficiency. For more information, please visit www.englishprofile.org.

CALD
The Cambridge Advanced Learner's Dictionary is the world's most widely used dictionary for learners of English. Including all the words and phrases that learners are likely to come across, it also has easy-to-understand definitions and example sentences to show how the word is used in context. The Cambridge Advanced Learner's Dictionary is available online at dictionary.cambridge.org.

CAMBRIDGE
UNIVERSITY PRESS

University Printing House, Cambridge CB2 8BS, United Kingdom

One Liberty Plaza, 20th Floor, New York, NY 10006, USA

477 Williamstown Road, Port Melbourne, VIC 3207, Australia

314–321, 3rd Floor, Plot 3, Splendor Forum, Jasola District Centre, New Delhi – 110025, India

103 Penang Road, #05-06/07, Visioncrest Commercial, Singapore 238467

Cambridge University Press is part of the University of Cambridge.

It furthers the University's mission by disseminating knowledge in the pursuit of education, learning and research at the highest international levels of excellence.

www.cambridge.org
Information on this title: www.cambridge.org/9781108818131

First published 2022

20 19 18 17 16 15 14 13 12 11 10 9 8 7 6 5 4 3 2 1

Printed in Malaysia by Vivar Printing

A catalogue record for this publication is available from the British Library

ISBN 978-1-108-81813-1 Starter Student's Book with eBook
ISBN 978-1-108-81831-5 Starter Student's Book A with eBook
ISBN 978-1-108-81832-2 Starter Student's Book B with eBook
ISBN 978-1-108-86221-9 Starter Student's Book with Digital Pack
ISBN 978-1-108-86227-1 Starter Student's Book A with Digital Pack
ISBN 978-1-108-86229-5 Starter Student's Book B with Digital Pack
ISBN 978-1-108-81814-8 Starter Workbook with Answers
ISBN 978-1-108-81815-5 Starter Workbook A with Answers
ISBN 978-1-108-81819-3 Starter Workbook B with Answers
ISBN 978-1-108-81820-9 Starter Workbook without Answers
ISBN 978-1-108-81825-4 Starter Workbook A without Answers
ISBN 978-1-108-81826-1 Starter Workbook B without Answers
ISBN 978-1-108-81827-8 Starter Full Contact with eBook
ISBN 978-1-108-81828-5 Starter Full Contact A with eBook
ISBN 978-1-108-81829-2 Starter Full Contact B with eBook
ISBN 978-1-108-86223-3 Starter Full Contact with Digital Pack
ISBN 978-1-108-86224-0 Starter Full Contact A with Digital Pack
ISBN 978-1-108-86225-7 Starter Full Contact B with Digital Pack
ISBN 978-1-108-81833-9 Starter Teacher's Book with Digital Pack
ISBN 978-1-108-81810-0 Starter Presentation Plus

Additional resources for this publication at www.cambridge.org/americanempower

This page is intentionally left blank.

This page is intentionally left blank.

This page is intentionally left blank.

This page is intentionally left blank.